COLLECTED COLUMNS FROM 1956 TO 1990

THE BEST OF
DAN COOK

The Best of Dan Cook
1956-1990
by
Dan Cook

With a foreword by Frank A. Bennack Jr.

and

An introduction by Blackie Sherrod

Corona Publishing Company
San Antonio, Texas
2001

First edition 2001

Corona Publishing Company
P.O. Drawer 12407
San Antonio, Texas 78212
(210) 828-9532

Library of Congress Control Number: 2001094867
ISBN 0-931722-15-2
Manufactured in the United States of America

Visit out website at
www.coronapublishing.com

Contents

Acknowledgements

*The editors wish to thank Jason Gonzalez,
Leo Leija and Kelly Guckian for their help in
researching the materials for this book, and Nicole Sherman,
Benjamin Olivo, Elizabeth Standifird and Marie A. Martinez
for preparing the copy for publication.*

Frank A. Bennack Jr.
President and CEO,
The Hearst Corporation

It has been my pleasure to have worked with, or competed against, Dan Cook for much of the 49 years he has been associated with the Express-News. He is one of a kind and, as unhappy as he might find the term, a genuine institution. I hold him in the highest esteem and thank him on behalf of San Antonio newspaper folk for his contribution to the industry. There are some limitations to that esteem, however:

1. Thirty years or so ago, he could have done a bit more to help me defeat Bobby Riggs in a now-legendary match Dan and I played against the old master at Trinity. Riggs beat us (surprise!) despite the fact that he wore a muumuu dress and carried a valise in his left hand while playing us.

2. Dan could have been more responsive to my efforts to lure him to The San Antonio Light during my days there as publisher. Despite lavish offers that would have made David Robinson blush, Dan steadfastly refused to come over to our side. No thanks to Cook, I finally resolved that problem by buying the Express-News, although all of my associates thought that a bit drastic as a recruitment technique.

Blackie Sherrod
Dallas Morning News

For some time now — about 15 minutes in fact — I have been trying to remember how far I go back with Dan Cook. Rutherford B. Hayes was in the White House, I think, or maybe it was Abraham Lincoln. Suffice it to say, it was before Mr. Cook had his trademark wrinkles.

I knew Dan during his stays in Beaumont and Houston and, of course, the last century in San Antonio, where he is pointed out with only slightly less frequency and fondness than the Alamo. Whatever I say about him and this column collection will be highly prejudicial, of course, because of our long palship and possibly because I owe him money. Besides, if I act nice he has promised me a free book, or at least one with a ministerial discount.

Anyways, over the past half-century, we have waged a gallant-if-losing war on Texas journalism, in scores of press boxes around the land and not a few library reading rooms, the ones with reasonable wassail bowls. Suffice it to say, together we have left our mark on a half-dozen Lone Star newspapers, not unlike smallpox.

Two Cook attributes have always gained my admiration; one, an usual amount of industry in two fields – newspaper and television – and, two, the weird ability to operate on a minimum of sleep. No, really, how he kept enough energy to operate full blast at two different venues has always seemed a little amazing and some of us suspect he made a deal with the Devil. I have never known him to shortchange the customer, either in print or on screen.

Dan has never been a conventional writer and that probably explains his longevity. And any collection of his work over the past half-century could well serve as a Texas sports history, told in unique form. Personally, I have found Mr. Cook to be a loyal and generous friend and deem it a duty – nay, a privilege – to recommend this collection to one and all.

You won't be bored and, in the final reckoning of our business, that is the acid test.

This collection of columns is dedicated to

Katy, my wife of 49 years.

For more than a decade, she put the children to bed

while I helped put the newspaper to bed.

THE '50S

His position reminds me of something my Uncle Ray used to tell me when I tried to cope with him in a sporting contest called gin rummy. "Boy," he would say, "the sweetest music in the world is to hear a sucker cry."

November 29, 1956

The Maiden Voyage of Cook's Tour

This short chunk of type is to introduce a new column – probably the only column in the newspaper that is absolutely necessary. It is necessary to the author, not to the newspaper.

The first newspaper printed in the United States came off the presses in 1764 and the first column followed six days later. As a rule, columnists can be placed in three categories: (1) Writers who have something to say, (2) editors who have to say something and (3) reporters who have nothing to say but with enough extra time on their hands in which to say it.

This "author" falls into the latter category, having been caught with feet upon desk and Spillane's latest in full view. Thus, today we begin a new column but make no promises.

The space this bit occupies from time to time (and those times will depend upon how much time we've got) will be of no particular service. This column doesn't figure to educate or enlighten but the editor is working on the theory that if we have enough extra time to write it some weary hunter or perhaps retired polo referee will have enough extra time to read it.

Editors aren't always right but they have the power to make reporters feel awfully wrong. And besides, you'd be surprised at the number of weary hunters and retired polo referees there are in this city.

And now, just so your time won't be altogether wasted on an introduction, we offer you a couple of gems gathered from intelligent conversations, record books, gin mills and locker rooms that weren't locked.

■ Archie Moore, who fights Floyd Patterson Friday night for the heavyweight bankroll of boxing, announced his first retirement from the ring the same year Patterson started kindergarten. That was in 1941. But time changes all. In 1942 Archie made his first comeback and Patterson moved to the first grade. This proves absolutely nothing but it brings to mind a remark Moore once made about Jersey Joe Walcott. Archie said that Walcott would never be a big drawing card as champion because he was "too old." People who live in grass houses shouldn't throw lawnmowers.

■ Our libraries and museums are filled with statues of naked Olympic runners and wrestlers. Reason for this is simple. Athletes used to run and wrestle naked.

A couple of Greeks got this Olympic business started in the year 392 A.D. and in those days the boys wore loincloths, sheets or whatever momma could spare from the bed. And then in 720 A.D. along came a distance runner named Orsippus of Megara. He was about a 50-1 dark horse in the race but somewhere down the line he lost his loincloth. Orsippus continued on as naked as a jaybird and he shipwrecked the bookies of that day by scoring a surprise victory. Hence, athletes in remaining contests discarded their clothes and all ran naked for many years.

You see, there are reasons for everything.

And the reasons for this column are weary hunters and retired polo referees.

February 8, 1957

Some would do away with the old pool hall,
They say for the youth, it's a real pitfall.
While others still argue, with backs to the wall
Delinquency isn't hatched from a white cue ball.

A Champion Speaks

"What this country needs is a good five-cent cigar." Those are the words of Thomas R. Marshall, and ever since the vice president spoke them in 1920 people have been telling us what this country needs most — other than nickel stogies.

The main topic nowadays in the "what we need" department seems to be a way to combat juvenile delinquency. Everybody who has ever been asked has some sort of solution to offer and most of the answers hinge around sports programs featuring more ballparks, swimming pools and the like.

But now comes Harold Worst with his solution and if it doesn't work the idea may set law enforcers back half a century.

In case you've just returned from a three-year African safari and

3

haven't heard, Mr. Worst has won great fame with a black tuxedo and a slender brown stick. In short, Worst is the world champion for three-cushion billiards.

Just why billiard stars find themselves compelled to perform in black tuxedos has always been beyond me. Perhaps it's because the stiff tux gives the man enough "lift" that he can forget the dingy pool hall in which he learned his trade as a boy.

Be that as it may, Mr. Worst suggests "more old-fashioned pool rooms" for our teen-agers. He adds that "the pool halls kept young boys off the streets and gave them something more worthwhile to do than run around in souped-up cars and chase girls."

The billiard champ is very unhappy that civic groups and lawmakers are banning pool halls in more and more states each year. He insists that in the old poolrooms "even a kid looking for trouble couldn't do more than get into a short fistfight."

Now Mr. Worst may know of what he speaks, but if he prefers getting a punch on the snoot in a "short" fistfight to chasing girls in a souped-up car he's just nuts.

Eager to aid this juvenile delinquency problem in any way possible, we localized the pool hall situation by bringing it to the attention of Mr. Merald (Skinny) Grant, lifetime San Antonio resident who is reputed to be the city's nine-ball champion.

Mr. Grant does not own a tuxedo so he is somewhat handicapped when working. And too, he holds no official title.

His position reminds me of something my Uncle Ray used to tell me when I tried to cope with him in a sporting contest called gin rummy. "Boy," he would say, "the sweetest music in the world is to hear a sucker cry."

Well, folks, Mr. Grant has heard his share of sweet music in this world.

But that's another story and today we are dealing with juvenile delinquency and pool halls. Mr. Grant had this to say about the matter. "Outbreaks of juvenile delinquency come and go but pool parlors are here to stay. Parents are just looking for something or somebody else to blame for their own failures. Why blame pool? Kids can meet anywhere to cook up trouble, even at church parties."

Anyone for pool?

Now Dig This, Dad

They're teaching the English language today about the same as they did when hamburger meat sold for nine cents a pound, but for some reason or another kids just don't talk the same.

Oh, sure, they use the same words. It's just that they put them in different places. I'd like to see an English professor attempt to diagram one of their sentences.

This rock-and-roll stuff, they say, is for the cats. Personally, I think it's for the birds. But ever since Elvis wiggled onto the scene his weird-speaking followers have grown to great numbers.

Now, this newspaper is dedicated to community service and since the community is loaded with jive-talking gents, I think it's only fair to waste a little space on them.

"Gone With the Wind" has been translated into 28 languages, I'm told. "Forever Amber" has been reprinted in 26 tongues. Which only means that the Turks and Arabs will have to wait a little longer to learn of Amber's love life.

But these classic tales have been translated for all to read and I think some sports bits are worth translating and reprinting. So, for the benefit of the Be-boppers and Gone Cats, I offer a few items from yesteryear — translated especially for them in their language, of course.

Rockne's famous halftime talk: "Now dig me, men. Those Cats are mellow and they're hep to our stuff. They're wise to our tries so we gotta rise. We gotta improvise. I'm dialing you in on the right line now, men. We gotta play it cool this next half and change our ways with some new plays. They've had some square on the scene with a movie machine and I tell you the Galloping Ghost couldn't coast today. Now I want you Cats to dummy up and give some thought to Daddy-O Gipp. You dig me? All-reet, shuffle on out there now and rumble and roll for old George…Go, Go, Go."

John L. Sullivan's farewell: "When a goop like Corbett brings me it's time to dump this dodge. I'm shagging on out and may try that square job route — you know, 40 hours per. Sure, I'm a sad lad and all ironed

5

out in the financial department but I'm planning one last ball before I wagon the whiskey. This boxing has me bugged. You see, dad, I don't dig this jivey jig these modern squares use. I'm a guy who tries the short haul in a barroom brawl and get hep to this, I can still kill any louse in the house."

June 6, 1957

Harlon Hill, Country Boy

It's amazing, all of this talk about a depression.

Why, just the other night I ran into a bargain that couldn't have been matched when Grover Cleveland was in office.

For the price of one beer I heard a four-piece band play five numbers, watched 24 couples dance on a 22-foot floor and learned that when Harlon Hill was 9 years old his entire wardrobe consisted of a pair of overalls.

Now how's that for a bargain? And I could have heard that band play longer but I didn't have 40 cents more for another beer.

Hill, as you may know, is one of the hottest professional football players in the country today. During the season, George Blanda does the pitching and Hill does the catching to make Chicago's Bears a threat at all times.

But this, of course, is not during the season so when I shuffled into the Tiffany Lounge a fellow named Johnny Jowdy — owner, operator and bartender of the joint — was pitching in the absence of Blanda. Results were the same. Harlon caught everything that came his way.

But don't get the idea Hill is a wild sort of gent who hits the joy juice hard. Actually, he's one of the nicest guys in sports today. He just likes to relax and soak up a bottle of suds every now and then.

Somewhere between the band's versions of "All Shook Up" and "White Sports Coat And Pink Carnation," I discovered a country boy with big-city class.

He's the kind of guy who pays eight dollars for a T-shirt and $4.50 for a French-cuffed dress job. Now how much more big city can you get?

But things weren't always that way. Harlon was raised on a farm in

Alabama and if you've ever wondered how he learned to get downfield and behind defensive backs so fast you quit guessing right now and give a share of credit to a big red rooster.

Jowdy's band was "Rocking At the Cosmo" when Harlon told me how he used to chase chickens as a kid on his father's farm. Well, it wasn't really his dad's farm but they were working it and besides, that's another story. Anyway, Harlon would imagine himself a big-time grid star dashing after fleet ball carriers as he legged it around after the capones. He had a big red rooster that could outstep Red Grange but the chicken, like Grange, finally wore down and eventually it was nothing for Harlon to overhaul him three times a day.

Yes sir, Harlon was a real country boy. He chopped cotton and milked cows for work and rode bulls and broke plow mules for play. But too much rough stuff didn't pay off. As I mentioned earlier, he had only one pair of overalls to his name and when they needed washing Harlon had to hide his nakedness under the bed covers and get "while-U-wait" service.

Sometimes things were pretty rough on the old farm. But football has changed all that. And well it should. After all, the big guy caught 11 touchdown passes last year and four of those grabs won ballgames.

The frolicky foursome gave out with "Tea for Two" as a collegiate-looking youth named Bobby Lance joined us. "You'll be hearing a lot about this boy," Harlon said as he made with the introductions.

Lance, like Hill, is stationed at Fort Sam. Lance, unlike Hill, will be around to help the BAMC Comets this football season. Hill will rejoin the Bears come September. Still, the Comets should be happy to keep one of these gentlemen. Lance was a great quarterback for the University of Florida in '54 and '55. Of course, he belongs to Uncle Sam right now but the Green Bay Packers have the first lien on him.

Lance ordered a round of suds as the band hurled a loud rendition of "Rocking Shoes" at an unsuspecting audience.

Yes sir, there are a lot of bargains still around. You just have to know where to look.

October 31, 1957

The Bear Will Leave the Aggies

For lo these many years now wire services and newspapers alike have pushed on readers red-hot tips and rumor stories that always come from "reliable sources." Now, those sources of information can be from Denny the Dip or Bob the Bartender – it makes no difference. If the reporter believes the report, it came from a "reliable source."

So today I offer my tip story but you must keep in mind that it comes from a most unreliable source.

And now, the story.

The big Bear is ready to pack his whistle, chalk and cap, surrender his three-year supply of rear-window Aggie stickers and leave College Station.

That's right, a most unreliable source tells me that this is Paul "Bear" Bryant's last season as head coach of the Texas Aggies.

Yes, I know. Kathy can leave Bing, Sputnik can leave Andy but Bear should never leave the Aggies. Still, don't be surprised if the sweatpants that Bryant is wearing this time next year are labeled "Property of the University of Alabama."

Word leaked out last week that Alabama fans no longer enjoy fall weekends and have decided to do something about it. Those folks figure their Sundays will be happier if the present coach's Saturdays are spent elsewhere so that's exactly where he's going to spend them in 1958 — elsewhere.

It's simple arithmetic that if 50 teams win another 50 must lose but the 'Bama boys are growing weary of receiving so many kickoffs each game. So the SOS went out to Bryant and some folks will tell you Bear was happy to hear from his old alma mater.

It is well to remember that Bryant is sort of a football soldier of fortune and the fortune is always largest where the need is greatest. Alabama has a small fortune and a desperate need. And, too, Bear probably would like nothing better than to return his old school to the gridiron glory it once knew but has long since forgotten.

The wise word has it that Bryant was contacted by Alabama wheels

8

and offered the job but Bear denies all such reports and insists he is very happy at Aggieland. Maybe so, but will he be happy there in February of '58?

The Aggies will wave a contract and howl like never before but Bryant will wave only his hand and move on down the road. The Bear is a builder and he has built the Aggies into national championship contention. The challenge now awaits him at Alabama – the challenge and a name-your-own-price contract.

Why then, you ask, does he deny these stories of his departure now? Simply because a coach and his players are as one – a team – and knowledge that the boss was soon lamming out could strain the close ties so badly needed between player and coach.

Despite scholarship and extra help squabbles, college football is still basically amateur – all but the coach. Don't ever forget that the coach is a pro and with him it's a bread-and-butter situation.

If a pro can get a thicker slice of bread down the line he usually starts checking the train schedules. Which brings us to this important question. How often do the trains leave College Station?

NOTE: As predicted, several weeks after this column was printed the train left College Station with Bear Bryant on it. He became head coach at Alabama in 1958.

February 18, 1958

Soul-Saving Sharpshooter

The finger that suspended in mid-air belonged to Samuel Slotsky, and if you sighted over the back of it you could easily see it was aimed at an elderly man wearing the black suit and white collar of a Catholic priest.

"There stands the world's greatest gunman and big-game hunter," Mr. Slotsky announced as he pushed the finger deeper into a light rain. It still pointed at the priest across the street, so I followed its line and came face to face with the Rev. Oswald T. McGinn.

Introductions followed and an interview resulted and it might be well to pause here and state that Father McGinn is one of the most interesting and lovable characters I've ever met. To some it may seem disrespectful to call a 79-year-old priest a character but this would seem so only to those who have not come in contact with Father McGinn.

Father McGinn, a saintly Irishman with an impish twinkle in his eyes, is a soul-saving preacher by trade but a moose-killing outdoorsman by hobby.

The rain had left his cigar in an idle state. He fumbled for a match. "Better to smoke here than in the hereafter," he said through a cloud of smoke.

"I'm pushing 80 now so I'm retired but once a priest always a priest," Father McGinn offered. "I say Mass every morning but I guess I do a little more hunting and shooting now that I'm sort of on my own a little more."

At 77 the good father was still pastor of Holy Name Church in Saginaw, Mich., and two years ago he celebrated his Golden Jubilee anniversary as a priest. During those 50 years he distinguished himself as an explorer of the Arctic, a lecturer, debater and scholar besides ministering to his beloved congregation.

Three years ago Father McGinn began wintering in San Antonio and on his big Jubilee E. A. Hatton of this city presented him with a beautiful, handmade .22-250 rifle. The only one of its kind, this gun has a gold magazine and is one of the sharp-shooting padre's proudest possessions.

"How much do you figure it's worth, Father?"

"Well, I'll tell you. I never look a gift horse in the mouth but I guess it must be valued at about $2,500."

Father McGinn has a room with the Frank Seidemans on Mission Street and it's a rather typical layout for a Catholic priest with a few exceptions. The holy pictures and holy water are there but atop the dresser are stacked seven boxes of Tampa Nuggets and over his bed is a painting of a big bull moose.

Personally, I would hate to look at this moose every morning upon arising, but to borrow an old one, to each his own.

Truly, Father McGinn is a most unusual man. He was born on Christmas Day. He has appeared on national television shows many times. He has been featured in many magazines, including Sports Illustrated.

Even at 79 he can flip a gun upside down or fire between his legs and still hit a tiny target some 50 yards away. He can place three bullets in a half-inch target at 100 yards and all three shots will pierce the same hole.

And among other things he can split a bullet on a razor blade causing the split pieces to hit small targets on either side of the blade. And all this without once changing the position of his cigar.

Father McGinn is as spry as a kid and his wit is razor sharp. But what are his plans now that he is crowding the 80 mark? "Why, I plan to make a long safari hunt in Africa sometime soon, maybe next year."

Father Oswald T. McGinn, with all due respect, is a wonderful character.

Television Messages

There will be only a short tour today. Things are not well at my house. I have a sore throat and a burning tongue. I have been smoking too much. My little girl also has a sore throat. She is only 4 and does not smoke at all. Her throat is sore because her tonsils were removed yesterday. They were lifted against her wishes, as is always the case with 4-year-olds.

While minding the home store I have spent more time with my television set lately. This machine box of electronics is very informative but you must stay on your toes to get it all. If you're the type who heads for the icebox or kicks the cat out during commercials you won't be as completely informed as those who remain seated for the whole show.

Just last night I was reminded that Mickey Mantle smokes a lot of Viceroy cigarettes because they are "so smooth." This came as a bit of a surprise to me since I was under the impression that Mickey did not smoke. Now I'm wondering if Mickey's tongue burns like mine. I imagine Mickey can afford to have a burning tongue for what the Viceroy people give him. My cigarette dealer doesn't even give me trading stamps.

Willie Mays and Duke Snider both smoke Camels and shave with Gillette razors. Cary Middlecoff puffs on a Viceroy before every putt. Bud Palmer drinks gallons of Florida orange juice and Doak Walker soaks his head with enough Vitalis to float the biggest craft at the San Antonio Boat Show.

Maxie Rosenbloom likes the piggyback refill his Paper-mate provides and Casey Stengel goes for a whole gob of shaving equipment. It's odd.

Casey should be the most closely shaved character in baseball yet the New York writers keep referring to him as the "grizzled old fellow with a day-old beard."

These are important messages if you are a sports fan.

My television set was about to tell me of Sam Snead's latest love but I had to kick the cat out. And besides, Marie – that's my little girl – was hollering louder than the television was playing. Marie was not crying because her throat was sore. She was crying because she wanted her tonsils back.

I lit a cigarette. It tasted good – even on my burned tongue.

M a y   2 9 ,   1 9 5 8

Red Just Likes Baseball

Red McCombs was leaning over the box-seat railing talking to ballplayers the first time I saw him.

He was obviously a happy man. You know, talking to the players and all. He was dressed conservatively but there was nothing conservative about the smile Red wore.

Billy J. (Red) McCombs thinks baseball is the greatest game going today and already he's done more than his share to keep it going.

We headed for the roof so we could talk without interruption. Red knows a lot of people and I figured the press box might be the best spot to chat. Besides, the drinks are free up there.

As we left the box-seat section Red aimed his finger at a big guy wearing Dallas' gray uniform. "See that fellow over there? That's Keith Little."

"Yeah, I know."

"Sure, but did you know he hit the longest ball ever tagged in Corpus Christi? It went over the left-field wall."

"That's not so far."

"It also went over the lights in left field."

"Oh."

Red is what you might call a country boy who made good in the big cities. He was born 30 years ago in Spur, Texas. Spur is near Lubbock. I forget just what Lubbock is near but it has no bearing on this column so I'll not bother to look it up.

McCombs has spent most of his adult life selling automobiles and today he's vice president and general manager of Hemphill's Ford Center. He's also a partner in the business with Austin Hemphill and he and Austin both will tell you that business is good.

Red was selling cars in Corpus Christi back in '53 when he received his first real bite from the baseball bug. Nothing more than a fan at the time, McCombs became interested in the push to save the city's franchise. The club was $40,000 on the wrong side of the ledger when George Schepps, park owner, pulled up stakes and retreated to Dallas.

"George Jones was owner of the Ford agency in Corpus where Hemphill and I worked," Red said. "We talked him into rallying businessmen to pay off the debt. He did, too. But only on the condition that I could find an operator for the club who would put in $10,000 to keep the team going."

Bob Hamric, an old schoolmate of Red's, agreed to buy controlling interest if the $40,000 back bill was paid off. But it seems that at the last minute Bob fell short of his financial goal. It was too late then to turn back so who stepped up? – why, Red McCombs the automobile man, of course.

McCombs and Hamric owned 54 percent of the team's stock until just last year.

"We still own the facilities — lights, stands and the such — but to this day I've never drawn a penny in salary or any other way," Red says.

"In other words, you got stung."

"Oh, no. I wouldn't trade the experiences for any amount of money. The realness of baseball — knowing the little things that affect every game and every player — are worth more than any cash I put up."

We left the press box and started downstairs. On the way out Red was telling me how he thought baseball was in a cycle and right now we were going through the unhealthy part. "But much better years are just ahead for the sport," he concluded.

Red McCombs was leaning over the box-seat railing talking to ballplayers the last time I saw him.

———

The Mystery Gun

I am the owner of the strangest gun in all America. It's a .32 caliber automatic pistol and it shoots all day on just two cartridges.

You'd think this odd feature would be a great money saver with the price of ammunition so high. But friend, that's not the way things stand.

I purchased this strange firearm from Mr. Gene Toudouze, a close friend who owns a hardware store. He thought the gun was empty and tested it before making the sale. He now owns a hardware store with a hole in the ceiling.

If this can happen to my good friend who is so familiar with guns I figured a greenhorn like myself should take extra care.

Arriving home with my pistol I circled the family around to give a short lecture on the danger of firearms. In great detail I told how all precautions should be taken with such a deadly weapon.

I then placed three cartridges in the clip and exhibited the proper and safest manner to handle a gun. Wyatt Earp would have been proud of me. Completing the talk I pushed back the business end three times and ejected three bullets.

"Now and only now is this gun perfectly safe," I announced. And with this I pointed my pistol toward the window and squeezed its trigger.

Unless some immediate adjustments are made at our house we're in for a cold winter. My bedroom window now sports a hole about the size of a quarter. As a matter of fact it's the same size hole that can be found in Mr. Toudouze's ceiling.

Somewhere in my demonstration I made a serious error. But it's all right. If a lecturer gets his point across in an impressive manner he has met success. Let it be known here and now that my audience was impressed.

Mr. Mike Henson was almost impressed. He's my next-door neighbor. Had he parked his car just a few feet farther to the left of his driveway he most certainly would have walked to work. By lining up the hole in my screen with the hole in the window it was easy to see I missed Mr. Henson's front tire by just a foot. That would have impressed him.

14

Recent stories about rabid dogs and mysterious coyotes prompted us to purchase the pistol. However, I hated to keep a gun in the closet because of my children. But that's no problem now. They're afraid to go near the gun. I'm afraid to go near the closet.

The manufacturer says this pistol holds nine shots. Just nine. No more.

I'd hate to remove nine cartridges from the thing and snap it at my other bedroom window. It could be a very cold winter.

September 3, 1959

Living Legend

He could live to be a thousand but as he strolled down modern streets or ancient roads small children and old men would still whisper his name while he passed – "That's him, Jack Dempsey, Jack Dempsey, Jack Dempsey."

The tough kid who started fighting in 1914 under the name of Kid Blackie today has no equal in the eyes of a hero-worshipping sports world. The magic web he spun about himself in the Roaring '20s keeps him apart from all others. Only the late and great Babe Ruth was ever on a par with the man from Manassa, Colo.

It was as if time stood still for a moment in the News editorial room yesterday at 2:35 p.m. Typewriters cooled. Work stopped. All eyes focused in one direction. On one man. Jack Dempsey was moving up the hallway.

Years have been kind to the former heavyweight champion of the world but weeks of heavy travel showed in his eyes. Long streaks of gray occupied both sides of his full head of hair. A fat cigar poked from his rugged but almost handsome face. Still a powerful figure at 64 he offered firm handshakes to all in the area. And then he sat down.

Thousands of interviews by some of the world's top writers have left Dempsey a confident, quick-thinking speaker. He anticipates the questions. He knows the answers. He talks clearly but fast. Almost too fast.

"Mr. Dempsey, why did you allow yourself to become so involved in the Johansson-Patterson promotion mess just when a lot of bad characters were being exposed as behind-the-scenes investors in the thing?"

"You've answered the question yourself. It was a mess and getting worse. A lot of people I've never heard of were getting into the thing to make it an even darker picture. I did it for boxing. No money on my part was involved. I just thought boxing deserved something better than the name it was getting."

"Then you received no money for your part as chief of negotiations for a return bout?"

"I got $500 a day for expenses and that included my plane fare to Sweden to see Johansson. We wrapped it up sooner than expected so I still had two days' expenses left. I told Johansson he could have that thousand to give to any charity in Sweden he liked. I kept nothing."

The man who became a living legend after two losing efforts with Gene Tunney refused to pick a winner of the next Patterson-Johansson fight. But he seemed to lean toward the Swede and he made it clear that he sincerely felt such a second bout would take place next year.

"I think Johansson is a much better fighter than most people believe. He bides his time and waits his chance. And he can hit with that right. I'll usually take a good puncher over a good boxer in 15 rounds."

More questions, more answers, a few pictures and Dempsey was ready to leave. His cigar was shorter by three inches.

Tall at 6-1 and heavy at 225 the former fighter greeted late onlookers, signed several autographs and moved to depart. Here to referee a wrestling match, Dempsey was on a busy tour.

Ad salesmen, copy readers and editors of all sorts strained for a last look as the big man legged it toward the elevator. It takes a pretty important celebrity to shake up veteran newsmen. Few indeed can do it. But this was different. This was Dempsey.

As he rounded the hall you could almost hear the hushed chant swell a few notes higher — "That's him, Jack Dempsey, Jack Dempsey, Jack Dempsey."

Inside Info

It's best, I'm told, to consider all sources and gather views from many folks before jumping to conclusions on weighty matters. At least that's what I've been told.

So it was with this in mind that I sought out one Benjamin Broadhind, better known in social circles as Benny The Book. It is a fact known to many that Mr. Broadhind has had a great deal of experience in selecting football winners. And that's what I wanted for today's column – winners.

Benny The Book was operating from the back booth of a tavern when I closed in on him yesterday. Copies of The Sporting News, Wall Street Journal and Sunbathers' Review were spread across the table that hid his oversized stomach. He was sipping the sweet nectar of a spirited beverage when I invaded his privacy.

"Pardon me, Mr. Book — I mean, Mr. Broadhind. But I'd very much like to discuss a little football activity with you."

"Sorry, son. I ain't taking no action anymore. I'm retired. And son, unlike Marciano, I did not retire undefeated."

"Yes sir. But I thought you might care to make a few guesses for the readers of Friday's News. No money would be involved."

"Little friend, you're way off base. I'm too old to lose my professional standing and turn amateur. That 'no money involved' statement you just made has terminated our conversation. Besides, son, I never guess. I know what I'm talking about or I just don't talk. Young fellow, if I tell you a mule rides double just put two on his back and beat him. Understand?"

Mr. Broadhind glanced through the Wall Street Journal. His trained eyes skipped over the tiny figures quickly. And then he traded the Journal for his Sunbathers' Review. This time his eyes spent more time on the figures. Benny The Book is a man of multiple interests.

And finally he spoke again.

"Tell you what, son. I'm going to extend to you a break. I read your prediction column last Friday and you missed three out of 10 in a most inexcusable manner. Seven were OK but somebody pumped weak information into your ear on the other three. I won't say you deserve a break.

But you certainly need one."

"Wonderful. Then you will allow me to print your selections?"

"Yes, I'm going to benefit you with some extra specials for the week. But just to retain my professional standing you will be so kind as to pick up my beer tab on your way out."

"That's very kind of you, Mr. Broadhind."

"Yes, it is for a fact."

And now to sum things up rapidly here is the information extracted from a dark den of drink.

Texas will defeat Maryland by seven points but only after a bruising, seesaw battle; Mississippi Southern will turn down Trinity by 13 points; Arkansas will nose Oklahoma State by seven; Baylor will whip Colorado by six; SMU will pass past Georgia Tech by a touchdown; LSU will edge TCU in an extremely close contest; Texas A&M will bow to Michigan State by three touchdowns; Texas Tech will slip past Oregon State and Houston will upset Alabama.

Here's a couple of real specials. Northwestern will knock off highly respected Oklahoma on national TV and Wyoming will upset Air Force Academy.

At least that's what the man said.

The Big Classic

For years now I've heard of the wild downtown celebrations after each Texas-Oklahoma football game in Dallas. But until Saturday I'd never before been in Big D for one of these contests. I was disappointed.

Oh, sure, there was a great crowd for a fine game. And they tore the goalposts down when it was all over. But the downtown mob that night was no wilder than a usual Saturday night gathering in San Antonio after a military payday. It was rather tame.

The gin mills did a landslide business and hotel lobbies were loaded. But it was all so orderly. A piano plunker at one joint ripped off "The Eyes of Texas" and half the folks joined in song and everybody clapped. Then he reeled through a chorus or two of "Boomer Sooner." The other half sang this one and again everyone applauded.

I thought he was a mighty brave fellow to take such a risk – playing both school songs before a packed house in a den of drink. But there were no jeers, hoots or fistfights. Just applause and song.

I shouldn't say I was disappointed. Because I really prefer it this way. But it was a bit of a letdown after expecting middle-of-the-street bonfires and free-for-all slugging bouts as in other years.

In the lobby of one major hotel a crowd of 30 or 40 huddled together and gave a college yell. Which college were they yelling for? Why, Missouri, of course. I'm not at all sure what Missouri boosters were doing in Dallas but no one else bothered to ask them and I personally didn't care if they sneezed their cheers for Kleenex Kollege.

Dallas police deserve a pat on the back for the way they handled details in general on the busy Saturday. But they also rate a chewing out for the manner in which they handled the "scalpers."

Tickets for the big game were all sold weeks in advance. So there figured to be a lot of scalping. But law enforcers, it seems to me, should set their sights on big professionals who make a habit of cornering several dozen ducats and pushing them at illegal prices.

If Joe Cluck is offered $20 for his lone $4.50 ticket as he approaches the stadium I figure it ought to be up to Joe to decide which he wants more – to see the game or pocket the twin sawbuck. After all, they don't tell Pete Smith, the merchant downtown, how much he can sell his overcoats for.

At any rate, about 150 folks milled in front of the Cotton Bowl prior to the game carrying signs such as "I need two tickets" or "Help, just one ticket, please."

Several of these sign bearers were policemen in civilian clothes. One officer offered a fellow $15 for a ticket but before a deal was closed the seller sensed a trap and pulled away. It might be that he spotted the bulge in the man's hip pocket. A bulge caused by a policeman's .38 revolver.

This was just one of the many little free shows offered in Dallas Saturday. They say the best things in life are free but most things in Dallas last weekend cost like thunder. Little book matches, usually given away, went two for a nickel.

Police looked in the wrong direction. They should have forgotten about scalpers and arrested that man selling book matches.

THE '60s

Actually, I'm no authority on basketball. Or anything else, for that matter. But I've got opinions on everything. When you come here for an opinion you've come to the right place. You might not get a good one but you'll sure get one.

Cuban Scene

The wheels are about to come off the Cuban sports scene. Cuban athletes alone are not enough to keep gates up, profits high and fans pleased. Yet the ever-present threat of mass violence makes the country unattractive to visitors and the resulting problem of economics may soon leave Havana a sports ghost town.

Take, for instance, the case of Danny McShane, a mean wrestler by trade but a nice guy to chat with.

"I'll never go back again. Fact is, I never thought I'd get out of there this last time," Mr. McShane said as he stroked his thin mustache. "I was wrestling a Cuban cop and for some reason or other there wasn't a person in the place pullin' for me. And you just know how hard they were pullin' for him."

However, that didn't form the base of McShane's problems in Cuba. But let him tell it, from the beginning.

"This is about the beginning of the tourist season so I was a little suspicious when my plane flight from Miami to Havana departed with only three passengers. It was a 40-seat plane but still I made up one-third of the passenger list. When we arrived, the airport was swarming with bearded soldiers. Everybody who owned a beard owned a gun and there weren't many clean-shaven faces around.

"Pedro Godoy, a Cuban wrestler, borrowed his sister's car to show me the sights. Naturally, he wheeled me by Castro's house, explaining that the man played a game very similar to musical chairs. Only this was musical houses. He owned about 10 houses and slept in a different one each night so his enemies wouldn't interrupt his sleep."

McShane, at this point in his tale, slacked off for a running start at the meat of his Cuban adventure.

"We had just passed Castro's house – the one he was supposed to be using at the moment – when a plane swooped down and hit it with a bomb. Windows cracked in our car – Pedro's sister's car, that is. I jumped out and slid beneath the auto and waited for the end of the world. It seemed like five full minutes before stuff quit falling.

"Funny thing, Castro wasn't in his house but I was just 200 yards from it. I guess there are a few wrestling fans who'd just as soon I'd been in it."

McShane's Irish mug, crowded with scars, clouds up when he discusses another reason he'll never return to Castro's Cuba.

"They won't let you take money out of the country to America."

"Why did you go over there to wrestle then?"

"Well, I got a real good guarantee and I was told my money would be sent to me by way of Canada. I don't like my money takin' such a long way home but they finally did send it. It went from Cuba to Canada to New York to Miami. I had about a three-week wait but it arrived."

"What was the idea of such foolishness? Or did you smuggle the money out?"

"Heck no, I'm no smuggler. They told me that was the way it was done. They just don't want any money leaving the country that's heading directly for America. I think it's part of Castro's cold war – or something."

And then my thoughts turned to one P. L. (Pinky) George, boxing impresario who guides the talents of Alejandro Lavorante. Mr. Lavorante is due to box in Havana this Saturday night. I can't help but feel that if Mr. Lavorante doesn't return to San Antonio and Manager George by early next week – with money in hand – Pinky most certainly will lead a Greek delegation against Castro in Cuba's newest and most unusual revolution.

M a y   1 8 ,   1 9 6 0

Spoiled Sugar

There is much to be said for Walker Smith, the man known to millions as Sugar Ray Robinson. And there is just as much to be said against this pugilistic wonder who defies the laws of Father Time as well as man-made rules.

No athlete in sports history rose to great fame from a lower beginning. Not even Babe Ruth's orphanage days can compare with Robinson's hot afternoons on the sidewalks of Harlem. For it was there that the ragged urchin named Walker Smith danced for pennies and those coins meant the difference between going a little hungry and downright starvation.

From such a humble start came one of the greatest ring-men ever to flash – and stay and stay – onto the boxing horizon. A master craftsman, the skinny-legged Negro compiled a phenomenal amateur record to become an immediate success. He had 90 bouts and won them all – 70 by knockouts in the first round.

In time he became welterweight champion of the world and when Robinson was just two days shy of his 38th birthday he won the middleweight championship of the world – for the fifth time.

The kid who danced for pennies grew up to dance in swanky nightclubs for $15,000 a week. And to dance in boxing arenas in a much more serious manner for many times this amount.

These things can be said in Robinson's favor.

Such fantastic success almost completely overshadows the fact that Robinson is a selfish, self-centered dictator who does exactly as he pleases with no regard or respect for the well-being or rules of others in his profession.

If ever a sport desperately needed an iron-fisted, just commissioner it most certainly is boxing. This latest Robinson stunt – failing to show up for a fight in Baltimore – gives only further evidence of the need.

As mentioned, Robinson's great success has overshadowed his dirty deeds that have sent more than one promoter in search of co-signers for bank loans. The public knows that Sugar Ray is a devastating puncher who has won more honors than any other boxer. The public has forgotten that Sugar Ray has broken more contracts and lied to more promoters than any other pug in boxing history.

The saddest part about it all is that he gets away with it each time.

Robinson has been around so long that few remember how he deserted the Army the night he was called for overseas duties. So perhaps it would take more than a boxing commissioner to straighten the actions of this man. Uncle Sam couldn't do it.

There's no secret to the method Robinson uses on his "skip-outs." George Gainford, a greedy old goat who manages the champ, checks the advance ticket sales two days prior to the actual bout. If sales are down it's an even money bet that Robinson will beg off with a hand or back "injury." If the gate is far off expected figures, it's almost a cinch

Robinson won't show. Such was the case at Baltimore.

A lot of fans are wondering just when Sugar Ray will retire. I only wish I were boxing commissioner for one day. I'd answer the question in a hurry.

Backward Glance

It was late Wednesday night. The ballgame was over. The last fan had long since departed. Only dim lights from beneath the stands prevented complete darkness. Only the low chatter and occasional laughter of two clean-up attendees broke the silence.

There are 64 steps from the press box down to the park's main aisle. I paused somewhere between 35 and 40 to rest my heavy load – the typewriter, scorebook, pencils and excess poundage a fellow gains over the years while sitting to use these other items.

Wondering about the Missions' home schedule, the date crossed my mind – July 6. The thought lingered and finally my mind galloped back 16 years almost to the hour. Back to another baseball park. To another city.

It was on July 6, 1944, exactly 16 years ago, that I got into this wacky, tiring, frustrating, wonderful business. My first assignment on that July 6 night carried me to Buffalo Stadium in Houston where I was to chronicle a baseball event for the Houston Post. This contest involved two Negro teams, the Kansas City Monarchs and the Cincinnati Clowns. It was only an exhibition but I was scared stiff.

"Let's see if you can write, kid. Get out to the ballpark and bring back a short story on the game," the man said. In those days they paid you exactly what you were worth and some on the staff thought I was overpaid when they awarded me a weekly salary of $25.

Sixteen years is a long time between ballparks and in all those seasons I haven't played four innings. I got a few hits and was charged with a few errors. But for the life of me I couldn't recall a single day that didn't supply at least a few hours of interesting pleasure.

Another light below the stands went off, making it difficult to find an ending to the curved sea of empty seats. A heavy, steady splash of water could be heard rising from the diamond area. Felix, the somewhat ancient groundskeeper, was applying a late coat of water to the thirsty infield. At least, I guessed it was Felix.

A fine business, I thought. Sportswriting, not groundskeeping. What other profession provides a ringside seat to a lifetime of thrills. And with a solid excuse for some to attend them all.

What other business, I wondered, could have brought me introductions to and conversations with such men as Babe Ruth, Joe DiMaggio, Rogers Hornsby, Dizzy Dean, Ben Hogan, Jack Dempsey, Joe Louis and Sammy Baugh. And such women as Babe Zaharias, the most fabulous female sports ever knew, and Florence Chadwick and Louise Suggs and Betty Jameson.

Felix was through watering and only the front office light and a cloud-hidden moon permitted any vision in the old park they call "Beautiful Mission Stadium." I gathered my typewriter, scorebook, and pencils to head back in and write another baseball story. Just as I had done exactly 16 years ago.

Not all things are changed by time.

November 4, 1960

Eyes of Texas

Many a goosebump dots the arms of spectators at Austin's Memorial Stadium when the Longhorn Band strikes up "The Eyes of Texas" just prior to the start of football games.

Many a drunk staggers to attention in nightclubs the nation over when orchestras hit the tune that once belonged to railroad workers.

It's the official school song of the state university but thousands of Texans who've never seen the halls of any college long ago adopted it as the musical introduction to stand and shout "Yowie" whenever it's played in distant territories.

But it started as a joke.

Perhaps you already know how the "Eyes of Texas" came into being. Perhaps. But it wasn't until just recently that I learned the true tale of how it was written in jest and received in laughter. I thought you might be interested.

Back in 1903 a member of the Longhorn Band, John Lang Sinclair, was requested to write a song for the university's annual Minstrel Show at the old Hancock Opera House.

Mr. Sinclair, a young man of many activities and various interests, was given only short notice and at that he delayed until the last hour. Finally, standing backstage and scribbling on brown wrapping paper, he hit upon the "Eyes of Texas" idea as a result of a saying used by the university's president.

Col. William L. Prather was then boss-man at Texas and he had a habit of starting most lectures with, "Remember, young men, the eyes of Texas are upon you." Often, when verbally chewing on a student for some deed of misconduct, he might start, "Your bad actions may have been covered by the dark of night but the eyes of Texas were upon you."

And so it was that Sinclair, strictly as a joke, penned the words to the tune of the "Levee Song" for that 1903 Minstrel Show.

When it was sung on stage students rolled with laughter and they say even the stern president allowed a broad smile. Wild applause greeted the song's debut and Sinclair, dressed in minstrel attire and blackface, was summoned for an encore. He sang the song in almost perfect imitation of President Prather's serious tone and solemn expression and students left the show doing the same with no feeling of school patriotism.

It was a hilarious joke, enjoyed by all.

But soon afterward death was to take the popular school president. Some students, knowing how much Col. Prather secretly enjoyed the song written to tease his talks, asked for the privilege to sing it at his funeral. Permission was granted and for the first time "The Eyes of Texas" was sung by sincere voices. Only then did the song achieve complete dignity.

Never since has it been a laughing matter.

Shamus is Back

Sure and 'tis another Fairy tale you'll be thinking of this but he was at me own desk this very morn, sucking on a wee clay pipe and drowsily humming the familiar strains of Galway Bay.

A full mug of Irish ale rested beside me Katy's picture. Saints preserve us. 'Tis grounds for dismissal and far from me liking to be getting a pink slip on the green start of St. Paddy's Day.

Faith and begorrah, without a doubt 'twas me old friend Shamus McGuire. An elf-like creature dressed in kelly green costume, Shamus was no bigger than a king-sized Coke bottle – and built along the same lines. This wee laddie stays bloated with blarney and ale but a leprechaun's visit on St. Paddy's Day should always be welcomed.

"I'll be thanking you to take your drink from me desk, Mr. McGuire, before one of our office wheels reports for duty."

"Indeed now, O'Cook. And what might your boss be called?"

"What he is called depends on who is doing the calling and who is doing the listening and who got the last raise. But his name is Kilpatrick, Charley Kilpatrick."

"Ayee. Kilpatrick, you say. Perhaps you be right, laddie. I'll be hiding me mug of ale for one with such an Irish name is sure to toast this day with drink."

"No, no, Shamus. Mr. Kilpatrick is not one to engage in drink so early. 'Tis a fact I'm telling you that he hardly engages at all."

Taking no chances, Shamus belted the full pint with one great gulp. The ale was well-hidden and only small traces of wet evidence remained about his white whiskers.

"Now it's business we'll be getting to," Shamus said after a rude belch. "I've little time left for it's off to the golf course today. The Fathers are having their annual Irish Open and it's me solemn promise I've made to officiate. Father Michael O'Holden is the favorite and 'tis me duty to follow the favorite. The good priests take this tournament with a serious tone and I'll be watching to see that no hand mashies or foot putters are used in the woods."

With this, Shamus pushed pencil and pad in my direction. "It's notes you'll be taking. I've got some choice words."

"But Shamus, last year you told me that San Francisco would win the National League pennant. What have you to say about that?"

"Well now, 'twas only a year early that I was. This Willie O'Mays will be having a grand season and the Giants will win in a walk this year."

'Tis difficult to argue with a leprechaun so Shamus continued without interference.

"You'll be proud to hear that Floyd O'Patterson will whip that Englishman Henry Cooper this summer and then take on Sonny O'Liston early next year."

"Do you know this to be true?" I asked as Shamus moved toward the exit door.

"True it is, laddie. I've got it on good word that the order is as I've given it to you. Just yesterday I heard it in confidence from the very lips of Cus O'D'Amato. Now are there any doubts you're having?"

I had no doubts. No thoughts. The strong odor of Irish ale had lulled me into a cozy trance. Shamus gets good ale but sometimes he puts out bad information.

May   24,   1961

From Zip-Guns to Ball Diamonds

The blue '56 Ford pulled in front of the Express-News building at 2 p.m. A ham-like hand reached over, clicked the handle and an inviting door swung open.

Owner of the hand, Sgt. Leonard "Toto" Salas of the San Antonio Police Department, was right on time.

Toto was to spend the next few hours proving a point.

It is the contention of Sgt. Salas that recreation on the fields of sport supplies the most potent knockout punch we have to offer in a fight with juvenile delinquency. It is also Sgt. Salas' contention that these fields are far too few – especially on the West Side of town.

Before starting this tour with the veteran policeman it's best that you know something about Salas.

He can be tough but more often than not his bark is far worse than his bite. In his office he keeps a heavy switch but usually it is waved in bluff to help illustrate a strong point of conversation. In his car trunk he carries an arsenal of confiscated zip-guns, switchblade knives and a few clubs. But mostly in his car trunk he carries softballs, bats, boxing gloves and basketballs.

Toto demands respect from the kids with whom he deals. And he gets it. Willingly or otherwise. But this only seems fair in that he harbors a sincere liking – a mutual respect – for the youngsters and they need only to meet him halfway. But friends, they'd sure better get to the halfway mark with this cop.

His car is free of all police markings but folks on the West Side know it well. Some men spend their lives looking for oil, gold or uranium. Salas makes a big strike when he locates an unused lot that can be converted into a ball diamond. Toto, you might say, is a professional field-finder.

Take, for instance, the Pony League field located on Martin and NW 24th streets. That was a rich strike for Salas. Not long ago it was a jungle of tall weeds infested with field mice and small snakes.

Salas investigated and learned that it was city-owned property, a forgotten wasteland.

"I can't take any credit for that one," Salas says. "I just checked it out and found we could 'borrow' it if we got it cleared. Father Carmona, who used to be at Christ the King Church, called a group of his kids together and they did most of the work."

There are other diamonds that we visited, like the St. Augusta Braves Field at 5700 W. Commerce and the new Gardendale Little League plant with beautiful brick dugouts and a big backstop. But more than likely the feature of our tour took us to Rhodes Junior High School.

Here is what "outsiders" might label the West Side's hot-spot trouble area. From this neighborhood there once came more than half of the zip-guns made in San Antonio. And in this neighborhood those homemade .22 caliber pistols were often put to use.

It would not be telling any secrets to say that nearly all zip-guns today are made from stolen automobile radio antennas. The hollow tube makes a fine fit for the small-caliber bullet. The firing pin problem is solved in dozens of manners, some crude, some brilliant.

Pointing to one particularly well-made gun, Toto mumbled half to himself, "If the boy who made this had spent just half as much time learning to make the double-play he'd probably be a fine infielder now."

Outside Rhodes Junior High School there breeds the scattered remains of many well-publicized gangs such as the Ghost Town group, the Detroit gang, the Altos and the Villagers.

Inside the school there is a man who has contributed greatly to the decline of such groups. From their ranks he has used sports and just common sense to lift several gang leaders into roles of useful citizens. His name is Frank Runnels, former coach and now principal at Rhodes.

As we entered the neat building Salas had high words of praise for the school executive. "He's doing a great job out here. He likes the kids and most of them like him. And more important, he's not afraid."

He tried to overlook my next question but finally admitted that he thought there were some San Antonio principals who were afraid of the "tougher" students. "Mr. Runnels," Toto explained, "just lets them know he doesn't really think they're very tough."

Runnels welcomed us into his office, surprised at our visit. "We don't have any trouble out here," he explained. "I can't remember when we last had a fight on the school grounds. And you should see our men's room."

Just what it was that was so interesting about Rhodes' men's room I couldn't imagine but Mr. Runnels led the way. With great pride he pointed to the walls. Not a single mark, no initials. The walls were free of any and all pencil scribbling, certainly unusual in this age of Kilroy.

The gangs still exist on San Antonio's West Side. This is not to insinuate that they have been stamped out for all time. But mostly they are now led by cowards who fear to walk alone and the real would-be toughs are making good use of baseball diamonds.

Before swinging back Salas and I visited St. Timothy's Church where Toto gave Father Kenneth Hennessy a basketball he had conned from some sporting goods salesman. Baseball uniforms, perhaps from the same salesman, were dropped off at the Westside YMCA. And somewhere along the way a little kid of 10 put the bite on Salas for a new baseball bat. Salas stopped to check on the boy who had been brought to his office the week before. As is his manner, he talked roughly to the boy and then told him to use the bat on baseballs, not his neighbors.

Salas is doing a lot of good with his work. His hours take him far beyond the call of duty but it pays off. The red tie he wore on our trip was well worn and his suit sports a split seam near the right shoulder but his thoughts stay on one track – finding enough equipment and fields to keep the boys busy.

Just meet him halfway and chances are good you can get some of that equipment he carries. But pal, you'd better get to the halfway mark with him.

Maris No Hero

I want to pull for him but he won't let me. It can be of little or no importance to Roger Maris how I root when he strolls to the plate in search of another step toward Babe Ruth's record, but it's a major item to me.

I've tried to become a small part of the most exciting chapter in baseball since the big guy wore a pinstriped uniform. But he keeps me out.

I've often attempted to hurl myself into the wave of rooters pulling loudly for a new homer record. But he pushes me back.

I've secretly questioned the wisdom of those writers who long ago took pot-shots at his chances, calling him a poor substitute for the mighty Bambino. I've even wagered a few bucks around the office, betting that he WOULD break the record. But now I don't even care to pull for my opinion – or my money.

It's becoming more and more obvious that the thundering bat used by Roger Eugene Maris – loud as it might be – makes considerably less noise than the mouth of its owner.

Maris, talented as he is, must be labeled as a brooding, immature crybaby who would have been run out of baseball by the sharp-tongued bench jockeys of Ruth's day.

I only met him once for a visit of a few fleeting moments but I'm sure that if he were here now Babe Ruth would be laughing in his soda pop, beer or hot dogs. He'd go to the games, sit in the stands, root for Maris and tell everyone what a fine kid he is. But then he'd retire to the privacy of his hotel room and roar with laughter.

32

The world held just two stages for Ruth – baseball and fun. For him the two were closely related. He would have found a lot of fun in discussing Maris' childish behavior. He might have chuckled and screamed upon reading how Roger hid from newsmen Friday night, not wishing to discuss baseball on his "own time" after working hours.

At this moment Maris stands on the very threshold of becoming a national hero. But he'll never make it. Oh, he could break the homer record okay. But never, for any period longer than it takes him to round the basepaths after hitting number 60 or 61, will he be a real hero. Real heroes are loved, respected and admired by all. Maris can't fill the bill.

Because of his extraordinary talent he certainly will gain the respect of many – especially opposing pitchers. But that's about the size of it.

By his own words he tells us he's no great competitor. At the very peak of his career he wants to quit and go fishing.

Maris is the only athlete in the world today who has the power to push war-like headlines off every newspaper's first page. But he doesn't want to play anymore. As a matter of fact he has already asked his manager to bench him for a "much-needed rest."

Home-run hitter? Yes. A great one. Competitor? Goodness, no. A diluted sustitute for the likes of Ty Cobb and Ruth.

Maris fans might have ignored his blasts at umpire Hank Soar for calling "bad strikes" on him as he pursued the record, claiming he was forced to "swing in self-defense." And perhaps they overlooked his first cry of "too tired to continue." Maybe they didn't care when he refused to be interviewed anymore and hid in the Yankee trainers' quarters. And it might be that they agreed with Roger when he blamed a few loud-mouthed fans for one dismal showing.

But no fair fan – no matter how dedicated – can stand by Maris in his plea to be benched.

Actually, this is Roger's way of trying to show how little he cares for Ruth's record. Always a rebel, he's attempting to get across the point that he can exist with or without the homer mark.

But all it tells me is that Mr. Maris doesn't have enough ticker to earn my continued support.

Arnold Palmer: Golf's Greatest

It was the afternoon of Feb. 26, 1960, a sunshiny Thursday. That was the day I first met Arnold Palmer. The Texas Open's first round was drawing to a close and I was searching for Frank Stranahan, a wealthy gent who was threatening to become wealthier. He had just shot a 64 to take the early lead.

Jim Gaquin, PGA field secretary, insisted upon introducing me to the one they called Arnie. "He's got all the shots. Before long they'll be calling him the greatest," the usually conservative Gaquin said.

If the truth were known, I didn't want to meet Palmer on that February day in 1960. He had come in with a 69 and was grouped with half a dozen others, five strokes behind. Stranahan was the story and I had hoped to collar him alone for a private chat.

But the sparkplug heir had slipped from the club so Gaquin and I looked up Mr. Palmer. He was not hard to find.

The man from Pennsylvania had just 30 minutes earlier come in with a 69 but was back on the practice tee stroking a six-iron with power, grace and determination.

Pausing only to shake hands, Palmer explained that he would be happy to chat but he'd like to do it while he continued his practice shots. "Or," he offered, "if you don't mind waiting, I'll be through here in about 20 minutes. But I've got to iron some wrinkles out of this swing while I've got the mistakes fresh in my mind."

That was Arnold Palmer in 1960. A big star even then – he won the Masters in 1958 – he had to correct the "mistakes" from a 69 round. And correct them he did. The following afternoon Arnie popped a 65 at the field here and he went on to win the 1960 Texas Open.

In about two weeks Palmer returns to San Antonio, hoping to become the first man ever to win the Texas Open three consecutive years.

There's absolutely nothing phony about Arnold Palmer. He's polite but firm, humble but confident. When he depreciates himself for something, he means it.

But perhaps the thing that draws Arnie closest to gallery hearts is the ever-present human element in his game of golf. Such descriptive phrases as "the man with ice water in his veins" and "possessor of steel nerves" are just so many words scrambled together by so many writers when used in Palmer's case.

He blows a few easy ones just like everybody else. And he doesn't chain-smoke on the back nine because of an agreement with the tobacco folks.

In one sense, Palmer might be compared to boxing king Floyd Patterson. Floyd has been knocked down by just about every foe he's faced in recent years. But he always gets up and that's why he's still champion. And so it is with Arnold. Quite often he'll string together two or three poorly played holes. But Palmer rises to his greatest performances when trailing by two or three strokes.

Palmer has been piloting his own twin-engine plane to and from recent tournaments. Chances are, he'll use that transportation for his Texas Open appearance.

Arnie, you see, is in a hurry. The guy who got his first set of clubs when just 3 and played his first 18-hole round when just 5 has established himself as the greatest golfer of all-time in just seven years as a professional. And he's still only 30 years old.

May 18, 1962

Cage Traveler

When I was a little guy of about 8, I wore tennis shoes that carried the name of Chuck Taylor. Actually, they were basketball shoes but at 8 none of us played basketball so we called them tennis shoes. But, come to think of it, at 8 none of us played tennis either.

At any rate, those rubber kicks I wore were endorsed by Chuck Taylor. I didn't know much about Mr. Taylor but it stood to reason that he was a pretty fair athlete or they wouldn't have stuck his name on my shoes.

Now, some 27 years later, it seemed strange to be chatting lightly in a bull session with that same Chuck Taylor.

His full handle is Charles H. Taylor and he's here to address the St. Mary's annual sports awards dinner Saturday night in the St. Anthony Hotel.

"What does the H stand for in your name, Mr. Taylor?"

"That stands for an argument between my mother and my father. They couldn't agree on a middle name so they just left it at H."

"I see. I remember your name being associated with pro basketball but for the life of me I can't recall which college you played for. Were you All-America?"

"No, it would have been impossible. I never went to college. Just jumped from high school to professional ball."

The white-haired but balding gent will be 61 next month but he travels more for basketball today then he did while playing for the old New York Celtics. Fact is, in 1957 an airline announced that Taylor ranked third among the most air-traveled men in the United States flying to foreign countries. John Foster Dulles and wrestler Louis Thesz nosed him out for the 1-2 spots.

Taylor works for the Converse Rubber Company and those folks give him a pretty free hand in helping to promote the game of basketball.

"I traveled all over the world and for two years the high executives at Converse figured their company was paying my expenses. I guess they just never bothered to look at my expense account," says Taylor.

"But if they didn't pick up the tab, who did pay for those trips?"

"The state department. I work for them, too."

Taylor, it seems, is one of this country's top goodwill ambassadors. He sells just two products – basketball and America. Of course, when he's at home in the States he also sells tennis sho … excuse me, basketball shoes.

It was in 1919 that Taylor enrolled at Indiana University. He enrolled but he never attended. Before he could even find his classroom the professional Fort Wayne team offered Chuck a slice of the gate to play with them. He decided to try it just for one night but when his pay for the evening turned out to be $103 he decided to stick with it and skip college.

Not too many years later the Converse company offered Chuck $50 a month to let them put his name on their shoes. For the $50 he was also supposed to make suggestions for a new type of basketball shoe they hoped to market.

He did and they did. And 12 years later I was wearing those shoes to school each day – along with 2 million other little guys.

You won't find Chuck's name in the record books anywhere. He played pro ball for 11 years but there was no league then. When the NBA finally was formed in 1930 it was decided that the New York Celtics would have to disband and no club could carry more than two Celtics on their team. That's how strong Chuck's old Celts were in those days.

It's been 31 years since Taylor has competed as a player but it's still a pretty good bet that his name can be found on your little guy's basketball shoes.

Giving Thanks

About every five or six years on this day some of us actually sit down and reflect on the things for which we should be thankful. The best beginning for such gratitude often hits around good health, fine family and either spiritual or financial security, if we happen to be blessed with any of these gifts.

However, for reasons of which I'm not at all sure, this time my gratitude seemed to center around the point that causes me most anguish, my work.

The unusual and sometimes long hours that may either end or begin early in the morning make it difficult to adjust into any true pattern. The ever-present pressure of a deadline that seems to advance with alarming speed has prompted enough cuss words to darken if not altogether blacken the soul.

But brother, it beats working for a living. And besides, when you add it all up, subtract a little and then multiply a bit, it's the best durn work in the world.

Who, may I ask, couldn't be grateful for a job that puts you in the best seat in the stadium for every big game in your area? For a job that offers access to the dressing rooms and the confidential conversations between coach and players? For a job that actually necessitates close contact with the high and mighty headline makers of daily sports pages?

Looking back on this day of Thanksgiving, I'm sincerely grateful for work that, at one time or another, has enabled me to rub elbows with, chat with and even drink with such people as Babe Ruth, Jack Dempsey, Don Carter, Jim Braddock, Phil Rizzuto, Arnold Palmer, Max Baer, Dizzy Dean, Jimmy Brown, Sam Snead, Babe Zaharias and other immortals of the sports world.

You don't realize it at the moment but such meetings – interviews, if you want – blend together to make a mesh of memories that wouldn't be traded for the highest commission of the slickest salesman.

An occupational hazard in this business is to believe those who would classify a columnist as an "authority" or an "expert." After lengthy conversation with a sports celebrity we might be better informed than the average fan but our singular role still stands as that of a reporter, merely one to pass along the words and deeds of the great and near-great.

Still, our part on the sports scene is just as important as the equipment players use to gain stardom. Only the exceptionally talented – such as Roger Maris – can afford a complete snub of the Fourth Estate. And their actions, minus the words, are also dutifully reported.

There can be no other profession for which doors open so widely and quickly. Rare is the businessman, no matter how high an executive, who will keep a newsman waiting long. Especially if they're in search of favorable information concerning the businessman.

There can be no other job where a middle-bracket income man is extended so many invitations to hunt, fish and lunch with the area's financial giants.

Sometimes, after an especially pleasant day on a fine fishing vessel or a private hunting range, it's difficult to slip back into reality and not only understand but face the financial problems of an everyday working man.

You can meet the richest and the poorest in this business and some strong and sincere friendships can be formed from both sides of the track. Over the years I've come to believe there's very little difference between the rich and the poor. Very little, that is, other than money.

The uncertainty of any news development and the strong, sometimes fierce competition to gain first knowledge, add strain to the job. But these ingredients act only as a crutch, to help cross whatever routine and boring lines the work might involve.

It's a living. You don't live way up in the high cotton where the charity drives plague you for handouts. But it's the best work I've run across in this land of plenty.

Like any other job, it introduces you to a few deadbeats. But it also brings you in close contact with the greatest group around, the classic characters and genuinely good guys of the sports fraternity.

Today, I'm thankful for my post as reporter for that fraternity.

April 24, 1963

Golf's Growth

Just what there is about a professional golf tournament that attracts so many non-golfing spectators might be something for the head-shrinkers to work on. But whatever the reason, tomorrow many hundreds who have never once played the game will join golf's light brigade in a four-day charge across Oak Hills' course.

It's a social event, an all-day outing, a photographer's delight, a lot of exercise and sometimes — usually on No. 18 on the final day – a lot of thrills.

To even the hardened pros it's still a fantastic thought that one tiny tap on that small white ball can mean the differencc of a thousand dollars or more.

And perhaps this is what attracts the uninformed, the high-rolling risk that rules on each shot.

For instance, it was about eight years ago that I watched Doug Ford lean over and give a quick tap to what you or I would call a gimme. His ball was just five inches from the cup and Doug strolled up to it, leaned forward almost without breaking stride and spanked it a quick shot. The stubborn pill rolled around the cup and hung on the lip.

Ford had missed from no more than five inches away. To make it an even more frustrating situation, Doug hooked 'em up, played steady golf from that point and finished second. He missed the big prize by one stroke. And so it was that a five-inch putt kept Ford out of a playoff for the Texas Open crown.

But whether fans come to see or be seen, by Sunday's final round there will be nothing but experts lining the fairways and crowding the greens. Fellows who've never lifted a putter will tell you how Doug Sanders might be taking too long to learn his line. Ladies who've never powered a wood more than 150 yards will explain why Mike Souchak's drives are displaying a slight hook on the tall end.

And these helpful fans will tell you such things at the drop of a Dixie Cup. Bonded together in a fraternity of mystic togetherness, they spread the word of outstanding performances like no other grapevine in all the world.

How some gent standing on No. 17 can tell you that a young golfer is making the front nine turn in 5- or 6-under fashion is beyond me. But once the message is relayed fans dash to the scene of this outstanding performance like starving chickens running for corn. No microphone announcement. Just a simple whisper in the right direction.

Whatever the reason, professional golf tours have shown great growth in the past two decades.

In 1934 Paul Runyan was the leading money winner on the PGA Tour. Mr. Runyan raked in exactly $6,787. By comparison, Arnold Palmer pulled down the same honors last year and walked away with $81,448.

The old guard – fellows like Sam Snead, Ben Hogan, Byron Nelson and Jimmy Demaret – did most to popularize the sport and make golf tours big business. Then, just as these names were pursued and caught by Father Time, a player named Palmer appeared on the scene to jolt still more excitement into the show.

For a few years there Palmer was to golf what Babe Ruth was to baseball. The only difference was, at the time, golf didn't need Palmer as much as baseball had needed Ruth.

But golf has a husky foothold now. The idea of thirty or forty thousand dollars in prize money is enough to stir the more curious out. And, as one city dweller put it, "Gosh, but it's nice to get outdoors and watch all this golf."

He was "watching all the golf" from the concession stand nearest the scoreboard.

Turf Trouble

I 'd like to use my next few columns to tell you about my vacation on the Caribbean. But it might bore you. And besides, I haven't been to the Caribbean. Fact is I used the past week of my vacation to play a small and insignificant role in a great struggle for survival right here in San Antonio.

Some months ago I planted 32 patches of carpet grass on my new front lawn. Many men wise in the ways of such things advised me that it was most unnecessary to cut or pull weeds. "Carpet grass is strong and tough. It'll chew through and crowd out the weeds once it takes a firm hold, " they reasoned.

Since the carpet grass had a medium-sized hold and the weeds were a foot high, I took a week off to watch one of nature's spectacular wonders. Obviously the time was right for the carpet grass to devour the weeds and I sure didn't want to miss such a sporting show.

Armed with a water sprinkler and a desire to the curious, I sized up the sporting situation that would send my 32 patches of precious carpet green against the brutal battalion of wild weeds. It must be said that the weeds were impressive as they banded beneath their towering flag, a sturdy sunflower that figured to be a mouthful for even my largest chunk of carpet grass.

You had to feel a little sorry for the weeds. There they stood, a fine crop of assorted plants near the prime of life, about to be devoured by 32 tiny but tough patches of carpet grass. Had I not been told differently, I would have made the weeds about a 4-1 choice over the carpet grass. But the turf touts couldn't all be wrong so I made a mental price of 8-5, favoring the carpet patches.

Since it's an American custom to give the underdog at least an even break, I watered the weeds and grass evenly. It seemed the sporting thing to do for the doomed weeds.

Folks, you may find this hard to believe, but right out there at 1115 Cerro Alto Drive last week we had the greatest upset since Johansson unhinged Patterson. After three days of watering, the weeds somehow doubled their forces, surrounded the carpet grass, pushed the sunflower flag two inches higher and boasted not a single casualty.

I sent a late entry into the race, sprinkling two pounds of bermuda seed into the confusion. Now it's sort of like a battle royal, with bermuda rated a 5-1 chance for survival.

It's a fact known well by all turf touts that weeds don't devour carpet grass. But my 32 patches have dwindled to 22 and I can't believe the other 10 are off somewhere together planning a rally.

While all this front yard action was going on last week I noticed where Jim Piersall got himself traded to the Mets and Bo Belinsky also went to the minors. I don't know what this will do to the flag races but it's sure going to shake up the bubble gum folks who push picture cards with each penny pack. I have it on good authority that just three weeks ago one Bo Belinsky card was worth three Roger Maris cards.

Right now it would seem that Piersall has about as much chance of getting some World Series money as my carpet grass has of whipping the weeds. And that doesn't say much for the Mets. If I take another week off to work in the yard I'll match my weeds against anybody's carpet grass.

Anyway, weeds don't look so bad if you keep 'em green and have a nice sunflower in the middle.

June 20, 1963

Liz And Cassius

It's nice that Liz Taylor and Richard Burton could take time out from their busy routine to visit the Cassius Clay fight in London. But goodness, there was no need for her to get so excited and stop the fight. At least I don't think there was any need.

Liz, you must know, leaped from her seat and shouted "No, no, no" as Clay was banging the English bloke about his bloody eye. The crowd took up Miss – or is it Mrs.? – Taylor's chant and sure enough, the ref called a halt.

Of course, nobody is really sure just what Liz had in mind when she screamed "no, no, no." Richard Burton was sitting close beside her and although he wore an innocent look and had one hand wrapped around a bag of popcorn, his other hand wasn't visible. It may be that Liz's choice of words sort of shook folks. It would seem more in character for her to scream "yes, yes, yes."

But she didn't. She hollered "no, no, no" and thousands took up the cry to influence the referee.

It seems worthy to note that Sir Thomas Little, performing as referee, was about to ignore the fact that Henry Cooper was in dire need of a dozen stitches and a transfusion. Liz was nice to remind him, although Burton, probably occupied with other thoughts, did nothing to help.

But even though she assisted Cassius in winning as predicted, Liz still stole the play from Louisville's most famous slugger. She chose Clay's greatest hour of triumph to announce her most recent wedding plans.

And so it was that the following day newspapers the world over carried Clay's victory details inside on sports pages while Liz's next opponent was announced on page one.

Old Cassius probably felt cheated, scoring a fine victory and still being dropped to second place in the London news race.

Besides, Liz could have easily waited. Not many couples announce their forthcoming marriages when they're already married to other folks up the stream. The divorce announcement usually comes first. But since Cassius was hogging so much attention Liz just skipped her divorce bulletin and dropped the big bomb.

It may well be that Liz is finding it more difficult to keep her name in print now that the Cleopatra job has played out. Since Clay recently remarked how much he liked London and explained that someday soon he might book a few exhibition bouts there, Liz could pick up a bundle by acting as his adviser and assistant manager. Richard Burton could even carry the water bucket to add a little flavor.

As his career progresses Cassius is beginning to look more and more like Floyd Patterson. Both have quick hands, more speed than you figure to find in a heavyweight and a fair knowledge of boxing science.

Also, they both own weak chins. And while Patterson is a withdrawn, humble agent, Clay thinks humility is some sort of government handout.

In a way it's too bad that Patterson and Clay can't be matched before Liston ruins them both. A Patterson-Clay scrap would be a natural. But as things now stand Liston figures to retire them both, first Patterson and then Clay. Not even the screams of Liz Taylor will help these poor fellows once they crawl in against big bad Sonny.

The Recording Star

Cassius Marcellus Clay, grandson of an iceman and the coolest cat ever to grace the sports scene, has a long record. No, no, not the kind that Sonny Liston's got. This is a long-playing job, too, but it was released by Columbia instead of the police department.

The Columbia folks are asking $3.98 for the big platter and this request puts them at least on the same par with Cassius in the nerve department. It is to be assumed, however, that a husky hunk of each $3.98 will find its way into Mr. Clay's pocket.

If you play it at the correct speed the record will run for about 40 minutes, which has got to be 35 minutes longer than Clay will be able to run against Sonny Liston.

Cassius doesn't sing, play the piano or lead a band anywhere on the record. He limits himself to the thing he does best – talk.

The record is titled "I Am The Greatest." The flip side has a little variation. It's called, "I Am The Double Greatest."

Sonny Liston should get at least a piece of the royalties since his name is used more than Clay's. No less than three San Antonio record shops are already sold out of this one so it stands a chance of becoming a best-seller. But it's good for a limited time only. Just as soon as Liston takes Cassius apart the record will have a hollow sound and sales should drop faster than Clay.

There are a few good chuckles on the record, probably because Cassius claims to have written some of the script himself. And, of course, there's enough Clay poetry involved to ruin the dinner of any good poem-maker.

Cassius opens one side of the record with, "Friends, Romans, countrymen, lend me yo ear. I come to bury Liston, not to praise him."

After making a wild statement he backs it up with knee-slappers like, "If I tell you a mouse can outrun a horse you'd better put your money where your mouse is." And, "If Cassius says a cow lays eggs, don't ask how, just grease that skillet."

The mood, tempo and diction change often, giving the strong impression that Cassius is sometimes reading a ready-made script and sometimes winging it on his own.

Clay says he has nothing personal against Sonny. "He's really a nice old man. But he's got my job."

A little violin background music helps carry Clay through some of the lousier poems. Like the one that goes thusly:

Who would have thought,
When they came to the fight
That they'd witness the sight
Of a human satellite?

The crowd did not dream
When they put down their money
That they'd see a total eclipse of the Sonny.

All of this only goes to prove that Clay is no dummy. With this record Cassius is going to become the first non-champion to pile up money by not fighting.

Sure, he's really stuck on himself. But generally speaking, the whole "love thyself" bit is a pure gimmick designed to make folks hate him and pay to see him fight, hoping he'll get clobbered.

Throughout the record Cassius pokes a little fun at his "modest" attitude.

One of the better gags is on this line.

"Mr. Clay, have you ever been in love?"

"Not with anyone else."

While listening to the whole $3.98 worth I couldn't help but wonder what must have been moving through Liston's mind when he first heard the record. It's a frightening thing to dwell on for too long a period.

O c t o b e r   2 4 ,   1 9 6 3

Yogi in Charge

L awrence Peter Berra, the one they call Yogi, looked out of place 18 years ago when he first checked in with the New York Yankees. He was awkward behind the plate, with little or no idea how to set his feet before throwing to second. He also looked out of place in the batter's box, just barely staying within the chalk lines as he hacked and whacked at high, low and in-the-middle pitches.

And so it is today. To most baseball fans. I would imagine Yogi looks far out of place in the role of Yankee manager.

But despite his awkward appearance, Yogi did right well for himself as a player. For six years he led American League catchers in double plays — proving that he solved the problem of which way to step. And three times he was named the league's most valuable player — proving that his batting ability was above par, to say the least.

Still, it's difficult to imagine Yogi as a serious-minded manager of a multimillion-dollar operation.

For too many years Berra has been pictured as a team jester who in his more serious moments, digs deeply into dime comic books. Most of Yogi's funniest cracks are not intended to be funny at all.

Like the time he went to a certain café with other members of the Yankee team. Several of the boys — Yogi included — had never before been to the café even though it was fairly close to the stadium. Upon entering Yogi remarked, "No wonder nobody ever eats here. It's too crowded."

Berra's nickname is an excellent tipoff on the man. Born in St. Louis, boyhood pals pegged him with the Yogi handle. In those days – as now, I guess – a Yogi was considered a very odd character. The nickname stayed with Berra but he outgrew its original meaning. Now, with the Yankee veteran, it's considered a term of affection.

Of course this is a pretty good raise for Ralph Houk. As general manager his salary hops a bit and he no longer is bothered with the worry to win each time out. But it seems sort of strange that Berra would replace him as a manager. After all, it was this same Berra who kept this same Houk from becoming a first-string catcher.

Yogi, you'll remember, took over after Bill Dickey retired. Houk happened onto the scene just one year later. In the next seven years Houk rode the bench while Berra handled just about all the catching duties.

Fact is, Houk caught only 91 games in seven years and most of his chances came in doubleheaders. Now Yogi is taking over Ralph's managerial duties. But this time it's dealer's choice and Houk is the dealer.

As mentioned, it's hard to picture Berra as the Yankee string-puller. But I can't help believe that somehow or another he'll do a whale of a job. He always does. And one thing is certain. In no time at all he'll pass

Casey Stengel as the most quoted manager in the majors.

What newspaperman would dare pass up a trip to the Yankee dressing room to hear Berra explain a complicated play?

The Coming of Pay TV

It seems only right that California should be first with pay TV. The West Coast state has endured Art Aragon, Bo Belinsky, the Los Angeles Rams and Liz Taylor. Why not pay TV?

The men behind this new dodge claim that within 10 years 80 percent of the sets in America will have coin boxes attached for pay-as-you-see video. Maybe so. But I have every intention of remaining in that other 20 percent. It may strike you as a selfish attitude but I hope to get my set paid for before I start paying talent fees to actors and their agents.

When early reports of pay TV were kicking about I somehow got the idea it was going to be a two-bit operation. A charge of 25 cents for a regular-season baseball or football game with a 50-cent lick for the big ones seemed in line. Most anybody would pay a quarter to get rid of the cigarette, beer and razor salesmen. Not to mention the pushers of soap, cereal and salves.

The guys who peddle headache remedies on TV provide more cause than cure.

But let's face it, commercials don't really bother the viewing of sports events on TV. Oh, every now and then some idiot director will call for a commercial at the wrong time and while the winning score is being made we'll be watching some slob slick up his hair with a dandy new oil. But such cases are rather isolated and hardly worthy of mention.

That two-bits-a-game thought was erased last week in California when those plugged in for the trial run had to cough up $1.50 to watch the Dodgers, the same price an in-person bleacher seat would have cost.

Some sort of presentation on surfing – in color, no less – was offered for $1 while an Egyptian play of sorts carried a 75-cent price tag. The surfers got a little action but the Egyptians just barely escaped a shutout. The baseball game, however, was hailed by pay TV chieftains as an instant success.

One of the most glowing praises for the pay TV system came from a Los Angeles doctor – probably a plant. The doctor explained that the buck and a half was much cheaper than driving to the game, paying for parking and shelling out several more dollars for goodies from concession stands. Plus the bonus of no commercials to interrupt.

Well, that's one side of it. But how about the interruptions at home? Nobody can tell me that TV – pay or otherwise – will ever beat actual attendance.

I don't know about you but it takes me three innings to let my kids know I mean business and get 'em to shut up so that I can hear as well as watch TV. The next three innings are spent explaining to my wife that the game will be over in "just a little bit" and I'll be available for grass mowing and other women's work.

Of course, the final three innings run pretty smooth. Everybody in the house is so angry at me they wouldn't dare speak in my direction. Sometimes, however, the last three innings are ruined by "important" phone calls or visiting neighbors. But that's the chance you take at home.

No sir, 50 cents is the absolute limit I'll put out to join the pay TV corps. No matter what they're showing. The Dodgers could be racing the Egyptians on short surfboards and I wouldn't poke a buck and a half into the box to watch at home.

Most of us are rather spoiled. They're going to have a tough time collecting for something they've been giving away for years. Besides, they picked a bad place to conduct their trial run. Everybody knows that California is loaded with more unpredictable kooks than any other state.

November 25, 1964

Sweet Gridiron Symphony

Back before the turn of the century, when Ivy Leaguers dominated the American football scene, they worked out an offensive maneuver that became famous under the label of "Flying Wedge." For many years that "play" was considered the ultimate in drawing-board strategy.

It's obvious to anyone who's seen a game in the last few years that football has made tremendous technical advances in the past quarter century. I wasn't completely impressed, however, until the Sunday afternoon that I visited Victor Alessandro at his home.

Mr. Alessandro, as you must know, is a music man by trade. But he also digs football. Especially the kind that comes through TV sets on Sunday afternoons.

Victor's grass bears a circular trail worn thin by baserunners who've plunked a lot of homers in recent months. As we crossed the "diamond" to his workshop, Victor explained the whereabouts of home plate and first base when he and his young son tie up in a backyard concerto.

For some reason or other I'd always figured Mr. Alessandro came to this country from Italy or Austria where so many of those long-haired cats got their musical starts. But, gee, as a kid in Houston he got chased away from the same magazine racks at the same Cherryhurst drug store that I got thumbed from just a few years later. That store used to have the best comic books and the crabbiest manager in town.

Victor's backyard workshop is something to behold. In the middle is a large swivel chair surrounded by a piano, a tape recorder, a desktop and shelves loaded with records and books by just about every musician who ever fingered a flute.

"Golly, maestro, you really make an intense study of your work."

He offered a half nod. As if to say "yes," but not intense enough. And then he answered.

"A number of musicians work hard at their trade but we're still far beneath the study pace of less complicated things – like football."

"What do you mean? How can you compare a symphony orchestra with a football team?"

"I'm referring to the study. The homework. A good college or pro team is far advanced in technical study over us. They have first-class movies made of every performance – sometimes a film made on just workouts – and they study them carefully. When they make an error they know exactly who did it and why. They work for long hours to correct each error. They have end coaches, line coaches, backfield coaches, defense coaches, offense coaches and head coaches. They're far advanced over musical groups."

The comparison offered food for thought. And after thinking, I presented Victor with another question.

"Golly, coach – I mean, maestro – how can you correct the situation and catch up?"

"We won't be able to for a long time. The football teams take in far more money than a symphony orchestra and they can afford to spend more on preparation. But, if we had the money, I'd love to put a tiny tape recorder on or near each instrument during a performance. Then and only then would we be able to determine exactly who did exceptionally well and who committed errors during a difficult selection."

"That many recorders would cost a ton."

"Very true. But do you know that in just two or three seconds of some concerts several hundred errors could be committed?"

"Sounds like you ought to be redshirting some of your players."

"No, no, it makes no difference which orchestra you're talking about. There's that much margin for error and when you're dealing in the possibility of hundreds of errors in a two-second period, just imagine how many boots you might get during a lengthy selection. No, I'm afraid we're not nearly far enough advanced. Certainly not as far as professional football."

It was something to think about. But somehow or another I got to thinking how Victor must have read different and deeper comic books than I read at the old Cherryhurst drug store.

December 17, 1964

The Short End of Boxing

If you like the game – and sometimes, when I don't give it too much serious thought, I really like boxing – you have to sympathize with the fellows who keep it going in the small clubs.

They're not fast-buck operators who wheel and deal in the high cotton. They're little men, some of them far out of touch with big money, who love the sport and struggle on with an unreal sort of hope and faith that each show might produce a nice payday or a hot prospect.

Take, for instance, the situation here last Tuesday night. They could have held it in my backyard without disturbing my wife's flowers. And I don't have a big backyard.

It was rather obvious from the beginning that the show wasn't going to set an attendance record. But it did. An all-time low. Just 417 slipped out of the Christmas shopping mob and paid to watch.

The night before the bout Roxy Kalo called me at home. Roxy is a trainer of fair fighters and manager of not-so-good fighters. We've been friends for 20 years and during that period Roxy has owned only one main eventer. Needless to say, Mr. Kalo is not among the high-rolling ring managers you hear about so often.

"Dan, I need some help. We come in here on points, ya' know, percentage, and I unnerstan' the advance ticket sale ain't so good."

"Who is we, Roxy?"

"Me and Henry Dominguez, the state lightweight champeen. Henry is okay. But I need a little Christmas money. Things ain't altogether too well. Can ya' build a little fire unner this fight for us?"

"Roxy, I can't kid you. This fight can't do anything but lay an egg. It's not too hot a package even in the summer. But right now Christmas has everybody busy and busted. Sure, it figures to be a good fight. You and I could make a good fight. But who'd pay to see us?"

"Well, do what ya' can. Okay?"

"Okay. And, Merry Christmas."

"Yeah, Merry Christmas."

It worked out worse than I'd thought it would. You could have shot a six-gun in six directions without causing any casualties. Paul Alba came all the way from Austin just to be introduced and to challenge the winner. They could have introduced everybody in the auditorium and it wouldn't have delayed the show.

Nothing seemed to go right. Chato Herrera also hopped into the ring to challenge the winner. He sashayed around twice, drawing a little applause as he waved a cowboy Stetson. Then he hopped out of the ring. And fell flat on his face.

Dominguez evidently didn't take Mr. Kalo's advice on training. He ran out of gas in the second round and then took a terrific beating for the next six rounds. Since he was working strictly on percentage, Henry wound up minus his title plus a fat lip and sore ribs, all for $211.

But promoter Reuben Rodriguez took the real beating. Without catching a punch. He lost a little over $600.

Putting it all together, you hardly know who to feel for – Dominguez, who got walloped for peanuts; Roxy, who is coming up short at Christmas; or Reuben, the promoter who could have saved six bills by not promoting.

You hear a lot about the boxing men who wallow about in the big money. But there are two sides to every coin and that other side can be a rather pathetic sight.

Benny's Dancing in Miami

MIAMI – Holy mackerel, you should have seen it. Benjamin P. Broadhind dancing the Watusi on New Year's Eve at a swank hotel blast in South Florida. And in a clean shirt.

His partner for the happy occasion was a 22-year-old sweet swinger from Tampa. They made a lovely couple and a half. Benjamin, it seems, had informed the young lady that he was a big diamond dealer in Texas. Of course, it was a true statement. But Mr. Broadhind also deals spades, clubs and hearts.

"Benjamin, what are you doing here in Miami with the little pretty? I thought you were in San Antonio, trying to get pumped up after supporting the Baltimore action."

"Naw, son, I figured I might find a bigger pump handle over here. I'm still on the shorts in San Antonio but then ain't nobody ever got arrested for speedin' on the way to pay a bookmaker. I got until Monday to come up with the stuff so I thought I might score over here where the action is faster."

"Couldn't you borrow the money from your old friend, Animal Andrews? Or, maybe Circus Face Flanagan?"

"Boy, them two fellas wouldn't give a dyin' man directions to the Robert B. Green. Naw, this is somethin' I gotta do all by myself."

"Do you have any leads?"

"Yeah, everybody in town is bettin' the Packers will clobber the Cardinals here Sunday. I am of the reverse opinion."

"But do you have anything to put behind that opinion?"

"A small bundle. Not enough to pay last week's play on them sleepin' Colts, but enough to make a move with. I'm tryin' to drive a nail with a tack hammer."

"Where did you get the nail?"

"You won't believe it."

"Try me."

"Well, an old friend sent me a two-dollar bill in a Christmas card. He mailed it to my headquarters at the Flamingo Lounge and told me to buy the boys a rounda drinks. Since I was the only one there when it arrived, I called in a nine-team basketball parlay for two bucks."

"You're right. I don't believe it. Who sent the card?"

"A very respected businessman. Fellow by the name of G. Howell Hight. But he don't want no publicity."

"And you're going to tell me you hit a nine-team parlay?"

"They come in like trained pigs. It give my confidence a real boost. I thought I might come over here to Miami and sell stock in the Alamo."

"Have you tried?"

"No, son, Cuba is the big word here. Through some masterful negotiatin' I been able to push a few sugar cane fields in the suburbs of Havana. My profits is all ridin' on the Cardinals with a seven-point cushion to start."

The little lady returned from the punch bowl and Mr. Broadhind bid me farewell. It was worth a plane trip to Miami to see Benny do the Watusi to "Auld Lang Syne." Not to mention the tip on the Cardinals.

———

M a r c h   2 3 ,   1 9 6 5

A Visit With Ted Williams

He's one of those kind of fellows who never seems to get old. Just five months away from his 47th birthday he's still Billy The Kid, with coal-black hair, the youthful bounce of the great athlete he once was and a boyish grin that shows up more now than when he was playing.

Ted Williams, however, is no longer the Splendid Splinter. He's not fat – or even chubby – but the splinter has filled out. His seat, chest and stomach are gaining ground in the race to catch those great forearms he's always had.

Here to speak at the Hall of Fame banquet Sunday night, Ted checked into his room at the St. Anthony and tossed his bag onto the bed. He flipped open the snaps, raised the lid with a bit of ceremony and then dug around for a moment. Finally, he came up with a white dress shirt.

"You see, I do have one of these. I usually try and carry one for high-class banquets," Ted smiled as he waved the dress shirt. Williams is the original sport-shirt kid. Over the years Ted has endorsed a lot of products but never has he been approached by a tie manufacturer. That would be like Y.A. Tittle endorsing hair tonic. Or combs.

Besides "Billy the Kid" and the "Splendid Splinter," there's another handle writers hung on Ted during his heyday as a Boston slugger – "Temperamental Ted." Williams' running feuds with sportswriters made more than one headline. And since several sportswriters had heavy hands in the promotion of this project we couldn't help but give consistent thought to that last nickname.

Williams, however, displayed the personality of a hungry insurance salesman while here. He had nothing but smiles, handshakes and kind words for all he came in contact with.

There was only one shaky moment and the blame for that belonged to me. I had been told that Williams would consent to a press conference at 6:30 p.m. if the press so desired. And the press did so desire.

But Ted and his group were a little late in arriving. After spreading the 6:30 word to my colleagues I felt a little responsible so when we entered his room at 6:45 p.m. I made mention of the conference to Mr. Williams.

"Ted, I was told you wanted to hold a press conference at. . ." That was as far as I got.

"Who told you that? I've never wanted to hold a press conference. Now let's get this straight and. . ."

"Hold everything. Let me reword that. I was wrong. I wasn't told that you WANTED to hold a press conference. I was told that you WOULD hold a press conference. How's that?"

"That's better. I'll be happy to talk with the boys on anything they want to talk about. Ask them to come on up."

The banquet itself must be listed among the best ever held here. Nobody tried to set a speech marathon and Morris Frank, undoubtedly the finest master of ceremonies in this part of the country, was in his finest form.

Eddie Davis of the St. Anthony did a masterful job of setting the stage and even though Texas' Darrell Royal and Tommy Nobis played major roles in the program there were a lot of Aggies on hand. They might have been there scouting, just to see if Royal or Nobis let any secrets slip out.

Prior to the banquet Morris confessed that he wasn't sure how to introduce Williams. "I don't think he would like for me to go over all of his past deeds and I sure don't want to make him ill at ease just before his talk," Morris said. But when the time came, Morris handled the job brilliantly. He simply said:

"There's no sense in me introducing this next speaker. Anybody who hasn't heard of Ted Williams hasn't heard of Elizabeth Taylor. And there is a comparison. She broke up homes and Ted broke up ballgames. She has the curves and Ted hit the curves. Both have great batting averages in their respective sports."

Ted was still smiling when he stood to speak.

April 13, 1965

Opening of the Dome

He was worried about Vietnam and I was a little concerned with last month's light and gas bill, but Lyndon B. Johnson and I just pushed everything aside last Friday and went to the ballgame.

Of course, we didn't sit together. He had a much better seat. I was about 60 yards up, located between home plate and first base. On my left was Steve Perkins of the Dallas Times Herald. Lyndon was about 40 yards up, directly behind the right fielder. On his left was Roy Hofheinz.

The more I think about it, my seat was much better than the president's.

You'd think they would have given Mr. Johnson a better seat to watch the game that officially opened Houston's Domed Stadium. But then, the contest between Houston and the Yankees had been sold out for weeks. Since the president just made up his mind to attend a few hours before post time I guess he was lucky to get any kind of seat. Especially since Lady Bird and about three other birds were with him.

The whole night seemed a little unreal. The things that happened and the people there to meet should be taken in small doses.

For instance, it isn't every night that you chat with the Yankee manager, interview Roger Maris, shake hands with Mickey Mantle, watch a game with the president of the United States, meet former space traveler Alan B. Shepard, sit beside and write with such noted scribes as Red Smith and, all the while, enjoy the services of a velvet-suited waiter who mixes strong drinks and slices roast beef thick.

It's a little too much to take in one long session. Especially for a slob who's used to a cold hot dog, a cool Coke and self-service at sports events.

The big trouble with the new stadium – besides its ceiling that won't allow day baseball – is that few fans will ever really see it all. And you've got to see it all to really appreciate the splendor of the thing.

For instance, less than 10 percent of the fans who visit the stadium will ever set foot inside the Astrodome Club.

An even smaller percentage will ever get the opportunity to drop into the more exclusive club on the sky deck.

I've never seen that Skydome Club but – at great expense to somebody else – I ate in the Astrodome Club. For the life of me I can't imagine how the other club, four stories higher with prices to match, can be more elaborate.

The Astrodome Club is furnished with rich reproductions from the era of the Hippodrome Theatre and the bawdy Barbary Coast. It's plush. And if the surroundings don't knock you over the menu prices will.

Prime roast beef at $5.50 was the cheapest dinner I could find. Pheasant under glass came at only $7.50 a throw. What an age in which we live. Where a fellow can sit under glass and eat pheasant under glass while looking through glass windows at a baseball game.

There are other fascinating items that will be viewed by only a small percentage of Domed Stadium visitors these first few years. The 53 private club rooms are harder to crash than the safe in Hofheinz's right-field suite, and the sixth level Trail Blazers dining room won't catch much of the two-dollar trade.

Of course, the brokes – the real baseball fans – can always feed their faces in the Countdown Cafeteria on the third level, or one of the concession stands that features 30-cent hot dogs, 40-cent hamburgers and potato chips for a mere 15 cents. And if they really want to go hogwild and throw around a buck or so they can visit the ground floor Domeskeller.

No, you can buy a ticket and watch the event and say you "saw the Domed Stadium," but durned few shirt-sleeve fans will ever see ALL of that magnificent playpen.

But don't feel badly. From that seat in right field I'll bet Lyndon couldn't even see the game too well, much less the whole stadium.

Clay-Liston a Bold Robbery

When you compare the two great events – that fight last night and the Black Sox scandal – you've got to feel sorry for the poor ballplayers. They got caught and never collected a dime.

Sonny Liston and Cassius Clay, by far the boldest bandits ever to rob the public, laughed all the way to the bank today. And why not? They've got the funniest act since Laurel and Hardy. Abbott and Costello had to work a year to make as much as these two clowns got for one minute's work. And they probably rehearsed a lot longer.

Liston, appearing slower than a tax refund, must go down in history as the most courageous boxer of all time. It must have taken real guts to pull off that job before thousands of eyewitnesses and countless cameras. Especially after getting away with the bum shoulder plea he copped his last time out.

Here's a man who once fought with a broken jaw and never staggered. A man who caught Cleveland Williams' hardest haymakers flush on the chin and never batted an eye. A man who was battered by police billy clubs and graduated with honors from the school of hard knocks – and was never knocked off his feet. Until last night.

And then a light poke on the cheekbone – a punch too fast for the slow-motion cameras to catch – sent Liston reeling to the canvas. The iron man ran up the flag after making a comfortable, four-point landing.

It was only right and fitting that Jersey Joe Walcott would get into the act as referee. Maybe he got the job as sort of an anniversary gift. After all, it had been 12 years almost to the day since he stirred up a little stink of his own by melting before Rocky Marciano in round one of another heavyweight title fiasco.

Of course, poor Walcott never did find out what was going on last night. From the beginning he seemed as frustrated as the golfer who got a hole-in-one while playing alone.

Immediately after the fight Jersey Joe admitted he "never did see the knockout punch." He said that on a national radio hookup. But half an hour later Joe collected his wits (and pay), polished his memory and then described the devastating power punch in great detail.

Nothing went right from the very beginning. I got the idea that perhaps when they rented that Lewiston hall on short notice they promised to be out before 9 p.m.

Robert Goulet, the singer of songs, couldn't handle the "Star-Spangled Banner" even though he was reading it from notes: "Oh say can you see by the dawn's early night." But Robert got off lighter than Liston. They didn't replay his part on videotape.

Walcott appeared more stunned than Sonny when Liston did the el foldo. Clay himself was a little shocked. Walcott counted to eight or nine and Sonny pulled himself up – almost. And then tumbled over. Jersey Joe wasn't ready for that. He started to count again and then raced over to the sidelines to get some professional advice.

While Walcott was finding out what to do, Liston, discouraged by all of the indecision, got to his feet to see what was holding up the finish. He and Clay waltzed the Watusi for a few steps and by then Walcott got back with the message that the show was over.

It was left for the timekeeper, however, to pull the mother of all errors made on that night of many errors. He swore – and still does – that just one minute elapsed from the opening bell to the final count. He says he and his crew had two watches on the fight.

Actually, the thing lasted a lot closer to two minutes. So it's well that it did end early and wasn't carried the full distance. Had they gone on to a decision by the timekeepers' clocks we might just now be approaching round 14.

Like I said, it's as if the whole promotion were thrown together on a few minutes' notice for a few minutes of entertainment. No sense in hiring expensive help when you only need part-time workers.

After the first meeting of Clay and Liston I sat at this same typewriter and started a column with, "If last night's heavyweight title fight doesn't kill boxing then the sport will be with us for all time to come."

Obviously, it didn't kill it. In fact, a great number of fans swore that it was an exciting bout.

But I was wrong. Boxing won't be with us for all time to come. The federal government has been reluctant to step in and assume command, leaving the sport in the bold and ruthless hands of greedy gangsters. It runs wild, like a rudderless ship on the high seas.

But die it shall. The cause of death will be self-strangulation – at the box office. Only the curious, idle rich will plunk down money to see future title fights and there just aren't enough of the curious, idle rich to feed boxing's mob in the manner to which it is accustomed.

November 12, 1965

The Soft Sell On Football

It was Lady Holland who first said, "Troubles, like babies, grow larger by nursing." Or maybe it was Lady Chatterley who said that.

At any rate, it's true. I've compounded my large troubles by nursing the small ones. My problem was – and is – those two games in Houston this Saturday.

My dad and aunts, who live in Houston, have tickets for all Rice and Houston home games. Upon learning that I would be covering the games they decided my boy and girl might want to take in one of the games.

So it was decided that one – either the boy or girl – would go with the family in the afternoon to see Rice and the Aggies and the other would go at night to see Houston and Kentucky. Reasonable enough, huh?

Well, you guessed it, they both want to go at night to the Domed Stadium. Being the clever father that I am I began to do a selling job on the Rice-Aggie game. I took the boy aside first. He's 9 and his name is also Dan.

"Now look, son, you've never seen the Aggies play a game, have you?"

"Nope, last year when I wanted to go you said I was too young to watch our future Army officers get slaughtered."

"That was last year. They've now got a new coach and a new team. Besides, you're a year older."

"I'd rather go to the night game."

"Danny, I'm telling you this because I don't want you to miss one of the greatest moments of collegiate football. Son, when the magnificent Aggie band strikes up with that old familiar bugle call and the 'Aggie War Hymn' follows, 10,000 or more Aggies send up a great cheer. It gives you goosebumps."

"So, who needs goosebumps?"

"Look, boy, every Aggie stands up the entire game and cheers madly for the football team. It's something to watch. It's real spirit that you just don't want to miss."

"Yes, I do. I wanna go at night and see Houston and Kentucky."

I released the boy and went to work on Marie, my 12-year-old daughter.

"Honey, I wouldn't let your brother in on this but I know how much you like marching bands. The Aggies just happen to have the greatest marching band in the world today. Are you sure you hadn't rather go to the day game and see the Aggies march?"

"What's the Rice band like?"

"Well, like nothing you'll ever see again. It's not molded in the old John Philip Sousa tradition."

"Who does he play for, Rice or the Aggies?"

"Who does who play for?"

"John Philip Suzzy."

"He's an Aggie linebacker. Now, honey, have you ever heard 10,000 cadets cheering wildly while standing throughout an entire game? No, I didn't think so. It really puts those old goosebumps on your arms."

"I got goosebumps at the Domed Stadium when we went to the circus. The air conditioning was up too high."

And that's the way it went. It did, that is, until they put their scheming little heads together and bounced back to me an hour later. My son was the spokesman.

"Dad, we've been thinking and we both wanna watch the Aggies at the day game and get goosebumps."

"No, no, only one can go. The other has to go to the Domed Stadium and get goosebumps there. Remember?"

"But we wanna see that band that stands up and hollers. And Marie wants to watch John Philip Suzzy play linebacker. We don't wanna go to the Dome and see . . . ."

I wonder if Lady Holland was taking her kids to a football game when she thought of that bit about troubles and babies nursing.

January 11, 1966

Houston's New Kicker

Maybe you heard about it, how Bud Adams sashayed by a party Friday night in a Houston hotel and wound up signing his waiter to a $10,000 contract. And he wasn't even the headwaiter.

Mr. Adams, who owns the Houston Oilers, wasn't particularly impressed with the service given that night but the waiter told him he was a good kicker of footballs.

"I am a good kicker of footballs and if you would like to make me a favor I will kick footballs good for you." That's what the waiter told Mr. Adams.

"Just how good?" asked the interested Mr. Adams.

"Good like Pete Gogolak of the Buffalo Bills," answered waiter Eduardo Lloret, who was about to become an ex-waiter.

Now Mr. Adams didn't get to be a millionaire by listening to bongo drums when opportunity was banging in his ears. "Come to my office tomorrow morning and we'll go out on the field and see what you can do," Adams offered.

And so it was that Eduardo Lloret, an amateur soccer player who once played as a semi-pro in Argentina, checked in Saturday morning for his first close look at an American football field.

He kicked for about two hours, using the side-step, soccer style. They say from about 25 or 30 yards out, he was as certain as your mother-in-law's visit.

Finally, kicking from mid-field, Eduardo got some real professional help. Adams, who had watched silently on the sideline, explained that they were not holding the ball properly for Lloret's long tries. You can explain things like this when you own the football – and the team.

"Here, gimme the ball and I'll show you how it should be slanted," said Bud.

Eduardo held his breath for that important kick. Mr. Adams was wearing a wristwatch that cost more that the whole Oiler backfield. Had he missed the ball and booted the watch through the uprights Houston would have had the only diamond-studded practice field in all of football.

But, with Adams calling signals and holding the ball, Eduardo punched it through the uprights from 50 yards out. And with that kick Eduardo traded his waiter's badge for a football suit.

Lloret might have done better had he taken a lawyer along to negotiate a contract. Or, at least a headwaiter.

As things developed, Mr. Adams asked him how much he wanted and Lloret answered, "Nothing, I just want to play."

But, what can you expect when you send a waiter to do a football player's job? The only time a pro football player says he doesn't want anything is when a doctor or a judge is asking the questions.

Adams, however, decided that $10,000 would be a fair price for Eduardo's first season of kicking. He probably found that amount lying around in his office floor after talking to Tommy Nobis.

It could be that Adams will get a lot of publicity and nothing more from this latest move in the recruiting field. Eduardo's contract, like most signed these days, depends upon whether or not he makes the team next year. George Blanda, the Oilers' top field goal man the past several seasons, is on the way out so that should leave an opening.

If this thing works out the Oiler coaching staff might face a real problem. I can just hear the coaches talking now.

"Bones, we got to have some help at guard. Did you mention it to Mr. Adams?"

"Yeah, he said he's gonna see about it tonight."

"Who's he gonna see?"

"I'm not sure, but he's going to the horse show. You don't suppose he's gonna bring back one of those society jockeys to play guard, do you?"

"I don't know, but don't suggest it. A 90-pound guard would be worth headlines everywhere in the league."

Sometimes it appears that the pro football race for headlines is more interesting than the race for rookies or the title race itself.

April 19, 1966

A Visit With Mantle

He's 34 years old and in the twilight of a great but injury-plagued career. Still, at times – especially when he smiles or laughs – Mickey Mantle doesn't look much older than when he first became a New York Yankee back in 1951.

It might well be that Mickey is destined to someday occupy a berth in Baseball's Hall of Fame. He's certain to be remembered among the all-time Yankee greats.

But you just can't help wondering what a tremendous slice of everlasting fame this man from Oklahoma would have cut for himself had not injuries and ailments followed his every step along the baseball roads.

Mantle had all the equipment to be king of the superstars. And high on his list of necessary tools was a heart that pushed him out day after day, sometimes taped like an Egyptian mummy. The guy can't remember when he played a whole week without a single sore spot.

In 1951 – his first with the Yankees – he injured his right knee in the fifth inning of the second World Series game.

That was his first major ailment in baseball. Many dozens were to follow.

And now in 1966 – perhaps his last in baseball – he's nursing the scars of a recent shoulder operation. When they rolled him onto the cutting block back in January some said he was through as a player. Even high medicos for the famed Mayo Clinic listed June as the earliest possible date for his return.

But when the season started, Mantle did too.

And now, here to look over his holdings in an insurance company, Mickey smiles and tells you how things are going to be okay. After all, he's a switch-hitter and his shoulder only hurts when he bats left. No pain at all when he bats right. And he can almost throw hard every time.

"I'll be fine, no pain at all, in about another week," he smiled.

"How many more years do you plan on playing?"

"Oh, I dunno. Maybe one or two. This depends on a lot of things. But right now I feel fine."

Of all the questions fired his way Monday this was the only one that he stumbled on a bit before answering. And for good reason. He's got a better idea than any one but not even Mantle knows for sure how long Mantle will play. Chances are, he'll play just as long as it's physically possible and he can still win a starting berth with the Yanks.

Mickey has a large bundle tied up in Morris Jaffe's First Financial Life Insurance Company. They didn't add him to the board of directors just as a publicity gimmick.

"How many outside interests do you have, besides this one?" someone asked.

"This is it, I've got a large investment in this."

Oh, he still pushes soap and shaving equipment on TV commercials. But those things will vanish when he hangs up his spikes. Mickey is pinning a lot of his future hopes on this insurance venture.

He'll tell you about the company's Mickey Mantle Youth policy. And he'll ask – in a half-kidding and half-serious manner – why his picture wasn't included in the bulky report to stockholders.

But he's really more at ease when the talk returns to baseball.

"Sure, we're off to a slow start, but it's early. We've got some problems, a few injuries in key places. But don't count us out," Mantle said here yesterday.

And then he recalled how a sportswriter visited the Yankee dressing room after the season opener a year or so back.

"It was the first game, the very first game of the year. We had just lost to Minnesota and we had made five errors. This guy comes in and asks, 'Well, boys, do you think you've got a chance this year or is it all over?' Imagine, after the very first game."

Mantle the businessman is serious enough about the world of Wall Street to fly here between games for a stockholders' meeting. But Mickey the player, the sandy-haired gent with flashing blue eyes, still thinks baseball first when given a choice of thoughts.

Chinatown's Bare Facts

Chinatown, San Francisco's answer to New Orleans' French Quarter, is an unusual tourist attraction that boasts some most unusual features. For one thing, the place is loaded with real Chinese. For another, just about every entertainer in every Chinatown joint works naked from the waist up. It's rather difficult to enjoy the music and not stare while a five-piece topless girls band works over a bouncy tune.

The girl with a steel guitar draped around her neck seemed to stay in great danger of suffering an accidental but self-inflicted wound.

The old strip joints are things of the past in San Francisco. They've reversed the whole plan. They now start out naked and wind up getting dressed at the end of each act.

The Houston Oilers faced an 11 p.m. curfew Saturday before their Sunday game with Oakland so most of the players went across the bay early in the afternoon to take in the 'Frisco sights.

It was in front of the Co-Ed Cork Room that our party of writers caught up with a party of eight Oilers. The Co-Ed barker was telling us – in loud tones for all to hear – that his joint boasted "five college co-eds and one high school dropout on the next bill of farc." Naturally, that show was going to start in just two minutes.

"Don't let him kid you," an Oiler advised us. "That high school girl dropped out 15 years ago."

"Yeah? Then where should we go?"

"Try Mrs. Shuenberg, mother of eight."

"Mrs. Who? Mother of what?"

"Over there. Where the crowd is."

Sure enough, across the street in large letters there was a sign for all to see. "Mrs. Shuenberg, Mother of Eight." A smaller neon sign over the door modestly remarked, "She's fantastic."

Mrs. Shuenberg did not have her children with her Saturday night so we had to take the management's word that she had eight. But certainly they wouldn't lie about anything such as that. Besides, Mrs. Shuenberg did seem to have a lot of experience in handling crowds.

Mrs. Shuenberg did a little dance and sang some nice old songs.

Personally, I didn't think she was exceptionally talented but when a poor widow of 24 tries to scratch out a living for her eight children you've just got to applaud. Besides, Mrs. Shuenberg did measure up well in other departments.

It was an interesting evening, to say the least. But I found it difficult to conceal my embarrassment. After all how do you maintain a normal look when you're surrounded by dancers, singers, waitresses and musicians with bare chests? And your wife is sitting beside you the whole evening.

The greatest entertainment of the trip, however, came on the plane when the Oilers ate. Folks, it's something to see. Two pretty little hostesses moved groceries from one end of the plane to the other for a solid two hours and still they called, "Hey, miss, got something else back there to eat?"

You all knew that Ernie Ladd is a defensive tackle, pro wrestler and statesman of sorts. But did you also know that he's a magician?

He can palm two turkey sandwiches in one paw and still have room for a gin rummy hand. I looked out the plane window for a moment and when I glanced back big Ernie had made both sandwiches disappear. He's really a great magician.

The team has rather quiet trips home. Wherever they go. They just can't get their hands raised on the road. These are grown men, of course, so they don't sit around and moan. But they play cards quieter and even chew their food a little quieter.

They even seemed to snore a little softer on the six-hour plane ride home.

December 30, 1966

Dallas-Green Bay Thrills

No single sports event in Texas history, in my memory, has generated more overall deep interest than Sunday's Dallas-Green Bay game for the NFL title. Pick any building and from the elevator to the men's room the conversations all center around that one professional game.

Holiday party-givers, lacking knowledge of the big sports scene, have had to juggle the hours of their ginfests Sunday or stand prepared to face empty rooms.

Jack Onion, recently elected associate justice, court of criminal appeals, somehow settled on a 4 p.m. Sunday time for his official swearing in ceremony. Invitations went out before someone reminded the judge of that Cowboy-Packer tussle on TV.

A wave of whispered protests followed, many backed by threats to bring TV sets to the ceremony. Onion, not eager to be upstaged by a TV set on the high note of his career, today changed the starting time to 1 p.m. Now he's only bucking the AFL title game.

Charles Barrow, stepping up as chief justice of the 4th Court of Civil Appeals, is handling the situation a little differently. He's going to the home of retiring chief justice W.O. Murray to watch the game on TV and at halftime Murray will swear in Barrow in the living room. Then it's back to the TV set for the second half.

The Dallas game will answer many questions. Besides the obvious one of which has the better team.

Can the Cotton Bowl cleanup crew get things back to normal in time after the Georgia-SMU contest?

Will Green Bay's Golden Boy, Paul Hornung, roar back into the high headlines with another clutch performance? Or will he ride the bench most of the way, offering more evidence that he'll soon be traded?

Can Don Meredith, a guy once tabbed a "loser" who recently was voted the NFL's Most Valuable Player award, rise to the occasion with a great performance?

Or will Bart Starr, the old pro some say should have received the award, give a lesson in strategy and passing to his younger foe?

And finally, how often will the fleet Bob Hayes outleg the defensive backs to pull in long strikes? Or will Meredith be allowed enough protection and time to ignite the bombs to Hayes?

In boxing circles this game would be billed as a ring-wise boxer against a young slugger.

Green Bay, wise to the ways of sound strategy and rough play, would be the boxer willing to pile up points on short strokes and then use the clock to its advantage.

Dallas, offering a polished attack that can strike anytime from anywhere, would be the puncher. But this puncher also has a durable defense.

In attempting to predict the game my mind strays back to the boxer-puncher line. I've seen far too many punchers grow desperate — and, eventually careless — trying to land the big one.

For that reason I'll take Green Bay. The Packers feed on the desperate and the careless. If Dallas can score first the Cowboys may well have things their way all afternoon. But if the Packers punch in the initial touchdown the Cowboys could come apart at the seams.

The winner, I think, will be the team that doesn't lose its composure and the Packers seem to keep a husky hammerlock on their composure.

NOTE: Green Bay did score first, racing to a 14-0 lead before the Cowboys offense even ran a play, and the Packers held off Dallas in the final minute to win, 34-27.

Preacher of Hate

It was just 48 hours before the heavyweight title fight in Houston and main speaker for the program was Rev. Muhammad Ali. He got top billing over other speakers who had more titles in front of their names and a few initials and abbreviations behind their handles.

Houston's Black Muslims were not too active in 1966. As a matter of fact, they were very inactive, owning the lowest attendance record for meetings in the nation.

But alas, the natives were restless on this night for prayer and preaching, and a full house filed into the large meeting room.

Not all were Muslims, black or white, and it was very difficult for ushers to distinguish a true believer from a curious visitor. After all, what's a fellow to do when attendance jumps from 8 or 9 to over 200?

Well, for one thing, the "ushers" frisked every person who entered the room. Not for money. For weapons.

One Negro man had a pair of fingernail clippers in his pocket and the huge usher needed a consultation to handle the matter. He called in the chief usher and after the two carefully weighed the situation they let the fellow keep his clippers and pass on in.

Every man who had a ballpoint pen in his shirt pocket got the same treatment. The usher took the pen, pointed it at the owner's head, about two inches from an eye, and pressed the button. This eliminated any chance of someone smuggling in tear gas or a single-shot gun in the form of a pen or pencil. When the Black Muslims meet to discuss the world's weighty problems they don't want any hanky panky.

It's believed that all of this precaution at the front door started after Malcolm X got interrupted during a sermon one evening. Poor Malcolm X was discussing the evil white man and the hereafter when a couple of Negro gents rushed up and shot him full of holes. It was a very exciting meeting that attracted a lot of publicity. So did the funeral.

At least 30 white men attended the meeting and most were reporters who were in Houston for the fight.

A hush fell over the crowd when Rev. Ali stepped up to do some serious preaching, the kind which he hopes will keep him out of the draft. Rev. Muhammad devoted his opening remarks to the lowly pig.

Some of the better business minds in the audience probably looked upon Ali's address as a game effort to harness the price of pork. With choice ham going for about a buck and a half a pound the Rev. Muhammad really bombarded the pig.

"The pig is the dirtiest animal in all the world," he remarked. "Anybody that would eat of the pig couldn't possibly call himself clean. The pig has about 15 locations on its body that are full of pus," Ali shouted as he warmed up on pork chops and ham hocks.

Before the boxer-preacher could settle down to the more important business of verbally dealing with the white man he took a brief break while ushers asked "all visitors" to leave. They didn't come right out and tell the whites to scram but since they weren't in the market for any white converts they motioned to the door at the few lingering "visitors."

It may well be that Cassius Clay is a convincing preacher, a point he's attempting to make with his draft board. In all fairness it should be mentioned that none of the "visitors" rushed out to get ham sandwiches.

Many Negroes in attendance refused to embrace the Black Muslim beliefs and merely dropped by to look and listen to the world's greatest heavyweight boxing champion. So it wasn't too difficult to get the word on what happened after reporters left.

Muhammad Ali, the man who just 48 hours later was to be cheered as a "world's champion," went into great detail about how all white men are "devils created by a mad scientist."

When you think it all over it's a sad, sickening situation. Cassius Clay, a remarkable athlete who has the power to be America's greatest goodwill ambassador when the nation needs unity more than at any time since the Civil War, winds up being an immature preacher of hate.

His logic and thoughts are so childishly stupid that he could hardly be considered dangerous. Except for one important thing. We listen to him. When the heavyweight champion talks, people listen.

The boxing world doesn't need a "white hope." Just a sane champion.

April 4, 1967

Banning of the Dunk

A number of basketball fans have written or called asking for my opinion on the new rule that bans dunking or stuffing. Sgt. Fausto Gutierrez of Brooks AFB, for instance, wrote a three-page letter to request opinions on the matter.

Actually, I'm no authority on basketball. Or anything else, for that matter. But I've got opinions on everything. When you come here for an opinion you've come to the right place. You might not get a good one but you'll sure get one.

It is my uneducated but studied opinion that the new rule is one of the worst things that could happen to basketball. It is a direct slap and penalty hurled at all tall men who play the game. It is also a post-season insult to the national championship team and its star player, Lew Alcindor.

Even before Alcindor and his UCLA teammates could accept the nation's applause for an undefeated season the NCAA fathers met and handed down the ruling that, in effect, said, "Okay, you won this time with the 7-1 Alcindor but we're changing the rules to stop you next season."

If the basketball bosses are allowed to get away with this piece of law-making, Randy Matson and others who weigh over 240 should handicap themselves a few yards when they put the shot against smaller men. Faster football ends like Bob Hayes should have to start five yards behind the line of scrimmage, pass receivers who stand over 6-7 should have to catch the ball with one hand and tall tennis players should not be allowed to crowd the net, or when serving, stand near the baseline.

The tall basketball players are in a minority and when they stuff a basketball they're displaying a natural shot – for them. They're reaping one of the rare rewards their unusual height provides. And now that's being taken from them.

Basketball authorities made a mistake. Those who know the game best and love it most should speak out soon to correct that mistake. At least, that's the opinion from this corner.

Add another sports name to the automobile business here. No less than 10 fellows who used to make sports headlines are now selling autos here.

The latest to join the ranks is Jennings Anderson, former Brackenridge and Texas Aggie star who opened the North Star Dodge agency out on San Pedro.

Anderson is built like a tall pool table but he once stepped the century at 9.9 for the Aggies. He used to be a halfback but some extra weight now makes him look like a retired field goal kicker who doubled at tackle.

––––––––

Moment Of Glory

It was difficult to believe Saturday, when they announced the scores of the Masters golf tournament. It was as if the pages of time had been rolled back. Back to another era. Back to the heyday of the mechanical marvel, bantam Ben Hogan.

At 54, the ice that once nestled in his nerves had dropped to his putter, leaving the tiny Texan with a cold blade and a jumpy, sad stroke on the greens.

Oh, in his time he'd snaked in more than his share of long ones for the big money but some say that most of Hogan's putts were willed in, through sheer concentration.

It becomes harder to concentrate on a game after you cross the half century mark. Even a game you know and love so well.

That's why Ben was ashamed as he practiced on the putting greens just prior to the Masters. He actually apologized to a writer he didn't even know. Twice he paused and studied for long moments before tapping at three-footers. And twice he missed by half a foot or more.

He seemed embarrassed as he caught the writer's eyes and remarked, "I just can't do it anymore."

Then he putted again. And missed again.

"It's my nerves. That's all. Just bad nerves and I don't know what I can do about it," he said. And then finally, after a full hour of such practice, he gathered his gear and moved back into the clubhouse.

At that moment he looked like a million-to-one underdog for this year's Masters title.

The man who had won four U.S. Open tournaments, two Masters titles, two PGA crowns, the British Open and countless lesser honors, moved through the crowd dejected and unnoticed.

Gene Sarazen, another old pro from yesteryear, signed autographs and had the time of his life. Like Hogan, he was in Georgia to once again play in the Masters. But, unlike Hogan, he harbored no hope of winning.

Ben Hogan never teed up in his life without earnestly seeking a first-place finish.

Some thought it was a minor miracle when Ben stayed close with opening rounds of 74 and 73.

"He can't get there but he just won't quit," one local pro remarked.

But then came the third round and the old magic that followed Hogan for a dozen years returned stronger than ever.

Somehow, somewhere he found the strength to once again out-drive his younger, larger foes. His irons were as accurate as a rifle and the chill was gone from his putter. For 18 holes the "Wee Ice Man" was back in form. The "Texas Hawk" was on the prowl. From out of the past came Ben Hogan to offer his challenge to the new greats that were not of his time.

And when he'd spun his old magic over the long layout the crowd was wild with excitement. Hogan had blazed a 66, the best round of the tournament, and moved within two strokes of the leader.

It would have been nice had Hogan been able to hang on Sunday for just one more fabulous round.

But all who read fairy tales know that magic has a time limit. The beautiful coach returns to a pumpkin. The footmen become mice again and a kiss from the right lips awakens the sleeping princess.

And so it was at the Masters this year. Hogan's magic was gone Sunday, overtaken and erased by the galloping gait of Father Time. Saturday's challenger became Sunday's also-ran as bantam Ben found jumpy nerves behind a cold putter to struggle home with a 77.

The hour of glory had passed, perhaps never to return. And when it was over the golfing gods seemed to have their personal satisfaction for there, tied in 10th place with Hogan, was another face from the past, Ben's old rival from a hundred golfing wars, Sam Snead.

July   28,   1967

Drag Queen

She's got blue eyes, long, straight, honey-colored hair, freckles on her nose and a small smile stays on her thin lips. She's 26, weighs 120 and stands 5-4. As a housewife and the mother of three Mrs. Arlene Oaulline doesn't have much spare time but what little there is she devotes to oil painting and — now get this — motorcycle drag racing.

Oddly enough, Mrs. Oaulline had never even been on a cycle until a year ago and she now holds a national title and is gunning for a national record. Since very few women race motorcycles Arlene competes against men.

"How did you happen to take up motorcycle drag racing, Mrs. Oaulline?"

"My husband, Jack, bought one a little over a year ago and for a long while I didn't even want to ride with him. But he finally talked me into it and I liked it. Then I began to ride by myself. Finally, on the first of this year, I entered a race here at the San Antonio Drag Raceway. I found that it was real fun."

"How fast do you go?"

"It's a regular quarter of a mile drag strip. We're hitting over 100 when we reach the end. On a good run we get up to 110 before shutting down."

"Do you open it up all the way?"

"All the way, all the time. From the instant you start you twist the throttle wide open and leave it there. It's fun."

"Yes, sound like loads of fun."

"Would you like to try it sometime?"

"I'd love to. But I'm very busy this week. Maybe in the winter when it gets a little cooler."

Mrs. Oaulline is the "new look" fostering the new image hot rod and drag clubs seek. Once she dons her street clothes you'd never guess she could jockey a big 'cycle to near record speeds.

Even her conversation seems foreign to the dragsters I've known. When asked if she'd ever taken any spills Arlene replied, "I had a few minor spills at first when I was learning but once I became proficient it was different. I haven't encountered any problems like that in months."

But on my next question she fired a change of pace. When asked what she likes best about drag racing I figured Mrs. Oaulline would come back with something like the thrill of the high speeds, the wind whipping her face, the spirited struggle to stay aboard the roaring monster and all that sort of jazz.

Instead, she blushed a bit and announced, "I guess it will sound terrible, but I just love to win."

Mr. Oaulline, owner of the big 750 CC charger Arlene rides, doesn't compete as a dragster. A construction worker, he stands 6-2 and weighs about 200. That's too husky a load to stay in contention for more than a few yards of that quarter-mile strip.

"And the kids? Do they ride on the hog?"

"Please, it's a 'cycle. No they don't ride. Of course, they've all been on once or twice for brief rides but I don't let them on often. It's too dangerous. Besides, Jack and I agree that just one person at a time should ride."

Arlene is hungry for more national titles – plus the record – after tasting victory in the spring nationals at Odessa. She's making plans to compete in the national motorcycle meet in Indianapolis in September but she's not yet sure Jack can take off from work.

The record is 12.97 seconds for the quarter mile and Arlene has made the trip in 13.05. Close, but no cigar.

"It's getting to be a thing with me. I want that record badly. I try for it almost every time out. Everything has to go perfectly and some night I feel it will."

Mrs. Oaulline races on the drag strip here almost every Saturday night but she stays away from the oval races. "It's rough and very dangerous. Even the veteran racers spill a time or two during a long race and they often get their legs cut up. I don't want my legs all chopped and scarred."

This makes sense. Especially after you've seen Mrs. Oaulline's legs.

Principle Swallowed

The International Olympic Committee lost its guts over the weekend. Also, its authority. But because it did perhaps we're all breathing a sigh of relief today. We now know the show will go on as planned. It'll just go on without South Africa.

For a long while it appeared that the whole Olympic Games plan, plus millions of dollars in preparation, would go down the drain in order to admit a team that probably couldn't win a fourth-place handshake if all the invited guests appeared.

It boiled down to principle and you began to wonder the true worth of a principle.

More than likely, most of the nations threatening a boycott if South Africa were admitted were bluffing. But the Mexicans, who have already coughed up many millions to prepare for the games, were in no mood to call such a bluff. Neither were high Olympic officials from other countries who honestly felt the games would lay a magnificent egg if South Africa were admitted.

So the principle has been discarded – and South Africa with it. Because – aside from the boycott threat – there's no real reason why that nation should not be permitted to compete.

South Africa is segregated, they say. And it most certainly is. But the South Africans have given their solemn word that their Olympic team would not be segregated – that all their athletes, black and white alike – would be housed together and given equal treatment. Wouldn't that be a great step toward total integration?

But now the Olympic Games have been converted to just another political football.

The next step might be to threaten a ban against the U.S. if we use any athletes from Alabama, Georgia or Mississippi. Or even a trainer from Memphis, Tenn.

Or to get away from the racial issue perhaps we should call for a boycott against the Communist countries because so many of them use forced child labor.

And to get back to the racial issue maybe we should call for a boy-cott against the Congo. There are tribes in that area that still practice cannibalism. It's one thing when a Negro is scolded for drinking from the wrong water fountain but it's something else when big bwana winds up at the dinner table on a plate.

The point is, Olympic officials should be interested only in the treatment the various teams give their athletes and not the customs and policies of the countries. The UN can't even solve those problems but the Olympic wheels now seem ready to try.

It was Russia, you'll recall, that started the outcry against the admission of South Africa because of that nation's racial policies. So it strikes me as rather strange that not a single Negro ever makes the Russian team.

In the past two decades a great number of Negroes have migrated to Russia but so far not one has emerged as an outstanding athlete. Do you suppose they are getting a fair shake over there? It's something the Olympic committee should look into between checks on South Africa.

Personally, I'm glad the Olympic muddle is clear and the games will go on as scheduled. But I'm afraid the sacrifice was far too great. There are so few principles left in this old world. It's sad to see another one swallowed by greed, selfishness and fear.

May   16,   1968

The Forecasters

One of the main complaints society has against sportswriters is that this breed of newsmen has become notorious for incorrectly forecasting the outcome of major sports events.

Yet, one of the main reasons so many pay to witness the big athletic contests is that they are so unpredictable and the unexpected always happens.

A football takes a wrong bounce, an umpire misses a third strike, a dime bolt works free on a speeding race car, long putts suddenly drop for an unknown kid and an eager youngster lands a lucky punch on a confident champion. These are just a few of the strange ingredients that work the word "upset" into newspaper headlines — and leave informed sports-writers red with embarrassment.

"How you gonna pick this next one so I can bet the other way?" is an age-old taunt sportswriters must endure a thousand times a year. Oh, how I would love to answer, "I'm picking me to clobber you with a 2-by-4" and then whip out a big board. Instead, you laugh with the crowd and always leave smiling.

That way they might remember you as a "good sport." Not a good sportswriter. Just a good sport.

Misery, they say, loves company.

So today I seek the companionship of our nation's top political writers. These guys haven't picked a winner since Roosevelt knocked out Wendell Wilkie.

For reasons I'll never understand these newsmen usually are held in high esteem by the general public. This might be because the general public is so busy arguing over the deeds and misdeeds of the politicians they overlook the writers.

Still, the noted scribes who report on political science from the White House drawing room can't even predict a starting lineup, much less the outcome. And they're dealing only in men, not footballs, bolts or near-sighted umpires.

Four months ago, according to all reports, LBJ was a lead-pipe cinch to get the Democratic nomination and Gov. Romney was a light favorite for the Republican job. These two horses weren't left at the gate. They wouldn't even come out of the stalls.

Rockefeller "positively" would not run a few weeks ago according to reports. Now he's in the race although he still hasn't taken off his warmup jacket.

Bobby Kennedy was content to wait and "would do nothing to oppose LBJ." Now he's two furlongs in front on the Democratic derby.

Ronald Reagan couldn't even promote reruns of "Death Valley Days" in Nebraska, political writers claimed. But he gathered 41,000 write-in votes and that was about 30,000 more than Rockefeller.

Sen. McCarthy was just rocking the boat when he boldly stepped into the big leagues for the New Hampshire primary. Experts claimed he was merely lodging his own protest against the establishment. But he socked it to 'em and that one "protest" promises to change the course of history. It opened a whole can of worms and now political writers can't even agree who the contestants are, much less the favorites.

About the only time the political scribes have been right lately was when they reported that Nixon would run. Man, they didn't go out on a limb there. That was like revealing that IBM has computers. Or Richard Burton has fun.

And so it goes, armed with assists from Mr. Gallup and other opinion takers, the Washington writers still struggle for a .500 batting average in the political league. This, while the poor sportswriter boasts a .700 percentage and endures great suffering from the few we missed.

"Hey, fathead, who you like in the Preakness? I wanna be sure and not bet on that horse." And, "You cost me money last week. You couldn't pick your daddy out of a carload of apes."

June 14, 1968

Athletic Bodyguards

A little research has revealed that for many years athletes — or former athletes — were aides to top public officials and at their sides when attempts were made on their lives. But only one actually prevented death and to do it he used his ability as a football player.

Such research was prompted by the actions of Roosevelt Grier, the big former Los Angeles Ram who disarmed the gunman who shot and killed Robert Kennedy.

Twenty years after President James Garfield's 1881 assassination, President William McKinley was fatally shot. A former wrestler was at Garfield's side and McKinley, blasted at close range during a public hand-shaking session, had a former football player positioned behind him when he was hit.

Vice President Theodore Roosevelt moved into the top office when McKinley died eight days after the shooting on Sept. 14, 1901. Teddy was the one who was saved by an athlete.

TR went out of office in 1909 but in 1912 he was campaigning for a return on the Progressive, or Bull Moose, ticket. Unknown by Roosevelt, a nut by the name of John Schrank had been thinking of killing him for years — ever since he dreamed that McKinley's ghost came to him and accused Roosevelt of murdering him for the presidency.

Unfortunately for Mr. Roosevelt, the ghost made a comeback in 1912 and it was too much for Schrank. He decided to act. But fortunately for Roosevelt, his top aide was a former football player for Detroit University.

Elbert E. Martin had played right tackle for Detroit and it was known that he was quick as a big cat.

When Schrank caught up with Roosevelt, the candidate was on his way to Milwaukee Auditorium to deliver a speech. Just as he stepped into his car the would-be assassin raced to within six feet of Roosevelt and shot him in the middle. He used a double-action revolver but after the initial shot he calmly cocked the gun and took aim again.

Before he could get off the second shot Martin lunged from the car and downed him with a flying tackle. Witnesses claimed that Martin cracked the gunman in the stomach with a shoulder and slammed him to the concrete.

The one slug that Roosevelt took first penetrated a metal case (for his glasses), then tore through his 50-page speech that was folded double in his pocket. The slug fractured one rib and came to rest deep in Roosevelt's chest. He carried it there until he died of natural causes seven years later.

Just for the record, Teddy Roosevelt was every bit the tough guy historians still picture him.

Immediately after the shooting his friends tried to take him to a hospital but he insisted on first delivering his speech. And he did, too. "It takes more than a shot in the chest to kill a Bull Moose," Roosevelt roared and with that he departed for the Milwaukee Auditorium.

Records show that it took him 50 minutes to deliver the 50-page talk but it's suspected that he skipped over a few items. Especially those blanked out by the bullet hole.

The incident increased Roosevelt's popularity so much that he almost overcame the odds but he did miss and Woodrow Wilson stepped up to the presidency.

Until his death in 1956 Mr. Martin carried a handsome watch that was engraved, "To Elbert E. Martin from Theodore Roosevelt in remembrance of Oct. 14, 1912."

And because of that incident President Wilson immediately got himself a former football player as one of his aides. And even though

Teddy's near-assassination has been almost forgotten the policy of hiring athletic bodyguards or "aides" has been generally followed through the years.

———

Anyone For Big Leagues?

Say, do you trust me? I mean really trust me. If you don't then there's not much reason for you to read any deeper today. This might be the most important column I'll ever write and it's one that requires a lot of trust on your part. You've got to believe what I'm telling you is the absolute truth. And then you've got to react. And fast.

San Antonio has dabbled in minor-league everything at one time or another and although some of the ventures have been very successful we now seem to be reclining in a sort of restful limbo.

We seem too big and sophisticated to accept and support minor-league sports and we're not big enough and rich enough to support major-league sports. So here we sit on the sidelines, ignoring our own and too far away from the hot action.

You can believe that or not. It's only an opinion and it's not important that you agree or disagree.

It is important, however, that you believe me when I write that a man here in town has a positive plan to bring an NBA franchise to San Antonio — for next season.

You've got to believe blindly because I can't reveal names. I can't even mention the name of the NBA franchise that would be coming here but I can tell you that the plan sounds very workable.

The general idea is to sell 2,000 season tickets, the best seats with added comfort, and then scale general admission for each game way down to meet the budgets of all.

Think of it for a moment, a National Basketball Association franchise right here. The world's greatest players — Wilt Chamberlain, Jerry Lucas, Bill Russell and all the others — would be playing here every week.

And think of this: there is no other NBA team in Texas. San Antonio would lead Houston, Dallas and all others in this field. Big-league, big-time basketball.

Such a franchise could do more than HemisFair to draw national attention to this city.

Also keep in mind, this team wouldn't be started from scratch with new and young players. The whole franchise, with the team stars intact and signed to contracts, would be moved here.

Those are the things I'm asking you to believe.

Now comes the most important part. You've got to react.

Please, how many of you would be willing to pay $2 a game to see at least five NBA games here in San Antonio next season?

That's the question I've agreed to ask and your response will play a great role in deciding whether the franchise will come to San Antonio. Your response, of course, would not be binding and you're not asked to send a dime or sign a contract.

No long letters on the matter, no personal opinions on whether the franchise can or cannot be obtained. You've just got to believe me when I say it positively can be obtained.

The price is right and the contacts are tight. But this city has suffered through several failures at various box offices and the man who holds the key to it all wants to know just what sort of response he might expect.

No, he's not a fast-buck promoter. And he's not a visitor who just dropped in from the East to test public reaction for the future. He's a San Antonian who wants to put a big-league sport here. He wants to do it right away because the opportunity may not return for many years.

I'm convinced to the point that I've agreed to ask for your opinion but we only want honest answers to a simple question.

Again, would you be willing to pay $2 a game to see at least five NBA games here in San Antonio next season?

It's important that you answer right away. A postcard and three minutes of your time may do more than you realize to push San Antonio onto the big sports map.

From experience I've learned that people don't write newspapers unless (1) somebody's made a bad error, (2) somebody's voiced a lousy opinion or (3) something free is offered.

I'm offering you nothing but the firm belief that we can move San Antonio into the big sports picture. I hope that belief is worth a brief reply.

NOTE: Read the next column to see what kind of response Cook received.

November 27, 1968

Now, About That NBA Team

How do you write "thank you" and impress upon folks that you really mean it?

A simple "thanks" seems insufficient for the many hundreds who took time to write cards and letters — and hustle up petitions — in response to a request here last week.

At the last count 1,233 had written to say yes, they would support an NBA franchise if one could be obtained for San Antonio. And from that number they requested or "pledged" a total of 4,800 tickets for at least five games.

Also, there were 27 petitions sent in, the largest one from Joe Garcia of Joske's (carrying 178 signatures and addresses) and the second largest from Kelly Field, with 102 signatures.

It was interesting and heartwarming to glance through the cards. Cards that said, "yes, sock it to me, baby." And, "you asked for penny postcards but they went out with 50-cent haircuts so will you accept my yes vote on a nickel postcard?" And, "put me down for three season tickets to anything that's big-league."

Oddly enough, the most negative reply said, "I don't think it'll work but if somebody tries I'll buy two season tickets."

Twenty-one people mailed checks for tickets while two others sent cash. All of that was returned, of course.

Approximately 300 included personal notes that really should be answered. But I can't. It would take me three years to write 300 letters. And that's only if I got a secretary for the last year.

You're entitled to know more about the setup and the possibility of actually getting that pro basketball franchise here. As mentioned before, I'm not at liberty to reveal everything but I'll tell you all I can.

1. There is an NBA franchise that's for sale although it has not been placed on the open market, and a San Antonio man — a close friend of those who control interest in the team — has been given the option to purchase the team for $3 million.

2. The San Antonio man does not have $3 million but he feels certain he can put together a syndicate that does have that kind of cash.

3. Before he tackles the organizing of a monied syndicate he wants to be sure the operation would be successful in San Antonio.

4. He feels that he can sell 2,000 tickets at $5 per home game — with not too much effort. But he is not at all sure he can go beyond that. He's afraid that after he sells the higher-priced season tickets there might not be enough interest left to sell many general admission tickets at $2 a game.

That's why he came to me. He wanted me to ask you if you'd be willing to pay $2 a ticket just for five home games. There would be many more home games, of course, but he believes anyone willing to try five would wind up seeing one.

He also believes that anyone willing to take time and effort to write — and receive nothing in return — must have genuine interest in such a project.

I think your cards and letters will convince him that there is great interest in such a project here.

In all probability I won't hit on this subject again here for a good while. This afternoon I'll dump your response in the man's lap and then it will be up to him to get the wheels turning — if they are to turn at all here.

December 24, 1968

A Christmas Eve Poem

'Twas the night before Christmas
When all through the house,
Not a creature was stirring,
Not even a mouse.

The stockings were hung
By the chimney with care,
In hopes that Saint Nicholas
Soon would be there.

But up at the Pole Nick froze in fear

To make his deliveries he'd need high gear.
He'd waited too long, but he clinched his fist
And pondered again this strange gift list.

From Clay there was a request from the soul
He'd written old Santa for a legal loophole.
And a man named Floyd made Santa a dare,
He wanted two judges, both decent and fair.

And from Dandy Don came an unusual request
A gimmick to allow him to play at his best.
Have the league brass, those wheelers and dealers,
Put Dallas down for 8 games with the Steelers.

Roberto the golfer stood alone with his plea,
Old Santa could hang this on anyone's tree.
The simple request put Santa to dance,
Ten dozen golf cards, signed in advance.

But Unitas' order gave Santa a whirl
'Twas a place on the bench for a guy named Earl.
A request from Wilt, called in by phone,
He wants a coach he can call his own.

Old Santa sat down and poured a slug of juice,
He was ready to pass, to call a truce.
For baseball batters filled him with appall
They wanted a livelier, yet bigger baseball.

The folks in Kentucky had a rare request
But it put old Santa to a mighty tough test.
No Derby results for the coming year,
It's the '68 winner they're waiting to hear.

Now none of this loot was in Santa's bag
But he was far off schedule, no time to lag.
So into the sleigh the old gent hopped,
A twitch of his hands, the ancient whip popped.

So Santa is coming, he's on the way now,
And from me to you I'll make one vow.
No more poetry here, not from this stall,
After I wish Merry Christmas, to one and all.

———

January 13, 1969

Namath Proves Super Boasts, Sinks Colts

MIAMI — Joe Namath spent much of last week using his mouth to stir interest in the Super Bowl and then he spent much of Sunday afternoon using his arm to back up the boasts of his mouth.

It's now debatable as to which was more accurate, his mouth or his arm, because football history will prove that neither was ever far off their true targets.

Namath and his surprising New York Jets, rising far higher than most fans figured possible, shocked the once-proud Baltimore Colts 16-7 in the third annual Super Bowl here yesterday in one of pro football's most stunning upsets.

Namath, who had so much to say last week, chatted a little before a TV mike after the game but then clammed up around reporters. And Matt Snell, who gained 121 yards on 30 carries for the Jets, probably said it for Joe when he chased reporters.

"I didn't even get a vote for the AFL All-Star Game and all you guys could write about was how great the Colts are so don't try to talk to us now. Go on over and talk to them," Snell said. And he said it often.

There was, of course, celebration in the winners' dressing room but they came away from the game resentful and angry, just like they entered it. Only an angry and talented team could have destroyed Baltimore like the Jets did Sunday.

A capacity crowd of 75,377, including the three moon astronauts, Vice President-elect Spiro Agnew, Ted Kennedy and his father, Joseph Kennedy, watched as the 18-point underdog Jets scored first in the second period and then ran up a 16-0 lead before the Colts could dent the scoreboard.

To say that Namath entered the game confident would be like saying Elizabeth Taylor likes men.

But Namath's confidence didn't all stem from his own ability. He had confidence in his receivers and his offensive linemen and that trust was well-placed.

George Sauer, the former Texas star, caught eight of Namath's hot pitches for 133 yards while the Jet quarterback got better protection than a presidential motorcade. He had to eat the ball once when his receivers were covered but on only one other occasion did the Colts break through and grab the object of their daylong search.

The Colts, some experts claimed, formed the best pro team in football history because they did so many things so well. But Baltimore was trumped by the Jets in every one of those "do well" departments Sunday and the key behind this monumental upset probably was the four interceptions the Jets produced.

Baltimore, with its highly publicized secondary, failed to pick off a single Namath pass although the Colts can blame only their clumsy fingers, for there were several solid chances missed.

Both teams used two quarterbacks as Baltimore called the old pro off the bench in the third period but Johnny Unitas did only a little better than starter Earl Morrall.

Namath injured his throwing hand in the third period and Babe Parilli came on for the Jets but after one series of downs Namath was back in business.

Baltimore opened the game just as expected, rolling through the white-shirted Jets for three first downs but then the drive was stalled. When Lou Michaels missed a 27-yard field goal the tide turned and an exciting afternoon of the unexpected unfolded.

The Colts got a good chance early in the second after Ron Porter grabbed Sauer's fumble on the New York 12. On the second play, however, Randy Beverly intercepted Morrall's end-zone pass as the ball bounced high off the shoulder of Ron Mitchell, the touchdown target.

Then the Jets went to work for their only touchdown, moving 80 yards in 12 plays. Namath took turns hitting Snell, Sauer and Bill Mathis and finally it was Snell who raced wide to score from four yards out. Turner kicked and the team that "couldn't win" was ahead 7-0.

Tom Matte, who got 116 yards on 11 carries for Baltimore, almost pulled the Colts even before halftime but he was half a step too slow for

Bill Baird. Matte broke over tackle and found daylight down the side-lines but Baird cut him off at the pass, making the stop at the Jets 6 after the day's hottest foot race.

After one try at the middle Morrall went to the air again and it was a mistake. Johnny Sample swiped it on the 2 to further frustrate the Colts.

In the third Turner added field goals of 32 and 30 yards to make it 13-0. Early in the fourth, after Baltimore got tough in the shadows of its own goal, Turner booted his third three-pointer, a 9-yard kick.

With Morrall on the bench and Unitas in charge Baltimore took the following kickoff and drove 50 yards to the New York 26 but then the old Colt miracle-worker of years ago saw one of his passes stolen by Beverly in the end zone.

Three penalties helped the Colts go 80 yards for their lone score as Jerry Hill climaxed the march by driving over tackle from a foot out with just 3:19 left in the game.

Then Baltimore pulled an onside kick to fan the fires of hope but Unitas was far off target when it counted most and the drive fizzled on the Jets 18, leaving each New York player with $15,000, twice the amount each Colt will get.

Colts coach Don Shula said after the game, "They played better than we did so they deserved to win." He found no argument on the score.

The Jets, with several NFL rejects and a coach who was fired by Baltimore in 1963 (Weeb Ewbank), Sunday brought the young American Football League its greatest triumph in its first Super Bowl victory.

J a n u a r y   3 0 ,   1 9 6 9

Baseball's Hall Pickers

Judging from all past performances it might be safe to assume that no player shall ever enter baseball's Hall of Fame on a unanimous vote. You see, sportswriters do the voting and 340 sportswriters wouldn't all agree that King Kong had hairy armpits.

Never in the history of sports has one man dominated a game as Babe Ruth dominated baseball during his long career. His tremendous power and huge bat made fans forget that he was once a great pitcher who set records just as some of his home run records stand today.

Still, when it came time to vote on whether Babe Ruth should enter baseball's Hall of Fame no less than 11 sportswriters left him off their ballots. Imagine, the game's all-time career home run champion being snubbed by 11 men who were paid to report on baseball.

So why all the excitement in some quarter because Stan Musial failed to enter the Hall on a unanimous vote?

Ty Cobb didn't go in as a unanimous pick and Walter Johnson, once a pretty fair pitcher, got left off of 37 ballots. So why should Musial become the first to get named on every ballot?

After all, Musial just set or shared 64 major or National League records. And he only got 475 home runs and he must have concentrated on weak pitchers because twice he got three homers in one game. Also, you can overlook the league endurance record Musial set by playing in 895 consecutive games because he didn't play all those games at the same position, sometimes leaving his outfield post to try first base.

Everybody knows why Ted Williams wasn't a unanimous choice. He thumbed his nose at too many sportswriters and we sportswriters don't forget. No sir. Give me a bad time when you're in the minors and I'll fix your clock if I have to wait 30 years. You could hit 10 tons of homers and I wouldn't vote for you for batboy of the Bloomington Bloomers.

Of course, with some sportswriters, it's not an altogether personal matter. Exactly 72 writers failed to name Joe DiMaggio on their ballots and he didn't even enter the Hall on the first vote when he became eligible. Let's face it, not everybody likes Italians, no matter how well they might have performed.

Years ago I remember reading how one writer, a solid pillar of Christianity and a leader in his church, boasted that he didn't vote for Ruth because the Babe drank too much, went with too many wild women and was a bad influence on the youth of America.

Of course, the writers are only asked to vote after judging a man on his baseball performances. If they ever run box scores on each player with space for "booze consumed" and "women dated" the interest in baseball might pick up considerably or die altogether.

Actually, the only thing anyone connected with baseball could hold against Musial is that he once was a sore-armed minor-league pitcher who almost gave up the game to become a salesman. If they care to go back far enough they might discover that his brief pitching career — in the minors

— wasn't too impressive. But his 22 brilliant seasons in the majors should have taken care of that "blemish" on his record.

Some now say that Mickey Mantle or Willie Mays will become the first to enter the Hall on a unanimous vote. But don't you believe that for one minute.

After all, out of 540 voters there's bound to be at least one Yankee hater and one who won't be fond of Negro players.

NOTE: As predicted, neither Mantle nor Mays were unanimous picks into the Hall of Fame. Mantle entered in 1974, getting 322 of 365 votes, and Mays was elected in 1979 with 409 of 432 votes. Closest player to being unanimous was Tom Seaver in 1972 with 98.84 percent — 425 of 430.

J u l y   4 ,   1 9 6 9

Chicago Story

P hil Wrigley, the chewing gum man who owns the Chicago Cubs, can be a stubborn individual who likes to live with his own ideas. He has, however, been known to back off when some of those ideas spring obvious leaks.

Like when he decided to have rotating managers for the Cubs. Mr. Wrigley got himself about nine managers and they all took turns bossing the Cubs and then moving down and around to run a Chicago farm team. We all wondered what would happen if a guy got on a 15-game winning streak and his time with the Cubs ran out. But the Cubs, being what they were in those days, never forced that problem on Wrigley.

That idea had some merit because when a team plays like the old Cubs played any manager is an 8-5 favorite to get axed before the All-Star break. Wrigley didn't have to fire anyone. He'd just rotate the coaches around. One day a fellow might be running the Cubs' team and the next night he might be turning in lineups for Wenatchee in the Northwest League.

Nobody seems to recall just when that plan went down the drain but it's rather common knowledge that Wrigley is now overjoyed at having Leo Durocher in complete charge of his Cubs.

But Leo's current success in Chicago only hardens another idea that

Mr. Wrigley has been stuck with for many years. As far as he's concerned the darkest day in baseball history came when Thomas Edison discovered the light bulb.

Wrigley hates night baseball. He firmly believes that baseball was intended for afternoon enjoyment and people should all be home chewing gum when the sun goes down. So Wrigley Field in Chicago is the only major-league park in existence without lights.

Some thought Mr. Wrigley was beginning to weaken when attendance dipped through some of the Cubs' really low years but an old night owl named Leo rushed in to save the day. Day games, that is. Durocher prefers day games because they allow him more time to pursue his other hobbies at night.

At any rate, with Durocher leading the Cubs toward a possible World Series date, attendance at Wrigley is up 70 percent over their crowd figures for the first two months of last season.

It's hard for some of us to understand how 20,000 fans would attend a routine major-league game that started at 1:30 p.m. on a weekday afternoon. But that's what the Cubs averaged for four such weekday games just a week ago.

Chicago is one of only two cities that still have more than one pro baseball team (New York, of course, being the other) so it's safe to assume that when the Cubs prosper the White Sox suffer. And vice versa.

Some thought the Cubs, with their day baseball, would never again outdraw the White Sox. But that theory is being shot full of holes as Durocher's merry men march up victory road in broad daylight with thousands of new witnesses each month.

Now rumors are being circulated that the White Sox might soon be packing and moving to greener pastures in another city. Arthur Allyn, president and part owner of the Chisox, says he has no intention of moving. But he does admit that his club needs a few more colorful heroes, not to mention a few more victories.

"We need one good, exciting player as a drawing card and we haven't had one since Minnie Minoso," Allyn recently admitted.

It could be that everyone else is wrong and Wrigley is right. After all, about 90 percent of today's major league games are played at night but when they get around to the biggie — the World Series — they revert to day games no matter which clubs are involved.

Some say that Mr. Wrigley is too much of a tightwad to buy lights and they point out that he saves about $8,000 a season on electricity alone. That not only isn't true but it also isn't fair.

The little savings wouldn't mean as much as two days' sale of Spearmint chewing gum. And then there's always Juicy Fruit.

NOTE: Second-oldest stadium in the major leagues (behind Boston's Fenway Park), Wrigley Field got lights in 1988. Oh, and despite winning 92 games in 1969, the Cubs finished second behind the late-charging Amazing Mets.

J u l y   2 3 ,   1 9 6 9

O.J. Weighs S.A. Offer

When you sit at home and say it slowly, $50,000 for six months of football sounds like a lot of money. In fact, 50 thou for six months of anything should keep your shoes shined through the off-season. After all, you've still got the other half-year to peddle encyclopedias or toil as a greeter in one of the nicer watering holes.

On the other hand, $240,000 sounds like much more, even if you say it fast with the tub water running.

The flying finger of football fate has twirled up an odd set of circumstances that pits our San Antonio Toros in a price-bidding war against the Buffalo Bills — with the Toros four furlongs out front.

Most folks laugh and say "it's ridiculous" when they hear that the Toros are bidding $15,000 a game for the services of O.J. Simpson for 16 games this season. But O.J. isn't laughing. And neither is his manager, Chuck Barnes.

Look at it this way, which is the way the Toro owners looked at it before making the offer. The presence of Simpson should add at least 4,000 to the gate of every Toro game. At $5 a copy that's $20,000. Or, if they decide to up the ticket price to $6 should Simpson sign, that's $24,000.

The Toros get all their home gates but nothing from the road games, so Simpson, at 15 thou a pop would become an expensive item when the Toros go visiting. But, as Henry Hight put it, "I'm sure we could work out something with the other clubs."

Simpson, he of Southern California and Heisman Trophy fame, is the most-publicized football player ever to not play pro ball. Any minor-league operator would give his homecoming queen and six baton twirlers to have O.J. play in his park, no matter whose uniform he wore.

Hight is one of the Toro owners who came up with the idea of pursuing Simpson and although his offer was a sincere one he had no idea what size can of worms he was opening. As he put it, "Man, just hours after that story broke I had CBS-TV, sportswriters from all over the country and six radio stations calling me."

Most important, however, was the call from Los Angeles that carried the voice of Chuck Barnes. Mr. Barnes is Simpson's manager and although he admitted that both he and O.J. were "very interested" in the Toro offer he said that Simpson was also interested in a movie career. Seems that he's been a card-carrying member of the Actors' Guild for the past two years.

What a shame it would be if a running hoss like Simpson wound up in the flickers. That would be like putting Richard Burton in as a linebacker for the Packers.

Fifty thou really isn't a fair price to offer a guy like Simpson and since two minor-league clubs — the Toros and Indianapolis — have decided to offer him more than double that amount it's evident that the Bills are using the draft system in an effort to save money and shaft O.J.

In all fairness, however, Mr. Simpson started the financial tug-o-war when he attempted to put the hooks to Buffalo.

The first bid that tumbled from O. J. was a calm demand for $500,000 plus the loan of another $500,000 on a three-year contract. He didn't even say whether he wanted to repay the borrowed money in monthly installments or a big chunk here and a little dab there.

That's rather stout requesting from a guy who has never made a first down against a pro defense.

Buffalo argues that there's absolutely no way such money to Simpson could be justified because he couldn't possibly pull enough extra fans. And the main reason he couldn't is because the Bills' stadium seats just 45,748.

Pete Rozelle seems to be doing okay without all the free advice tossed his way but maybe the commissioner should appoint a three-man board to arbitrate such salary debates between drafted players and pro teams.

Some say Simpson is bucking the system, trying get Buffalo to trade him to one of the West Coast teams. But, at any rate, the player and the team are about $350,000 off on salary, give or take a few thou, and that's a long way off.

Some sort of guidance should come from the commissioner, especially now that he's sold Joe Namath's joint and has a little time on his hands.

THE '70S

And so it was that we wound up with Bobby and Billie on one network and Bonnie and Clyde on another. Heaven only knows what NBC offered Thursday night but it's a known fact that Bobby, Bonnie, Clyde and the NBA all got slaughtered about the same time.

Meredith, Help!

No, it's not true, the Dallas Cowboys are not disbanding and calling off the rest of the 1970 season. It just seemed that way Sunday when the defense wandered off to look for that offense that's been lost for so long.

Of course, they better not put it to the coaches for a vote this week because Tom Landry probably would rather be off deep-sea fishing in Mexico with Reuben Rodriguez. And Tom doesn't even know Reuben.

Cowboy fans have been arguing for weeks over whether Craig Morton or Roger Staubach should be the starting Dallas quarterback. It's been the contention here that Morton's experience gives him a slight edge but neither of these men has the ability to lead the Cowboys to great heights. Not even when they are healthy, which they don't happen to be at this time.

Do you suppose Howard Cosell could handle the TV color all by himself for the rest of the way so Dandy Don Meredith could put on his pads and get the Cowboys rolling once again?

A lot of fans who hated Meredith might reject this idea and Dandy Don might not cotton to it himself. After all, he's been sitting in the press box for almost half a season now and he hasn't received a single fractured rib or busted beak. This is the longest Meredith has gone in a football season without an ailment since he smoked corn silk behind his daddy's barn.

But the way things stand it could be that the best healthy professional quarterback in Texas wears a San Antonio Toro uniform on weekends. That might not be the finest compliment ever paid a Toro since all the other field generals are now out of the field and taking turns with doctors.

Houston's hope for a fine success story this season, Charley Johnson, owns a busted collarbone while Dallas' Morton has fresh pain in an old knee injury and Staubach is sporting an infection on his elbow.

Staubach's ailment wouldn't be considered too serious if it weren't necessary to hang a big bandage on his passing arm. Yet, that bundle of rags and tape does handicap his accuracy.

No matter how long you move around athletes you sometimes never know which items are worthy of reporting.

Take, for instance, Staubach's arm.

After the Cowboys' first home game on Sept. 27 — against the Giants — I followed the Dallas players into their dressing quarters and tagged behind Staubach as he left the Cotton Bowl field.

You didn't have to be Sherlock Holmes to notice that there was a skinned place just below his right elbow and a thin stream of blood trailed all the way to his hand. I moved a little closer to get a good look at the wound and it obviously was a minor matter that needed nothing more than a Band-Aid.

Skinned places, bruises and little streams of blood are as numerous as strong odors in a pro team's dressing room after a tough game so it was decided that Staubach's bloody arm wasn't worth a paragraph. And it really wasn't then.

But that was on Sept. 27 and now, several weeks later, that small injury has become infected and even the team trainers "aren't real sure when Roger got that AstroTurf burn." If it's any help, I can tell them the exact date. It was the same day I put my trained eye on it and decided it wasn't worth mentioning.

Landry really is in trouble with the boo birds now. For years they concentrated on Meredith and this season they've divided their jeers between Morton and Staubach, saving a few specialties for Tom.

But now they're all gone or wounded so Landry figures to be the center of attention when the Cowboys return to the unfriendly home grounds on Nov. 1. The natives should be very restless by then because after that 54-13 loss to Minnesota the Dallas team journeys to Kansas City this weekend for what could be more of the same.

Landry might find some consolation in the fact that his next home opponent will be Philadelphia. Tiny Tim could quarterback the Cowboys and beat the Eagles if the defense regroups.

The Generation Gap

Yeah, there's a generation gap, okay. There always will be. For instance, I'm much older than my children. As a matter of fact, we're a whole generation apart but from all I can gather that's about the way it's supposed to be.

Everybody winds his motor differently but I'm not the least bit eager to bridge that gap. I don't want to look, act or think like a teen-ager and I sure wouldn't expect any of them to envy my looks, deeds or thoughts.

All this jazz about "trying to understand" the kids is fine to a point but the more noise we make over the issue the more complicated they're apt to become. If I were a kid again I think I'd enjoy all the confusion caused by the great inability of the old folks to understand me.

And all this simply leads to a New York high school principal named Dr. Gilbert Weldy.

You must have seen the story in the News yesterday. It was about the high school football player who refused to take off his helmet for the national anthem, was kicked off the team by the coach and then got backing from Principal Weldy.

Weldy, you'll recall, told the coach to take the kid back because, after all, he was just expressing a personal opinion so the coach was infringing on his constitutional rights. The coach refused so Weldy canned him. Then the rest of the coaching staff decided to quit and the whole football team announced similar plans if the coach wasn't given his job back.

All of the adult educators were running in a wild and complicated circle of never-ending confusion when 17-year-old Forrest Byram rushed forth with a solution. Forrest, you see, was the kid who started it all by protesting American policies with his helmet, and not necessarily with his head.

And what did Forrest do? Why, he called a press conference, or course. He told the newsmen that he had decided not to go back to the team — even if they would have him (which they wouldn't). Instead, he was going to play the tuba in the band.

And would he blow the right notes on his tuba when time came for our national anthem? Certainly. After all, Forrest says he sees it as just another piece of music and he's going to give it his best efforts.

Maybe I'm being hard and shallow but to my way of thinking this is a classic example of some pseudo-intellectual claiming understanding of a 17-year-old who doesn't seem to understand himself. The boy was shocked to hear that his teammates didn't want him back and if he can't figure that out he's really not ready to tackle the world's problems.

We're now living in an era in which the high school football coach is, by some, cast in the role of a bully who spends most of his time checking haircuts and chasing dropouts who love to hang around schools after surrendering student status.

Maybe so. This could be a small part of their duties in some cases.

But it's about time that parents and all educators realized that football is a game that demands unity and strong discipline. There can be no halfway measure or compromise on either of these demands if any degree of success is to be realized.

If a boy isn't willing to be disciplined and doesn't intend to fall in step with the others he should not report for football. If a father doesn't want his kid to be put to the task and required to conform then he shouldn't allow him to go out for the team.

Like it or not, that's what much of football is about and when one boy threatens to destroy the unity of his team with a solo protest he couldn't be more harmful if he intentionally dropped passes.

Sure, a few of the pros do as they please and get by but in that league there's such an abundance of talent it sometimes overcomes everything. Nevertheless, the late Vince Lombardi offered a lot of evidence favoring unity and discipline. And then there's the Minnesota team, perhaps the best pro club around right now.

The Vikings are so completely disciplined that they have a certain way to stand for the national anthem, with their helmets in their right hands.

This, according to the Supreme Court — and because of the Supreme Court — is the age of freedom in America. Freedom to do about anything from preventing prayers in schools to showing the most revealing sex movies to a sometimes-shocked public.

Sure, there's a generation gap to be bridged. But it sure would be better to meet out in the middle of the bridge rather than keep rushing to the other side and searching in all directions.

June 2, 1971

Mays Still Going Strong

Last month William Howard Mays Jr. turned 40 and last Monday he gave one of his most sensational overall performances, displaying all of his fine talents and at an unfamiliar position, first base.

In case you missed it, the one they used to call the Say Hey Kid leaned into a 3-0 pitch and cracked a homer that tied the game at 1-1. He was brilliant at first, twice robbing the New York Mets of base hits in the ninth inning with spectacular infield play. And it was his darting, daring base-running in the 11th that finally paved the way for his winning run and a 2-1 victory.

Not bad for an old guy who was playing professional baseball before some of today's big leaguers were born. Not bad at all for a fellow who is forced to talk about his "possible retirement" with each new interview.

It wasn't altogether accurate to say that Mays was at an "unfamiliar" position when he moved over to first Monday night to fill in for the injured Willie McCovey. Mays has played third, shortstop and first on numerous occasions for the Giants but the outfield is his regular area.

But Willie, as we all know, is one of those rare superstars who can do it all and do it well. He's one of the last of the great ones who has somehow maintained his amazing stride despite advancing years and numerous problems in private life.

Some say he's the greatest player baseball has ever known. Others are not willing to vote him that singular distinction but nearly all will rate him somewhere among the game's all-time top 20.

Yet, despite his fame and lofty position, the only true changes in Mays' even disposition and personality have been improvements that stemmed from maturity. He's never been a prima donna type, a moody man who broods and pouts when things go wrong. He just digs in a little deeper and makes things go right.

Willie has never sought publicity in any of his endeavors. By the same token, he has always made himself available to newsmen and never once has he been short, rude or difficult in any manner with the public or the baseball writers who have made many demands on his time.

Several years ago, at the All-Star Game in St. Louis, about 50 of us news types gathered in a large hotel meeting room for an advertised press conference with the baseball commissioner.

After 15 minutes of light chit chat and waiting it became rather obvious that the commissioner was out of pocket and running on the wrong schedule somewhere. The guy in charge was embarrassed as he "begged patience" and told us "a surprise was on the way."

What he had done was rush an errand boy up to Mays' room to ask him to please report on the double to the meeting room. Ten minutes later Mays appeared, still half asleep from an interrupted nap.

The league official then announced, "Gentlemen, the commissioner is running very late and might not make it so I've asked Mr. Mays to come down and answer a few of your questions." With that Willie looked up and said, "I'm sure glad somebody explained what we're all here for because I didn't have the slightest idea."

Then Willie added, "Tell you what, I'll answer any of your questions that I can if you'll let me ask some questions, too."

Everybody laughed and the most enjoyable, relaxed half-hour of the whole St. Louis trip followed.

It's nice to know that a man like Mays, evidently in the twilight of a brilliant career, is still a very capable performer and a valuable asset to his team — as well as to the game of baseball.

July 16, 1971

The Homing Pigeons

This great period of progress — an age of computers and other ingenious electrical machines — seems to have taken us full cycle.

We in the communications business are at the point where our stories and columns can be transmitted great distances in just seconds and high-speed typesetters convert the written words into hot metal in a matter of minutes, ready for the master mold and then the huge, complicated presses.

But despite all this progress we stand ready for a return to 1939 and Bill Goodspeed's homing pigeon service.

Western Union has been on strike for many weeks and now the telephone people are shutting down to join the picket parade, demanding something or other they haven't been getting.

So, maybe it's back to the birds.

Goodspeed, however, might be reluctant to retrace the steps of his youth as he toiled to become a member of the Express-News photography staff. After all, he's won about 20 state and national awards for his pictures and now stands just a few years from retirement.

It was in 1938 that Goodspeed was hired by the Express-News, as a pigeon trainer.

Then, as now, his hobby was racing homing pigeons and he became a major part of an experiment after getting the promise that the job might work into a position in the photo department as a cameraman.

Newspaper work is a never-ending battle to beat deadlines as well as the competition. Thus, the idea to take homing pigeons to Austin for Texas' home football games and release them at halftime, with action film of the first two quarters strapped to their legs.

Flying time from Austin to the Express-News rooftop loft was a little over an hour so Goodspeed often had his pigeons collected and pictures developed before the game ended.

One bird usually carried the film but a companion pigeon was also sent back, just to encourage the film-bearer and to discourage him from any unscheduled pit stops.

This pigeon express worked well for two years and only once did Goodspeed lose a messenger, and some film. A farsighted hunter near San Marcos mistook Bill's bird for a dove and shot him dead. The film, with regrets and a brief explanation, was mailed in three days later.

So now I'm wondering, if film worked with pigeons 32 years ago, why couldn't the birds handle typewritten stories today?

Of course, the way some writers go in for length it might take a husky bird to make it back from Seguin without getting a double hernia. Our political writers would need bald eagles or whooping cranes to tote their loads back home.

And there's one fellow here who'd need a pelican. Editors claim they don't measure his stories. They weigh 'em.

It could be that some of those park pigeons that have been building muscle for years on peanut handouts could handle the average job. But we newsmen are going to look awful silly walking around in strange cities with pigeons under each arm.

Maybe the telegraph and phone people will get their business straight in the next few days so we can continue along the path of progress.

But if this is not to be, well, we'll just have to improvise.

Okay, Goodspeed, back up on the roof.

––––––––––

Ali Needs a Crowd

It's probably true that Cassius Clay no longer enjoys the ring, neither the actual fights nor all the gym drills that precede each outing. Still, he needs boxing. And for more reasons than the financial rewards it brings him.

Muhammad Ali is an incurable ham and he loves the crowds and all the fanfare they create for him. They're his joy, his comfort and, perhaps too, his strength.

While most celebrities grow weary of the continuous adulation fans heap their way, Ali thrives on it. While so many men of great fame seek to slip in and out of hotels unnoticed, Ali works to stir interest, to generate bigger mobs.

Four or five days prior to his fight with Jimmy Ellis, Clay's car was parked smack dab in front of the Astroworld Hotel where he was quartered. It seldom moved. When it did, it returned to the same, central parking spot.

It's a most unusual car. An Oldsmobile Toronado, loaded with every gimmick known to the Detroit auto workers. It's colored a deep brown and when the sun hits it just right it sparkles, like gold. The hubcaps and bumpers are a brilliant gold color. Some speculate that the car actually does have gold bumpers but that's real long-shot speculating.

On the day before his fight with Ellis, Sunday, Clay decided to visit Astroworld, Judge Hofheinz's answer to Disneyland. Joey Bishop, the TV comedian, led the front guard that accompanied this journey and drew crowds of hundreds along the way.

A special tram returned Clay to his hotel and, although he had a handful of aides and lieutenants on both sides, he strolled to the front desk to inquire about his mail.

The crowd was slow in forming in the hotel lobby so Clay paused for a moment and studied an envelope the desk clerk had given him.

This lured a few autograph seekers into a short line and the fighter chatted with each as he signed "Muhammad Ali" to scraps of paper. Still, no mob.

Moving toward the elevators, Clay spotted an old colleague from the bash business.

Archie Moore, the former light heavyweight champion who is enjoying some success as an actor, was sprawled on a table intended for lamps. As Clay approached, Moore held up both hands, providing targets for shadow boxing.

Clay began jabbing at Archie's big paws. First some quick punches and then a fast series of combinations. The crowd began to form.

"No, no, back up, boy. I've told you before not to get too close to your work. Back up some," said Moore.

"I can punch good up close or way back. Don't make no difference once I get untracked," said Clay. "Get those hands up again. Come on, get 'em up." Everybody in the lobby jammed toward the small aisle in front of the elevators.

The fleshy splat of fists whacking into open hands could be heard over the crowd that now pushed and jammed deeper into the small area. Nobody could get off the elevators. Nobody could get on. But then, nobody seemed to want off or on. The show was under way and they had ringside seats, of a sort.

Clay whistled some big ones into Archie's palms, said something about "taking up a collection" because he doesn't like to work before big crowds for free and then stepped through the open jaws of the nearest elevator. The crowd roared with laughter.

The act was over and most in the crowd rushed off to tell others what they had just seen and heard. It was five full minutes before the lobby returned to normal.

Training for a big fight can be a horrible drag. And boxing itself can be downright painful. Even dangerous.

So when Clay says he's "sick of it all" he might be 100 percent truthful. And when he says he'll have enough money for life after one more Frazier fight, he might well be correct.

But without boxing he will be, in time, without the crowds. He might need them far more than he realizes.

Clay can change his name, personality and occupation. But there's so much ham in him he might never get it all cured.

A Guide for the Women

It has come to my attention that a great many housewives have recently become addicted to football and many of them are still unfamiliar with the game's language and technical terms.

Okay, folks, I'm here to help.

We all realize that Howard Cosell and his colleagues start dozens of little stories each Monday night during crucial plays. They even finish some of them, also during key plays. But too many announcers take too much for granted, not considering the fact that thousands of new fans don't dig the lingo.

After 20 years of marriage to the same sportswriter, my wife, Katy, has a keen insight on the game and the terms most women would most want defined.

So, at great expense to the management, I've arranged for Katy to pinch-hit here today and offer her football definitions. Here, as a public service for women fans, are answers to football questions you've always wondered about but never been able to interrupt a game long enough to ask. Mrs. C. is handling the typewriter from here on today.

NOSE GUARD: Face mask, of course.

FAIR CATCH: She's not real pretty but a lot better than nothing.

QUICK KICK: Opening remark after seeing bill for breakfast at Houston airport.

SIDELINE PASS: Sometimes used by reserve players on cheerleaders. And vice versa.

DELAY OF GAME: No poker until team plane takes off.

BACKS IN MOTION: Chubby cheerleaders during fight song.

STAYING IN POCKET: Newspaperman's wallet when wife wants to go "someplace nice" for a change.

DRAW PLAY: Front-office term that denotes player seeking salary advance. Usually a player who pays a lot of alimony or child support.

HIP PAD: Sleeping quarters for Joe Namath.

WIDE RECEIVER: Fat girl who hangs around team's hotel lobby.

QUICK PITCH: Usually done on date 20 minutes before player's curfew.

SECOND EFFORT: This comes 10 minutes before curfew after quick pitch resulted in slapped face.

SCREEN PASS: Like when a player slips a note to the hat check girl while checking out his wife's coat.

CLIPPING: What players get on road trips when they visit small nightclubs with large go-go girls.

DRESSING ROOM PASS: Special section used as meeting place for friends of team owners and athletic directors after games. On some occasions photographers and sportswriters use these, if there's any room.

OFFENSIVE END: How sportswriters close stories on games they incorrectly predicted.

Now then, after you've studied and learned these you should be ready for the more technical terms like umbrella defense, red dog and splitting the seam. We'll graduate to those at a later date.

J a n u a r y   2 8 ,   1 9 7 3

The President's Friend

In recent days the heads of many great nations have eulogized the late Lyndon B. Johnson, offering rare and sparkling praise for the tall Texan who once held this country's highest office.

However, most of the kind words heretofore resulted from friendships that stemmed from political bonds. Among those hit hardest by Johnson's death was a special friend who enjoyed a special sort of acquaintance with the former president.

He rarely spoke of such visits but Texas football coach Darrell Royal spent many hours many times with Johnson. Royal was one of the very few who had a standing invitation to visit the LBJ Ranch. With this in mind I called Coach Royal and asked if he would share some "Johnson stories" now that the big man is gone. Basically, this was his answer:

"First, I think you should know that I always treasured my friendship with President Johnson and I made it a strong point never to discuss it much with anyone. He was a warm, wonderful person and I saw an entirely different side of him than most people got to see.

"I learned from him that you can be a common man and at the same time be a great man. I was totally relaxed in his presence but I was always proud and elated to be with him. Yes, that was the case. I never discussed our friendship with anyone outside our family simply because I felt he might prefer it that way. But now that he's gone, well, I can't see any harm in answering your question.

"You've got to understand that our relationship was just a spit-and-whittle sort of thing. To begin with, I'm not even politically informed enough to discuss the things he knew most about. But I've stood with him on his ranch and heard him talk some important talk with big people. I was just pleased to be there as a listener. And I swore to myself I'd never repeat a word I heard there. If they wanted their stories repeated I figured they knew how to get the word spread without any help from me.

"Actually, my friendship with President Johnson was a rather surprising thing. It's still surprising to me. All I ever did was vote for him and like him. Nobody ever asked me to do anything more and it doesn't seem that we had a lot of common grounds. But Lord, I enjoyed riding with him over his ranch and I think each tree had a meaning for him. Some of the pastures and hilly areas are just magnificent when the flowers are in bloom and he loved to show those scenes. I don't think he liked to do it alone but I always enjoyed being with him there, even when we'd visit the same place for the second and third times.

"Not many realize it but I don't think President Johnson missed but one Texas football game after he left office. I believe he missed our game with UCLA in Los Angeles in 1971 and that was all.

"It always thrilled me when we won a big one and he came to our dressing room afterwards. I felt like we were giving him some special pleasure, something to do, something to offer added excitement and interest in his late years.

"He was a big (Jim) Bertelsen fan and he had Eddie (Phillips) out to his ranch a few times the year before. I figured it might stimulate his interest and help him enjoy the games more if he knew some of the players so I suggested he have four or five boys out to the ranch at the start of last season. He took me up on it after two games.

"I picked our tri-captains and Julius Whittier. He particularly asked for Roosevelt Leaks so one weekday the five boys and I drove over to see him for lunch. We had a great time. You don't have to wonder where to sit or which car to ride in when you're with him because he'd tell you. And in a nice way. Like, 'Now you sit over there close to the food and Roosevelt, you come sit here beside me because I've got some questions I want to ask you.' I don't know who enjoyed that day more, me, the players or President Johnson.

"The last thing he said to me was more of an invitation but he seemed to be scolding me.

"He said, 'I get the feeling that you and Edith (Mrs. Royal) are waiting for an invitation before you'll come see me. I want you to call me like you'd call your momma. If I'm busy and have to be in San Antonio or Austin, I'll say so and we'll make it another time.'

"No, I can't tell you anything big or revealing about my friendship with President Johnson. There really isn't a great deal to tell. And yet, it was a very special thing to me and I can't describe the pleasure I had riding with him over his ranch, talking about little things that somehow took new importance when we discussed them.

"Like I said, he was a warm, wonderful person and the only regret I have is that everyone didn't have the opportunity to see him as I saw him."

So said Darrell Royal, the football coach who enjoyed "spit-and-whittle" visits with the late president.

February   15,   1973

Memories of Dad

It's strange how your mind works after you lose someone you loved a lot. Without even half trying you race back over rarely used memory lanes, crossing avenues long ago forgotten.

They must have been impressive moments at the time. Why else would they loom so important now and bid for such prominent roles in the hours of grief that follow death?

My dad was 84 when he died Sunday in Houston, so although his passing was no great surprise it still came as a shock. When I kissed him goodbye on the forehead the weekend before I knew it would be the last time I'd see the old man alive. I think he knew it, too.

Dad enjoyed amazingly good health until a stroke crippled one side about eight years ago. From that point on he went slowly downhill. But then, most folks do at 76.

But Lord, what a man he was until that sudden ailment. Over the years, from time to time, I've felt a bit guilty on the occasion that I would write about an athlete and refer to him as "one of the most courageous men I've ever known."

My father was a pretty fair football player many years ago and there has never been any doubt in my mind that he most certainly was the most courageous man I'd ever met. But then, courage comes in all shapes and sizes so I'll offer you an example of what I mean.

He was an electrician by trade. Some 22 years ago I drove out to pick Pop up from work at the Goodyear Rubber plant, located between Houston and Pasadena. His car was in the shop and a windy rainstorm had him stranded. When I arrived some sort of emergency developed, and three young men rushed to my father for advice. He told me to sit down and get comfortable for a few minutes while he "tended to a little business."

Then that 62-year-old man buckled on a belt load of tools, trotted out into the fields and began to climb a high pole that disappeared into the thick sky. I wanted to whip up on the three younger men who let him go but I watched in silence, too frightened to move. He came down after 20 minutes, repairs completed. He took off a rain jacket, motioned toward the door and said, "Come on, son, let's go get some supper."

My dad was retired from Goodyear when he was 65, thank God, but he refused to accept the easy life so he hooked on as head of the electrical department at Rice.

Those were the fun workdays for Dan Sr. He had to have an electrician at every sports event on the Rice campus so he picked himself for that chore. In short time he became the Owls' number one booster.

But there were problems there, too. Pop was 66 when half the stadium lights failed to come back on after a football halftime show.

I was listening here in San Antonio on the radio, working the Saturday night desk for the Express-News, when the announcer explained that the lights should be back on soon because "Mr. Cook, the

Rice electrician, is making his third trip up one of the high light poles, going to the top again to check things out." The old man never made much effort to distinguish between fear and common sense. The tough jobs just looked so easy to him.

As mentioned, it's funny how faded memories now flash by bright and clear. Like the time when I was 10 and dad took me to see the Cherryhurst Park champion, a kid named Walter Transeu, fight in an amateur boxing tourney.

Walter could whip anybody at our park but dad kept telling me that he couldn't take a punch. I was angry with dad when he laughed after a skinny, hungry-looking boy named Ramirez flattened Walter with the first left jab he threw.

On the way home dad explained that any one of us could whip Walter if we had the courage to trade punches with him. He was right, too. But then, he usually was. He was always right on matters regarding courage.

I'm sorry most of you didn't get to know my dad. He was a very lovable character. You would have liked him.

———

March 28, 1973

Wooden is the Best Ever

There are always a big bunch of unsuccessful folks standing around very eager to put a knock on the most successful. That's why John Wooden, basketball coach at UCLA, has his share of critics despite the most sensational collegiate coaching career in history.

There are many who say that Wooden simply does the best job of recruiting. Each year he searches high and low for an 8-foot center and then settles for the best 7-footer available. Then he locates half a dozen fellows who can pass accurately. It helps if they stand from 6-5 to 6-9.

But there's really more to it than that. Much more. Wooden has now coached UCLA basketball teams to seven consecutive national crowns and nine in the last 10 years. His teams have won 75 straight games and 94 of their last 95.

Someday Babe Ruth's home run record will fall. Some Saturday afternoon a slim athlete — perhaps now wearing short pants and playing marbles — will pole vault 20 feet. There will be a time when football produces an incredible brute with blistering speed who'll shatter the records of Jim Brown. And the future is sure to have a Knute Rockne or Vince Lombardi-type coach who will capture numerous titles as well as the hearts and imaginations of many.

Yet, it might be safe to say that no coach will ever top or come close to matching the marks Wooden has made at UCLA. He seems to stand alone, now and for all time to come, as the true king of the collegiate cage court.

Sure, recruiting plays a major role in Wooden's success story. Any coach in any sport will be quick to explain that you can't win many games without the hosses. But, as mentioned earlier, there's more to it than that. So, in quick, capsule form, let's take a look at the most important rules of Wooden's coaching philosophies.

Since nearly every coach who owns a cap and whistle claims to put emphasis on teamwork it's not enough to list that one factor as Wooden's most important goal each season. It might be wise to take a look at how he accomplishes this feat of molding a dozen men into a unit that functions as one.

If you watched UCLA beat Memphis State to win the title last Monday night you may have noticed that no Bruin player ever attempted a behind-the-back pass or dribble. Now that's a little unusual in big-time competition in this day of slick ballhandlers.

Wooden, you see, has a hard, fast rule against such stunts. He believes a behind-the-back dribble comes in handy only once every four or five games and an around-the-rear pass is necessary only once every 10 or 12 games. So why spend time working on such slick tactics? In short, Wooden will not permit that kind of play from any of his players, no matter how well they might do it.

Someone asked him, "But suppose a Pete Maravich type came to you at UCLA?" And Wooden answered, "He would have to play differently or he wouldn't play. It's that simple."

Wooden really is proudest of his first national championship team, 1964. It was his smallest, by far, and it was made up of a Jew, a Catholic, a Mormon, two Protestants and well-mixed with blacks and whites.

Looking back, Wooden will tell you, "Now there was a great team effort, a challenge from the beginning and together — all together — we squarely met that challenge."

There's just no way to get around teamwork when you discuss the successes of Coach John Wooden. To him, it's everything.

April 11, 1973

The Day the Spurs Were Born

Snowflakes splattered across windows of the big plane as we moved toward the runway to leave Chicago. It was a dark, cold, miserable day in the Windy City. And the moods of many who had attended a lengthy airport meeting moments earlier matched the weather, offering no evidence that the session might have produced the brightest moment in San Antonio sports history.

There was no shouting, no back-slapping, no fanfare, not even a few smiles Monday afternoon in Chicago when San Antonio received official league approval to operate an American Basketball Association team for the next two years.

It seemed a little strange that the meeting would even be scheduled in a small room in O'Hare Airport in Chicago, where there is no ABA franchise. Or, for that matter, that the meeting would be necessary at all.

More often than not approval of a new site for an old franchise comes after a lengthy investigation, and a telephone vote is all that's necessary. But two owners — charter members — insisted on an eyeball-to-eyeball visit and discussion before voting, so Chicago was picked as a central meeting place.

It goes without saying that some of the ABA team owners, wealthy men with many interests, weren't too excited about having to fly into Chicago on a day when eight inches of snow was predicted. But fly they did, to view and interview the six-man delegation from San Antonio.

The 28 S.A. investors were represented by three from that group — Angelo Drossos, John Schaefer and Art Burdick. And there was Francis Vickers, HemisFair convention director, who made the trip to tell the ABA gang about our wonderful facilities. And there were sports editors from the Express-News and the Light, playing dual roles, eager to report back home and tell folks about the approval but delayed first by the ABA group, as we reported to them our sincere interest in the project.

Questions along that line seemed slightly silly since our presence at the meeting should have told the true story. After all, San Antonio newspapers don't send men to Chicago each week to check on the weather.

For some of the owners, like Charlie Finley, who has the Memphis ABA franchise among his large collection of sports projects, the acceptance of San Antonio was almost a formality. But two doubters in the group arrived with many questions and they had no intention of leaving until the last one got answered.

People at the airport must have thought there was a sale on briefcases in that small meeting room, the way folks kept rushing in and out, all carrying assorted satchels.

The San Antonio franchise seekers kept getting graciously invited in and then abruptly asked out. After two hours it began to look shaky, anything but the "formality" so many of us predicted when we left sunny San Antonio that Monday morning.

Drossos had mentioned that he would be "a little put out" if they made us fly all the way to Chicago and then just shook hands and said, "Okay, men, you're in." Angelo did get a little put out, but not for that reason. Some of the ABA team owners almost got too nosy too often and the three S.A. representatives began to pop back questions of their own.

When the announcement did come, telling that unanimous approval had been voted to move the Dallas basketball franchise to San Antonio, Commissioner Robert Carlson blew his chance for a dramatic moment with the big bulletin. He simply said, "Your motion carried, gentlemen, so welcome to the loony world of professional basketball." And then he turned to other owners and asked, "Is there any more business we should discuss?"

Mission accomplished. The last leg of the long journey into professional sports had been successful. It didn't turn out to be a happy, hugging and hopping affair, and it wasn't easy. But the real tough part still lies ahead, when the pro pioneers seek a united homefront effort in generating interest and selling tickets.

Maybe joyous moments are yet to come and some evening we'll all hop and holler and dance around the box office — after the last ticket has been sold for the season opener.

August 25, 1973

An Open Letter to Tex

Mr. Tex Schramm
President/General Manager, Dallas Cowboys
6116 North Central Expressway
Dallas, Texas

Dear Tex:

First off, let me congratulate you on that slick deal you pulled with Duane Thomas. The Lord only knows how you managed to unload him on Washington, probably your toughest foe in the Eastern Division.

Man, before your Cowboys strap it on with the Redskins on Oct. 8 Duane should have them so screwed up they'll be using silent signals because the quarterback won't be speaking to the center. If George Allen isn't ready for a funny farm in two months it'll be because Duane is already there.

You've sure come a long way, Tex, since you were writing sports for the Austin American-Statesman. Man, what a staff you folks had — Tex Maule, Jack Gallagher, you and Wilbur Evans. A bunch of real hosses. Never could figure out why you decided to go straight and leave the newspaper dodge.

At any rate, what I'm writing you about concerns your rules committee for the National Football League. Last time your little group met I think you all sashayed around Hawaii and discussed the possibility of tiebreakers. As I recall, the motions were tabled and not a great deal was settled on games ending in ties.

Now then, for the meat of this letter. Tex, next time your rules committee gets together will you please give some serious thought to field goals? I realize how reluctant officials are to change scoring rules of any sport. It messes up records and traditions. But it's durned ridiculous for these professional field-goal kickers of today — all on a par with Lou Groza now — getting the same points for kicking 10 yards less than the high school and college kids boot.

Your extra points are about as exciting as a sun dial. For that matter, an 8-yard field goal generates less interest than a 10-man marching band.

For cryin' out loud, Tex, you guys must realize that when anything becomes first cousin to automatic it departs from the area of excitement and when you boil it all down that's all you're selling, excitement.

It's understood that the reason the pros moved those goalposts up in the first place was to emphasize offense and put more points on the board. But these European soccer refugees have sidekicked football into another dimension and it's downright boring.

So, please, next time you NFL rulesmakers meet in Acapulco, Bangkok or wherever, give some thought to placing the ball on the 15 or 20 for extra-point kicks. It would also be a durned good idea to eliminate all field goals once a team has reached an opponent's 10 or 15-yard-line. Or, at least move the posts back 10 yards.

That would give coaches, quarterbacks and fans something to think about on a third-and-one situation from the 15. It's really a knock at your game when half your fans go for a hot dog while a one-point conversion is being prepared.

Oh, yeah, regarding our phone conversation of last week, that guy here with the laser beam machine, Chuck Carlock, will be in Dallas around the middle of September to show you his invention. I'll write you more about that later.

I did, however, want to get this kicking bit out in front of other fans. You people are going to have to take steps on this matter and I want to be sure I can say "I told you so" when you finally get around to handling it.

Take care and give my best to Al Ward and Curt Mosher, those other sportswriter dropouts on your fine staff.

Regards,
Dan Cook

Behind the Riggs Scene

Now then, about that tennis match over in Houston.

First off, let it be said that Billie Jean King outran, outhustled, outplayed and, finally, outscored Bobby Riggs in the match that drew the biggest crowd in tennis history.

Secondly, the whole thing really just proved that (1) a good hustler with a fair gimmick and a loud mouth can still get rich overnight in this country and (2) the best woman performer in the world can beat the best 55-year-old male tennis player.

All that jazz about women's lib taking two steps forward might be true but Riggs admitted a day before the match he got into that area strictly by luck — good luck. Bobby knows — or, knew at the time — next to nothing about women's lib when he started popping off against female tennis players.

He came up with the line, "women should remain barefoot and pregnant" and followed with, "a woman's place is in the kitchen and bedroom, and not necessarily in that order." After that, he found himself on the crest of a wave that carried him, eventually, to defeat.

But talk about crying all the way to the bank. Look at it this way. One year ago 90 percent of all American sports fans under 35 couldn't have told you who Bobby Riggs is. His yearly income, counting all hustles, probably was under 20 thou. Now, one year later, his picture has been in every newspaper in the nation and he's at least $1 million richer. That's right, $1 million richer.

Bobby and Billie Jean were playing for $100,000, winner-take-all, and Mrs. King took it all. But what wasn't advertised too well was the fact that the two main eventers would also share in the TV money.

Riggs, hustler, scuffler and promoter that he is, endorsed everything from Sugar Daddy candy suckers to orange juice, and his agent admitted that Bobby's take for the whole shooting match will come to "slightly more than a million."

And he was the loser? Lordy, I'd love to lose a couple like that.

The funniest hustle of all, however, was not on the tennis court. That was the behind-the-scenes television struggle.

Everybody wound up angry at everybody, a rather common occurrence in the wacky world of the magic box.

You see, CBS recently outbid ABC for National Basketball Association TV rights, grabbing a package the ABC people had held for years. So ABC went to the bank and outbid CBS for the Riggs-King match. That burned the CBS people since they had started the promotion by televising Riggs' earlier match with Margaret Court. And so it was that CBS unloaded a big one, placing the movie "Bonnie and Clyde" right opposite the tennis match.

Howard Cosell played right into CBS' hand midway in the tennis match when he announced, "I understand we have a big movie opposite us on another network but folks, you can see a movie anytime and this will be your only chance to see this great tennis match."

It's been estimated that with that reminder, at least 25 percent of ABC's tennis audience switched channels to check on the "big movie." After all, they had already seen a full set of tennis and it wasn't exactly a goosebump raiser.

And so it was that we wound up with Bobby and Billie on one network and Bonnie and Clyde on another. Heaven only knows what NBC offered Thursday night but it's a known fact that Bobby, Bonnie, Clyde and the NBA all got slaughtered about the same time.

For that matter, so did all of us who picked Riggs to win in straight sets.

Aaron Goes One Up

It makes no difference whether or not Hank Aaron ever strokes another baseball out of anybody's park. With one stroke of a pen the other day he went one up on Babe Ruth.

In fact, he zoomed so far ahead of Ruth the figures aren't even comparable.

Maybe it's only right that Hammerin' Hank should become the first active athlete to sign a million-dollar contract for moonlighting services unrelated to sports. After all, just a few months ago he complained that, because he's black, he's received far too few offers to endorse products for profit.

He probably was right, too. Everybody in baseball and a whole bunch of folks with just a mild interest in sports kept watchful eyes on his every move as he approached Ruth's career homer output of 714. But only a small handful wanted to pay Hank to tell the world how well their razor blades worked or how great their breakfast cereal tasted.

He was second only to a dead man in the production of home runs but he wasn't even in the top 20 in the production of radio and TV commercials.

Some said his mild manner and rather sleepy personality went against him in that area of endeavor. But he came through right well on his one chance to push a man's cologne. Oh, I didn't rush right out and a buy a gallon of the stuff but I was pleased when someone gave me a small jug of it for Christmas.

Now, however, Aaron has passed all athletes, past or present, who dabble on the side for additional income. In the next five or six years Hank will receive more from the Magnavox Company than he got from the Atlanta Braves the last four years.

And you can bet that you'll be seeing a lot of Aaron on TV commercials, pushing Magnavox television sets, of course.

Ruth stormed across the baseball scene at a time when income tax put only the smallest dent in a man's paycheck. Phrases like "take-home pay" and "35 percent bracket" were then unknown to weary workers. The Babe deserved everything he got because he, more than any other individual, brought baseball back to the people — and vice versa — after the World Series Black Sox scandal. Yankee Stadium was known as the House That Ruth Built but he built more than that. He built a new foundation for the game itself.

Still, it's interesting to note that Ruth hit the scene before television and, in those days, it wasn't worth a rich athlete's time to drop by a studio and cut a radio commercial.

When sports stars were used to promote a product they usually made a deal with the league and got all the top hands on bubble gum wrappers or ice cream tops. You rarely saw one superstar, such as Ruth, pictured on a billboard, sipping coffee with Mrs. Olson.

The hottest product that carried Ruth's name didn't give a dime to the home run king. That was the Curtiss Candy Company's Baby Ruth, a chewy, chocolate-covered bar loaded with peanuts. It's still around and selling well.

According to the oft-told story, that candy bar first hit the market under the name of Babe Ruth. Since the Yankee slugger didn't have a slice of the action he went to court but Mr. Curtiss testified that the candy bar was named after his daughter, Ruth, and not the ballplayer. The judge then advised Curtiss to change his new candy bar from Babe Ruth to Baby Ruth. And that's the way it is to this day.

Who would have thought at that time the candy bar would have outlasted the life of Ruth and the career of the man who will someday soon break Ruth's record?

Hank recently said that he probably will quit baseball after this next season. Maybe they'll name a candy bar after him. It should be something with a lot of substance and staying power. Wonder how many folks would buy a 10-cent jawbreaker?

An Open Letter to Ali

Muhammad Ali
c/o Madison Square Garden,
New York, N.Y.
(Please Forward)

Dear Mr. Ali:

First let me congratulate you on your recent victory over Joe Frazier. I understand you'll wind up collecting well over $2 million for that bout, not to mention even more for an upcoming fight with George Foreman for the title.

You probably don't remember me although we've chatted several times. Usually I've been in a crowd of other reporters, just before or after one of your fights in Houston.

I'm the big, moon-faced guy who once asked you how serious you were in your role as a religious preacher. You answered with a question — you asked me how serious I was in my role as a sportswriter. Man, you really got me there.

If you're interested, you might check me out with your trainer, Angelo Dundee. Angelo and I have been friends for about 20 years. Of course, he'll tell you that I'm not one of your biggest fans or boosters. But I'm also not one of your hardest knockers. Not anymore, that is.

Maybe I'm mellowing in my advancing years, but I just don't get uptight about your deeds out of the ring anymore. You know, things like snubbing the draft, knocking the government and phony grudge buildups before every fight. Even that wrestling act you and Joe staged before your last bout failed to disturb me.

Besides, I'm a little weary of facing all the heat each time I toss a verbal slap in your direction. Some black fans seem to think that every white cat who doesn't approve of your deeds is a rednecked racist. But that's not the reason for this letter.

When the great Jimmy Brown quit pro football he announced that he was forming a business or group to show black people how to make money. As I understood it, his outfit was going to open a lot of big doors for little investors. But, to my knowledge, all Jimmy did was show everybody how to make money — for himself — as he became a good actor.

You've been in boxing long enough to realize that it's a game almost foreign to such qualities as loyalty and charity.

Oh, every now and then some old champ will need help and they'll stage a benefit card for him. But I'm writing you to offer a serious idea that should carry some appeal.

Several years ago I heard you preach a sermon in Houston. You knocked ham as terrible, unclean meat, unfit for human consumption. And then you made the statement that "black people have to help black people because white folks don't care." You said, "Black people with influence have to show more care for their own."

Okay, Muhammad, you might be right to some degree. If you still think along those lines, why don't you use your influence to spread millions of dollars among black people in every corner of this country? Hold on now, it won't cost you a dime.

It's always sort of chapped me that little boxing promoters around the country can struggle for many months, trying to keep the game going or get it started in their areas. They gamble their own money and some do good jobs.

But then, when a big closed-circuit fight comes along with the chance to make big money, the showing is almost always tossed to some group or individuals who have not the slightest interest or thinnest affiliation in boxing.

Your two fights with Frazier were real financial successes for everyone concerned. Nobody in boxing, black or white, in this state got the chance to earn a dime from the closed-circuit TV showings. Those fat plums went to music promoters, a big outfit that promotes rock-and-roll "concerts" around the state. How come?

I'm writing you and not Foreman, the champ, because I know you are, without a doubt, the most influential boxer in the world today and you're certainly not shy to use that influence. This is just a suggestion to use it to help your own.

Why not give the closed-circuit showings for your title bout with Foreman to the NAACP all over the country? They can keep some of their profits to help finance their ventures and turn the rest over for research on sickle cell anemia. Without costing you or Foreman a nickel this could be the greatest benefit fight in history and it would benefit all the black people in the world.

I'm not just trying to knock the rock-and-roll promoters out of another big payday. But they've already had two slices more than they deserve so they've got no kick coming.

Man, can't you imagine how loud they'd scream if the Beatles were to regroup and barnstorm through Texas with boxing promoters handling the shows?

Seriously, you must know that the biggest threat to all black people is sickle cell anemia, a form of blood cancer that cripples and then kills. Things being the way they are in this country, not nearly enough money is spent to research that problem. I'm offering you this plan to help before you negotiate any contracts with Foreman. If you don't care to involve the NAACP you could still demand that whatever promoters wind up with the TV rights that they give a percentage of profits to the research foundation.

I would close with a "good luck" in your fight with Foreman but, to be honest, I'll be pulling for George to whack you out early. But then, somebody always wins and somebody loses, except when there's a draw.

Best wishes,
Dan Cook

Lee Bypasses Masters

The Masters golf tournament might have a great overload of prestige and tradition but it doesn't have Lee Trevino — again. Lee has just about run out of excuses for skipping the big tournament so it's rather surprising that he doesn't go ahead and tell newsmen the real reason.

Those close to Trevino say he's often confided that his wife was snubbed in the rudest manner during their first visit to the Masters. He was treated okay but somebody or some group must have dropped some potent, sharp barbs on Mrs. Lee. Either that or they neglected to invite her to the pre-tourney style show for golfers' wives.

At any rate, Trevino stirred up a real storm after his initial effort in that big show. He told one and all that the course wasn't suited for his game and he wouldn't be back.

Lordy, that announcement really starched some of Georgia's more elite social groups. Imagine, the nerve of that former caddie, putting the bad mouth on staid old Augusta's finest facility.

After much yanking and a hard hassle, the great white fathers who run the pro tour finally managed to burp a small apology from Lee. He explained that his decision was nothing personal, but that the course was built for long hitters and golfers who hook well and those weren't two of his best qualities.

He might honestly feel that way since he hasn't exactly burned up the old course in the two years he's played in the Masters. As a matter of fact, 71 is his best round there.

But that's a lot of bull about the long hitters having the big edge. Too many little guys who couldn't lift a 50-pound grip have hogged more than their shares of major golf cash on layouts loaded with par-5 holes. Ben Hogan, for example, didn't keep weightlifters worried about his late entry in their meets.

And Sam Snead never gave any thought to joining Hogan to form a tag wrestling team but between them they won the Masters five times.

Those big dudes with rippling muscles very rarely wind up in the winner's circle in golf. Far more often it's the little guys with smooth swings and steel nerves.

Look, I'm a little over 6-1 and weigh 215 but without fail at every driving range I've visited some skinny teen-ager who would fit in my pocket takes a 3-iron and outdistances my longest drives. But that's another story for another day.

There's really no reason for so many folks in Georgia to get upset because Lee doesn't care for their golf course or golf tournament. It's just that they're not accustomed to having someone use one of their invitations to wrap leftover enchiladas.

Pro golfers are supposed to guide their careers in pursuit of an opportunity at Augusta. But Trevino tried it and didn't like it. More power to him.

If the truth were known the Masters might need Trevino a little more than he needs the Masters. But both are almost certain to continue and prosper, with or without each other.

In the past, when he balked at playing in the big one, Lee tossed out more acceptable explanations. You know, things like "pressing personal business at home" and the need "of two weeks' rest because of strained nerves."

This time Lee simply said he prefers to take his family fishing while the Masters is being played. You don't even have to read between the lines to get the full impact of that answer to an invitation.

A pro golfer leaving the tour to go fishing during the Masters is about like a jockey skipping the Kentucky Derby to go skin-diving.

Normally I labor under the opinion that the top-name golfers owe a certain debt to the sponsors of major tournaments and they should repay that debt with their presence.

But Trevino has cause to feel that the people who run the Masters owe him a little something and he intends to balance things out by not participating. I just wish he'd come out and tell the full story but evidently he feels that it's a matter too personal for publication. So be it.

My Most Interesting Stories

Next month, Executive Sports Editor Dan Cook will complete 30 years in the newspaper business as a sportswriter. He started at age 17 on the Houston Post and has been with the Express-News the past 22 years. Today, he writes of the most interesting sports stories he's covered in those 30 years.

* * *

It's not an easy task to turn back the pages in search of stories with the most interest or the most humor. Time has a way of reducing the new and magnifying the old. And sometimes vice versa.

In reflection, the last assignment, Houston's Super Bowl, doesn't seem as important — or as interesting — as the first assignment, an exhibition game in the old Negro American Baseball League.

The Vikings or Dolphins certainly didn't have an athlete with more talent or showmanship than that owned by the first baseman for the Cincinnati Clowns. You just can't find another Goose Tatum around these days.

Besides, the six or seven paragraphs I put together on that baseball game in old Buff Stadium 30 years ago clinched my first newspaper job, on the Houston Post. It wasn't an outstanding story but $25 a week wasn't an outstanding salary. Not even 30 years ago.

Nevertheless, that initial effort enrolled me as a card-carrying member of the working press, a seemingly non-profit, fraternal order pledged to dispense truth, entertainment and maybe even bits of wisdom.

The press card is a master key that opens many doors, a magic carpet that carries newsmen from the front row to backstage. It's one thing to watch artists and athletes perform. It's something else to hear them tell of their triumphs, explain their failures, replay the small details of big events.

In the last 30 years that press card has allowed me the privilege of lunch with Joe Louis, breakfast with Sam Snead, drinks with Rocky Marciano, a morning with Jack Dempsey, an afternoon with Willie Mays, interviews with Ted Williams and a whole day with Babe Ruth.

An impish Houston 3-year-old named Daniel John Cook Jr., sits still for the camera.

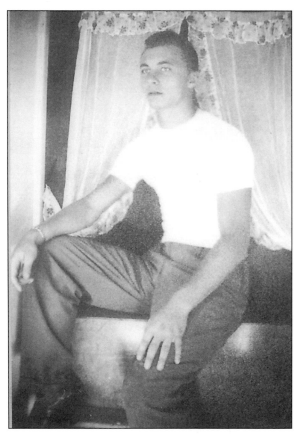

Top: Dan was an active athletic participant as a schoolboy, winning letters in several boys' varsity sports at Houston St. Thomas.
Bottom: Dan on his first day of work in the newspaper business at the Houston Post in 1944.

Above: As president of the Texas Sportswriters Association in the mid-1970s, Dan recruited Kansas City Chiefs owner Lamar Hunt (left) to help open the Texas Sports Hall of Fame. **Right:** Dan prepares to get a new perspective on South Texas as he boards a jet trainer at Randolph AFB in the late '60s.

Above: For many years, Dan (reclining at left) was a fixture among the sports scribes who meandered across Texas and Arkansas on the annual preseason Southwest Conference Football Tour.

Left: Caught in the flow of a phone interview — or a personal matter — Dan casts a wary eye at his photographic intruder.

Above: Dan goes to bat for the Express-News in a 1989 softball game against the rival San Antonio Light.

Right: Ever the showman, Dan gets spiffy and struts his stuff at a 1981 charity fashion show.

Above: With Express-News publisher Larry Walker (left) and Alamodome director Mike Abington (right) on hand, Dan is announced as a 1996 inductee into the San Antonio Sports Hall of Fame.

Left: Publisher Walker congratulates Dan on yet another honor, his 1995 recognition as the Express-News' Hearst Eagle Award winner.

Above: The Cook clan on a June 2001 cruise aboard the *Grand Prince*. Front: Granddaughter Britney. Middle, from left: Wife Katy, daughters Marie and Alice Ann, daughter-in-law Laura. Back: Dan, son-in-law Michael Gian, Alice Ann's companion Doug Beauchamp, granddaughter Dani, son Danny.

Right: A man in constant demand for community events, Dan joins Greg Simmons of KSAT-TV in dishing out ice cream during National Hospital Week in 1987.

After 44 years as sports anchor at KENS-TV, the fat lady finally sings and the curtain closes on Dan's career as a full-time broadcaster on Nov. 29, 2000.

Yeah, that's name-dropping. But that's what this is all about.

It didn't seem overly exciting at the time but now, looking back, that day with George Herman Ruth has got to rate high on my all-time chart. He was the king and from all walks of life they crowded before him in endless streams.

The great one was in fading health when he visited Houston in 1946, two years before his death. But he maintained a fast pace on a busy schedule, shaking countless hands along the way and signing autographs when the tour slowed. He was 51 but he could have passed for 60.

The huge, round face beneath the brown cap forced a smile much of the afternoon but it had to be a boring ordeal for him, the thousandth replay of an old act. Only the city and the sea of faces differed.

When we had a brief moment alone I asked him, "Doesn't this get to be a horrible strain, all this greeting and handshaking?"

His answer was, "Naw, keed, you get used to it. It's good to be remembered." I think he meant that.

Selfishly, the thing I remember most about that day with Ruth was my continuous effort to register my name on his mind. Nine of us were to wind up the day with supper together and I entertained hope that before dessert he might remember my name. But it was always "keed" — nothing more, nothing less.

At the tender age of 19, I didn't know that Ruth called everyone "keed," even old teammates. Only his wives and close relatives, very few on both scores, escaped that label that sometimes stunned politicians and shocked royalty.

* * *

A good newsman, we're often reminded, is partial, unbiased, cold to the warm passions that so often surround a good story. But this really can't be right. No man with compassion and understanding can help from being swept into the festive mood he finds while visiting the dressing room of a winning team. Nor can he escape the sorrow that grips a fallen champion, especially a boxer who gave his best but still absorbed a bad beating.

Sometimes, perhaps, we get too close, too involved.

And that leads us to the sad situation of a former boxing promoter who headquartered in Houston, the late Ralph Smith.

As it so often happens to Texas ring promoters, Mr. Smith was enduring a bad losing streak in the late '40s. It was the same old story that holds true today — great fights, poor attendance.

But Ralph came up with a brilliant idea to pack the auditorium for his next promotion. Panting for breath, he ran it past me and even then it sounded like the most incredible long shot in box-office history. But he durned near pulled it off.

Seems that on the outskirts of Houston a black faith healer named Elder Bonds was pulling bigger crowds than the Democratic convention. Rev. Bonds was on the outskirts because police wouldn't allow him any closer. Nevertheless, the healer was getting a heap of headlines and the more the papers knocked him the bigger the crowds grew.

Since Smith was promoting a black lightweight named Harry LaSane — Hurricane Harry, of course — he decided to invite Rev. Bonds, and all of his following, to the boxing match. The reverend could hold his regular prayer meeting at 7 p.m., rush through some healing, take up a collection and then lead a parade to the auditorium.

Smith was not known as a silver-tongued convincer but one of his associates, Freddie Sommers, was gifted in that department. With enough money at stake, Mr. Sommers could talk the chrome off a trailer hitch and he had more nerve than a one-eyed mongoose. He was assigned the task of making the pitch. I was invited to tag along to report the project's progress, if any.

We thought we might beat the crowd if we arrived before sundown, around 6 p.m., but it was like a July Sunday at Coney Island when we made the scene. Chartered ambulances, carrying folks in need of instant healing, took the first six rows in the parking area. Thousands of believers, nearly all black, surrounded the outdoor tabernacle.

Sommers pushed through the throng toward Rev. Bonds' personal tent and I followed. My nerve played out, however, when we reached the gate and a big gent with a crucifix on his neck and a gun on his hip demanded to know what we wanted. All of a sudden I began to wonder myself, just what did we want?

But Freddie was not easily sidetracked. He lied and said he was "press, Life Magazine," and then he flipped the gate latch as the big man watched. Fortunately, I hesitated.

The instant Sommers got both feet inside the gate a German police dog the size of a Shetland pony leaped from the shadows and sunk a whole bunch of teeth into Freddie's behind. My exit was blocked by the crowd that pushed forward, attracted by the chilling screams of man and beast in mortal combat.

Freddie certainly was at the right place. He was in great need of a healer because that dog was getting better grips with each growl.

For the lack of something better to do I turned to members of the congregation and began shaking hands. Some were beginning to wear rather hostile looks, "Good evening, brother, didn't we meet downtown a few weeks ago?" And, "Sure is a beautiful night for a prayer meeting, isn't it?"

I gave Freddie up for dead after his screams stopped but I decided to stay for the meeting. A little religion never hurt anyone. Besides, sooner or later, they were going to need somebody to identify the body.

Rev. Bonds was a tad late moving into action that warm evening but after a 20-minute delay he started toward his altar, leading 13 men. The 13th was white and he had the entire seat ripped from his pants. It was Freddie.

In due time Rev. Bonds explained that he usually had only 12 apostles, as all the faithful knew, but that evening he carried a spare, a man who had promised to help him build a permanent church of great oaks.

If Bonds had let that dog hang onto Freddie's butt for another moment he could have held out for green bricks with a red roof.

But the point is, Sommers sold his package. Rev. Bonds agreed to attend the fights the following week. All he wanted was 10 percent of the gate and 13 front-row seats for himself and his 12 apostles.

Promoter Smith was going to go for the 10 points but he balked on the front-row seats because they were already sold. Any promoter can sell the first two rows for a pillow fight. It's those back rows that are hard to push. The whole deal fell through when Rev. Bonds got insulted with third-row passes.

* * *

More often than not when you talk about "best" or "most interesting" stories you're referring to those rare ones that put goosebumps on both arms.

King of my goosebump games was that 1963 thriller between Brackenridge and Robert E. Lee, the unforgettable touchdown derby that featured Linus Baer and Warren McVea.

That 55-48 Lee victory will be told and retold longer than all that WPA labor holds Alamo Stadium together. There's really no need now to rehash highlights of those talented youngsters who made that night a bright chapter in Texas sports history.

Actually, it wasn't my assignment to cover that game. I was only a press-box visitor, there to do a column on a championship schoolboy game, if it lived up to advance billings.

For long hours after it was over dozens of us discussed each touchdown, recalling the ghost-like darts of McVea and the fleeting form of Baer. It was one of the few nights I've come home very late and awakened my wife to tell her of a sports event. At 2 a.m. she wasn't real interested.

At 3 a.m. I telephoned Tommy Powers of the Texas Theater and advised him to get the film. Thousands wouldn't believe what we saw and they'd certainly want to see the movie. At that hour Tommy also wasn't too interested.

Now those game films are worn, spliced and shredded in spots. They've been shipped halfway around the world, on requests from servicemen in Korea, Germany and Japan.

It seems strange that a guy would travel so far to cover so many major events — the 500 race in Daytona, all-star baseball in St. Louis, Super Bowls in Miami, New Orleans and Los Angeles — but the most memorable single event was a high school game here at home.

* * *

Before going any deeper with this 30-year jazz, don't get the idea that this is intended as some sort of swan song. That's not the case. It's just that after certain periods of time it doesn't hurt to pause and look back and 30 sounds like a nice pausing point.

I'm having far too much fun to back off. The real fun, of course, comes from digging hard and beating other newsmen to hot stories. If you stay around long enough you'll win some and lose some but you won't hear about any of those losses here today.

To be honest, I cheated on one of my sweetest victories. That came when I was on the Beaumont Enterprise, just prior to my arrival here 22 years ago.

Orange High School had chosen a new football coach on a Thursday afternoon but they refused to make an announcement until the following day. The Orange Leader, you see, is an afternoon paper and all the big news of that city, I was informed, got saved for the hometown sheet.

My boss in Beaumont told me not to waste time chasing the story because Cullen Browning, Orange Leader managing editor, had a lock on such announcements in his area. There was no way he would allow a good story from Orange in our morning paper before his afternoon paper.

It presented an interesting challenge. Five men on the Orange school board, plus Mr. Browning, knew the name of the new coach. But after four hours it became hopeless. The five school men were kind and patient but they wouldn't budge and drop the slightest hint. Browning had them too well trained.

Finally, 30 minutes before our deadline, I struck at the heart of my problem, Browning himself. I phoned my dad in Houston and outlined a plan. I had him call Browning, from Houston, and say he was Max Shelton of the Associated Press.

He told Browning that he needed the story because he wanted to go fishing the next day but was eager to get the story on the wire before he left. He promised he would not release the story until noon the next day.

After just 10 minutes my father, an electrician, phoned me back with all the details — name of the coach, his record, his family. We beat the Orange afternoon paper. For months Browning took turns accusing a different one of the five school board members of leaking the story.

That really wasn't a fair method of handling a story and when Shelton heard how I used his name in vain he was furious. But it was fun. And, under similar circumstances, I'd do it again tomorrow.

When you really hunker down to playing newspaper it's the most exciting game I know. Actually, it's about the only game I know.

January 21, 1975

Miller Too Good to be True

There's something mighty suspicious about this Johnny Miller. You never hear much about his home or social life. Just his incredible deeds on a golf course. Folks, I'm not sure yet but I think he's a mechanical man. He might even be the Six Million Dollar Man.

Really now, has anybody ever seen him bleed? Or cry? Or bust out laughing? There's just that same, pure, boyish smile each time he puts his hooks on the winner's check.

Which happens to be every time he competes.

At 6-2, he's rail thin and without half an ounce of fat to be found anywhere. So much so that if he were to swallow half a cream puff you'd expect to see a lump in his stomach. A $6 steak should bend him all out of joint, like one of those big snakes that swallows a pig and spends the next two days getting it down.

But hold on now. This isn't intended in any way as a slap at the new king of pro golf. Much to the contrary, this skinny young man might be the greatest thing to happen to sports since the round ball was invented.

Still, he's almost inhuman the way he cracks that little white pellet with such accuracy. He's downright unbeatable.

The other day John Mahaffey kidded himself into thinking that he could take Miller. Mahaffey was three strokes down after three rounds and he made the remark, "I know I can catch him and I know that he's not unbeatable. After all, he's only human like the rest of us."

That's what Mr. Mahaffey said as he got himself all psyched up. And he wasn't just whistling Dixie in the graveyard, either. The next day he started off with four birdies on the first seven holes — and lost ground.

Really now, sports fans, when Arnold Palmer made four birdies on the first seven holes five or six years ago everyone got excited about the great "charge," and Arnie's Army flocked to the scene to offer encouragement. But all Mahaffey did with his great charge was lose another stroke to Miller, who happened to open his round with five birdies on the first seven.

And while on the subject of Palmer, he played well enough in the Tucson Open last week but he never got close to Miller. On his final round he started with a birdie and followed with an eagle but after six holes he had lost two strokes to the eventual winner.

Second-place finisher Mahaffey, however, must have been the frustrated one. He tried to rally again late and birdied number 11 — but lost ground as Miller eagled No. 11.

Sears Roebuck made the greatest deal it's come up with since publishing that first catalog when the company signed young Miller to a multi-year contract to wear and promote Sears slacks.

That was a couple of years ago and when I first saw one of the early TV ads I wondered who Miller was and where Sears found him. So help me, I figured some yo-yo in Sears' promotion department just sashayed onto a golf course and spotted some slim dude who would look good in their pants.

Miller must have picked out a good fit because a few months later he won the U.S Open. And he's been winning ever since.

Winning, however, is one thing. It's the way Miller wins that causes so much concern. He smashes par, kills the course and strangles hope from all competitors long before it's time for the final nine holes.

The one bad contribution the 27-year-old Miller has made to pro golf is the lack of suspense. He's taken the edge off the most interesting thing in sports, the close finish. When he makes the turn for the final nine about the only thing that could knock him out of the winner's circle is a sunstroke.

Personally, I think it's high time that we in this country located a hero that all kids can look up to.

Miller is almost too good to be true. He might even be too good to emulate but it would be worth a try. The guy doesn't drink, smoke, curse or . . . let's see, I've forgotten some of those bad habits Miller doesn't have.

It's been a long time since such an all-around nice guy dominated a major sport in such a sensational style.

Muhammad Ali might be a great boxer but it seems a shame to name him America's top sportsman for 1974. After all, he hasn't had a nice thing to say about this country in 10 years and just a few years back he was on the verge of going to jail for draft dodging.

And Joe Namath is a talented quarterback but about all he writes or talks about are booze, broads and his bedroom conquests. At this stage Miller appears almost mechanical as he coasts to victories but he's still a breath of fresh air.

June 3, 1975

Pro Cagers Talk Strike in Rio

It's a good thing to be united, even if you must go all the way to Rio de Janeiro to get yourself united.

That's what the National Basketball Association players did. The poor fellows endured all sorts of hardships to hold their annual meeting in Brazil, and when they returned it was agreed by one and all that they got themselves united at the lengthy session.

Fact is, they're so united now they're talking about a players strike if their NBA league merges with the ABA.

None of the NBA players would speak for the record but no less than four admitted, off the record, that the blabber-mouth trainer for the Milwaukee Bucks was telling the truth when he told of the strike possibility.

It's difficult to get an accurate salary average in any league because the superstars are so far ahead of the bench-warmers. So it might be best to eliminate the richly rewarded studs as well as the not-so-dependable subs. Do that and you come up with an annual salary average of about $65,000 per player for six months of work. That doesn't count bonuses. The average would be much higher if you included all hands.

In order to win and get those playoff purses you almost have to have at least one or two wheels who earn well over $115,000 each. If you go all the way, the chances are good that your club has at least one giant pulling down more than $130,000.

These salaries, plus the growing expense of travel, are the two main reasons more pro basketball owners lose money every season. Since only the IRS knows for sure an accurate comparison is difficult but it's safe to assume that far more teams in both the ABA and NBA lost money than turned a profit last season.

Most players in both leagues are college graduates. At least, they have papers saying they attended classes and earned passing grades for about four years. So how come they're not smart enough to know that owners aren't dumb enough to tolerate a strike? Can't they see that a merger of the two leagues is the only move that will permit pro basketball to operate on a profitable basis? Are the players so stupid that they believe their high salaries will continue to grow higher even though their front offices are in financial binds?

Rio de Janeiro might be a nice place to visit but it must be a lousy spot to conduct serious business.

All contracts and legal agreements already signed would, by law, be binding no matter what the league bosses decided to do on a merger. That's as far as the players are concerned.

The NBA players are fools if they think they can strike and prevent a merger that some owners feel is the only solution to the wild bidding war that occurs each year. It's nice to have a wedge, for the players to be able to play one league against the other. But if the league bosses do, indeed, decide to unite that united front tossed together by the players in Rio isn't going to be worth two backcourt fouls if they stick with a strike as their solution.

―――――――

October 22, 1975

Bills Still Top Contenders

Don't be misled by Monday night's upset of Buffalo or any of that jazz that Howard Cosell put out about the Bills having a weak secondary and questionable linebackers. He didn't say those things until the Giants scored and moved close.

Buffalo has a solid ballclub and O.J. Simpson is, by far, the best running back in America today.

The Bills could get their plows cleaned again this Sunday because they line up against the still-improving Dolphins of Miami. Nevertheless, the Bills should be potent contenders for that AFC East playoff spot all the way to the wire.

Of course, these are just so many opinions but they happen to be some of my better ones this week.

Simpson collected 126 yards in that losing effort against New York so he didn't make too many mistakes after the game started. O.J. did, however, make one prior to the contest when he submitted to an interview and bubbled confidence as he told how the Bills welcomed the chance to play on national TV "to show all the folks why Buffalo will get to the Super Bowl this season."

Coming from him it didn't sound cocky or boastful. He was just confident that he and his teammates were going to strap it on the Giants that evening. And that's the way it looked, too, for about two quarters as Buffalo rolled right out to a 14-0 lead.

But when it was over that interview left the weary Simpson with some egg on his face. A 17-14 loss to the lowly Giants is not a classic example of how to get to the Super Bowl.

This isn't to knock Simpson, however. The man happens to be my all-time favorite carrier of footballs. He replaces Doak Walker on my personal chart. Doak almost got replaced by Gayle Sayers on that list but the Chicago great got his wheels busted and had to quit before his time was up.

We all realize that Jimmy Brown was king of the road during his career but although he had my full respect I never could rate him ahead of the Doaker. There were just too many memories of Walker's incredible deeds when he wore an SMU suit.

Like the time he dashed down the sidelines with 40 seconds left and his team trailing by three points. Doak slithered 30 yards, stepped toward the middle, shot a glance at the scoreboard clock and then raced out of bounds. Doak could compute the odds on a play in an instant. He was always thinking — and winning.

And don't think for a second that Simpson doesn't have sharp valves operating upstairs in his think tank.

O.J. happens to be one of the few superstars in this country who long ago mastered the knack of getting along with all of his teammates, his coaches, team owners, fans and even the reporters who sometimes aren't easy to get along with when they ask pointed or silly questions.

"Mastering the knack" might not be the best way to describe Simpson's ability to get along with those around him. That sounds as though he works hard at it, sitting up late at night, wondering what nice compliment he can drop on his offensive guard or assistant coach the next day. Should he say "Hi, handsome" to that creepy sportswriter with the beady blue eyes, the one who keeps asking about his love life?

Actually, Simpson's "knack" for getting along is just like his talent, pure and natural. The man is in love with life and he enjoys and appreciates all the people who form small or large patterns in his lifestyle. It's no act. He's just being himself.

When the player strike was under way O.J. was one of the game's few stars who honored the situation and stayed friendly with the coaches and owners. And by remaining on strike with the others he also stayed friendly with the players.

When Simpson was burning up the turf at Southern California he made it a habit of always including his offensive line and co-workers in the backfield in any interviews that featured him.

"Hey, how about Joe up there at right guard and Billy on the left side? Those guys opened holes that you could have walked through." That's what he'd tell reporters when they shoved his way to hear how he gained all that yardage.

Simpson learned a long time ago what Larry Csonka discovered this season in the World Football League. Fans and reporters can call you the greatest but there never has been one great one who could go very far very often without some fair blocking up front.

Simpson is also aware that his teammates realize that his total income is four or five times more than anyone else's on the squad, including the coach. That's why he said "thank you" in a private, personal way after last season. He didn't want the press to know about it but O.J. gave heavy, gold bracelets to all members of the Buffalo team. The total cost on those gifts was right at $25,000.

The one they call "Juice" has a lot of talent, personality and wisdom. But above all, the man has class. That's something he'll probably keep long after he hangs up his helmet.

November 7, 1975

Get Elected, Become an Expert

Biggest problem with politicians is they always act like politicians. Even the ones who can't find their way out of a closet stand ready to offer instant solutions to all the problems of others.

You see, politicians don't need degrees in engineering, knowledge of science, a fair idea about economics or even light loads of common sense. All politicians need are enough votes to get elected. Once that happens they automatically become experts on highways, bridges, nuclear energy, business administration and, most recently, all sports played by folks from 10 to 60.

A guy who couldn't make his own car payments in July gets elected to office in September and by October he's ready to tell Ford how to build and price cars. Then he'll tell the banks how to finance them. After that he'll figure out a minimum-wage law so dishwashers will be able to afford cars.

If you haven't suspected, this is leading to the government's newest invasion of the life — and perhaps death — of the National Football League.

To be honest, at first I thought it was a rather cruel blow when Pete Rozelle ruled that his NFL would not sign any players from the fallen World Football League until this season ends. That was at first.

My sympathies rested with many of the San Antonio Wings players who were knocked out of work with little or no notice. The ones talented enough to make it in the NFL, it seemed, deserved the opportunity. Nevertheless, after giving the matter more thought it seemed that Rozelle did the right thing.

The WFL did all it could to tear down the NFL in an effort to compete against the older league. Raids were made on the NFL's top team, Miami, and nearly every superstar was approached with a fat offer. Joe Namath, the NFL's number one property, was offered millions to switch jobs and leagues.

Okay, so now that the WFL died a natural death, without any dirty work from the NFL that it caused so much grief, why should the NFL change the balance of its current season and risk countless lawsuits from WFL owners who are being sued by many and stand ready to sue anybody?

Rozelle's ruling, I think, was the result of a wise decision. But now comes the federal government, again, to tell Rozelle that he can't, under law, ban or bar the WFL players.

The federal judge in St. Paul said, "Professional sports and the public are better served by open, unfettered competition." Well, that must be so because a government man said so.

Let's look at it this way. You're a small businessman and you've got a successful clothing store. You hire about six tailors and they're among the best in the business.

One morning you wake up to discover that some folks are building another clothing store right across the street from you. After it's completed you learn that your new competitor has lured three of your best tailors away, offering them higher wages, fat bonuses and expense-paid trips to Europe every other year.

Okay, you do the best you can and fill your jobs with the best available tailors. After three months the new guy across the street goes busted. Naturally, the hotshot tailors would like to return but you've got your business back in good shape with the new help. So you tell your store manager to go with the people he's got and, under no circumstances, take any of the tailors who worked for your rival of a few months.

You're not just being an unforgiving employer or a hard-headed businessman. You're interested in the morale of your whole organization. Those new tailors you hired on short notice to fill the voids weren't as talented as your old ones but they worked hard and got the job done. Now you're supposed to boot them out and take the old fellows back, right? Wrong, I think.

It's the same thing, only on a smaller scale.

Of course, the government doesn't say that an NFL team has to take WFL players. It simply says the NFL commissioner cannot have a ban on those players. He must allow his team owners to hire those unemployed WFL players if the owners so desire.

Well, as long as you have 26 owners there'll be one or two — people like baseball boss Charles O. Finley — who will grab whatever legal loophole is offered to benefit himself.

The others will follow in self-defense. The strongest law in the universe is still the law of self-preservation.

So what it amounts to is the government has again brushed aside a league commissioner to dictate decisions.

It might not happen in our time but I'm still waiting on a congressman, senator or federal judge who will offer the ruling: "That's a decision that can be best made by the authorities of your league who are more familiar with the problem and all circumstances surrounding that problem."

Of course, that would be the same as saying, "I don't know for sure," and you'll never hear an elected official or one appointed by elected officials say anything like that.

Watching Pele at Alamo Stadium

L egends don't come this way too often so it seemed like a good idea to hustle out to Alamo Stadium Wednesday night and watch one in action.

After all, they used to show film clips of Pele on movie house newsreels long before they got the big screens and added the dirty words.

The only trouble with legends, especially live ones still performing, is that folks come to expect a bit too much.

My first meeting with Titanic Thompson was over a poker table and each time the old hustle king cut the cards I expected the queen of hearts and jack of spades to jump out and sing two verses of "Wabash Cannonball."

And so it was with Pele here Wednesday night.

Ancient Alamo Stadium, still in good shape, took on an unusual air for Ward Lay's rare soccer show. The mariachis from San Francisco Steak House were strumming guitars and working over the chorus of "Guadalajara" in front of the main entrance when I arrived around 7 p.m.

Inside, about 50 usherettes, Orange Jackets from Burbank and 15 Red Jackets from Fox Tech, stood their posts, awaiting passengers from the traffic that was beginning to snarl. A tall guy in short pants was selling Schlitz beer from a Pearl bucket. The World Football League is gone but it did leave beer at the old ballpark.

About 7:30 the Shriners' pipe organ, a yellow job on wheels, rolled onto the sidelines and pumped out a few typical pipe organ tunes and then the mariachis moved inside and went to work on a mike.

In the special box-seat sections, Starr Rooney stood guard and saw to it that each lady, upon entering, was given a long-stem yellow rose. The men were offered a free beer and then Starr whipped out a small towel and dusted each chair a split second before a rear end rested. Starr's towel hand was quicker than some of the soccer feet.

Half a dozen large signs on the infield track faced the main grandstand. They were advertising Pepsi-Cola, the drink that refreshes Pele when he's slightly pooped, and a couple of radio stations.

One sign, however, simply read, "George Best, May 8." That didn't mean much to soccer newcomers. The unknowing might have thought that George was running for City Council or maybe even constable and it was a paid political ad.

But soccer veterans know George Best is the strutting, swinging, jet-settin' young dude who plays for the Los Angeles Aztecs. He and his Aztecs will be here May 8 and local team officials are planning to work up some sort of contest that would give a local lady a date with George.

That could involve some future complications. A few years ago George had a date with Miss Universe and four months later she was the former Miss Universe. She was also pregnant, which is a husky violation of the Miss Universe ground rules.

Let's see now, George Best, May 8 with or without a date contest.

At 7:45 p.m. the New York Cosmos trotted onto the field and with them, as advertised, was the legend. Pele was the last to be introduced and as he waved to the crowd of about 15,000 and acknowledged the great ovation he flashed the familiar smile that has been photographed a million times in many corners of the globe.

Moments later it was photographed again and again as everyone within a three-mile area with a flash camera suddenly appeared on the field. Pele was almost mobbed by amateurs who elbowed each other like professional photographers.

A loud voice on the PA mike and four policemen finally restored order and allowed Pele to continue the brief warm-up session. Then came the start, the kickoff that sent the legend into action.

All eyes focused on the black man wearing the number 10 uniform of New York each time the ball worked near him. You sort of sensed the magic about him and his talents, a guy with the feet of Bojangles with a motor in each leg.

But, to be honest, to me he didn't look any better — or worse — than a dozen other guys on the field. Later, those who know the game were to say that it was a below-par performance for the great man but that he didn't make any major mistakes. He just failed to score and only on rare occasions did he dazzle opponents and fans with fleet footwork and pinpoint passes.

However, when an athlete turns 35 and has logged 20 years of professional play there just aren't great gobs of dazzle left at his command. The masters know their arts and sometimes they can reach back and perform yet another so-called miracle play but as the years mount they more often reach back and fail to find the handle at the moment desired.

Father Time has a way of sapping speed, stamina and skill and after he becomes a constant companion to the mighty ones great deeds are not produced twice a week on signal.

But when we're treated to the opportunity of seeing a legend we shouldn't expect legendary performances. It should be enough just to see Pele doing his thing, the thing he did better than any other man for many years — and still does best once in awhile.

After all, Titanic Thompson bested every high-roller on Broadway at one time or another but in that poker game that I sat with him, when he was 71, he lost $75.

The Strange NBA-ABA Pact

When the four ABA teams crossed over into the NBA fold about this time last year there wasn't a whole bunch of hard, mature business sense applied to the packaging of the deals. Not from either side of the table.

That is, nobody sneaked a pocket calculator into the meeting. They didn't invite the CPA in to scan the figures and offer some plain and fancy advice. It was more like some hungry blokes trying to buy pecans from a desperate farmer on the side of a road.

Both sides had something the other side wanted and the trick was to swing a deal, just about any kind of deal, in time for the start of a new season. The four ABA teams each needed to get a foot in the door and the NBA fathers were bound and determined to make that entry as expensive as possible.

And that's exactly the way it worked out, too. It's sort of remindful of the dishwasher who pays $600 down on a new Cadillac and faces $800 monthly payments. He knows that he's going to ride to work in style for one month but after that about 800 question marks surround his transportation.

It could only happen in sports, in America. A multimillion-dollar deal involving civic and business leaders from dozens of the largest cities in the country and the major tools they used at all the meetings were jaw-bone juice, bluff, diplomacy, leverage and desire. The ABA teams desired in and NBA officials desired to make the entry as expensive as possible. Everybody won. Or did they?

Well, it seems that San Antonio won. Enough of the old backers coughed up new cash and the lure of the NBA brought in some fresh "owners" so the Spurs appear to be, by far, in the best financial shape of the four newcomers.

The other three, however, just made small down payments on Cadillacs. The New York Nets sold off all their talented players so they wound up with the lousiest team and the lowest payroll in the league.

Denver was dead from the start. Any kid who makes a B-minus or better in fourth-grade arithmetic could have put a pencil to Denver's game plan and figured that it wouldn't work. Nobody has a right to expect a full house more than 95 percent of the time — which was what Denver averaged. But the team houses three superstars so the payroll is somewhere between extravagant and staggering. It's the only place in the country where three aces beat a full house.

Indiana must have made a bum deal or did a lot of things wrong because the Pacers haven't been able to meet their payroll for many weeks.

That leaves San Antonio, and the biggest mistake the Spurs made was going for the knot that ties them in with the three other ABA refugees. But then, that was the only rope the NBA smarts offered, the one with the knot in the end.

At this moment all league officials are meeting in a small California city named Coronado. And that's another story for another day. Have you ever wondered how and why sports people pick their meeting sites? The owners are now gathered in Coronado and in August the NBA Players Association will meet in Africa.

Nevertheless, Commissioner Larry O'Brien is reported to be trying to iron out all the wrinkles in his NBA suit over in Coronado. It's no easy job but Mr. O' Brien has had experience in handling delicate matters. Be remindful that he was chairman of the Democratic Party when Watergate exploded. Anyone who can engineer a counterattack against the White House should be able to solve some double-dribble financial deals.

After all, they're only talking about millions and most of it is on paper. Not checks. Just paper. Jawbone and escrow, the things that made up the old World Football League.

When sports leaders get around to discussing "serious money" they're usually referring to a certified check for $200,000 or so and it's got to either be on the table or in somebody's pocket at the meeting.

The only time green cash is ever displayed at a meeting of sports leaders is when somebody sends out for a bowl of soup and the waiter won't accept credit cards.

Now don't misunderstand. This isn't to knock the deal that allowed the four ABA teams to enter the NBA. At that time the ABA was sinking in quicksand and the only way out was through the NBA door.

The whole point is, they made us an offer that we couldn't refuse but all sides probably knew that we also couldn't live with that offer. Several

NBA teams have been struggling for years even though they've enjoyed all the benefits that extend to all the regular members. The four ABA teams, already struggling before they were admitted, were denied a dime of television money, refused equal footing in the drafts and stroked with millions of dollars worth of admission debts.

We — the four ABA teams — knew that we couldn't live with it and we certainly couldn't live without it. They — the NBA clubs — were armed with the same knowledge. Yet, a deal was struck. Does that make sense? Yeah, about as much sense as most major sports deals of this period.

Of the four ABA crossovers the Spurs are the safest of all, by far. Fan following is somewhere between good and outstanding, the player talent is better than average and the payroll is lower than most. Besides, our guys have concessions and the popcorn, peanuts and beer sales can make up for a lot of empty seats on the nights that the Nets and Indiana come to town.

Don't envy Commissioner O'Brien at Coronado today. And don't be surprised if all four NBA teams are forced to stash some cash in escrow. Those who can't agree to that might be brushed aside and soon forgotten. After all, any club owners who can't promise a pile of escrow really shouldn't be in the big-time sports market today.

A u g u s t   3 1 ,   1 9 7 7

A Master of Razorback Magic

FAYETTEVILLE, Ark. — Lou Holtz is a most unusual man. Chances are good that you just haven't seen anything like this dude who replaced Frank Broyles as football boss of the Arkansas Razorbacks.

Lou is a golden-haired, quick-witted promoter. He's a slick salesman, a humorist, an amateur magician, a fiery-tempered coach and a highly respected gentleman.

He's also the first to leave a head coaching job in the NFL — the New York Jets last season — to take a similar post in the Southwest Conference.

Holtz has been in this neck of the woods only a matter of months and although his team has yet to go on public display, he's somehow managed to capture the hearts of Razorback boosters. He is swift.

Lou is not the sort of fellow who wears on you, the type you have to be around months before you form an opinion of likes or dislikes. He comes on strong in an easy, smooth style. You know you like him two minutes after being introduced.

And that's no rib about the magician bit.

Lou greeted about 30 members of the press tour here Tuesday with his best rope trick.

The way my luck runs it wasn't surprising when he called for me to act as his assistant, the straight man, the dummy.

"Good afternoon, gentlemen," he started, "I'm happy that you're here and before we get started talking football I'd like to show you a little bit of magic. Cook, step up here and give me a hand."

The guy is sharp. He took one look at the group and pegged me for a pure patsy, the easiest mark to fool. Then he took three ropes — each about a foot long — and placed them in my hot hand and said some magic words. Naturally, when I opened my hand as ordered the three ropes were one long rope.

But an even neater trick was the way Holtz convinced fans that "every Arkansas home game ticket will be sold long before the season starts." He told one and all that if they wanted a little behind room in the arena they had better "buy now." Did they go for it? Like flies swarming honey.

End-zone seats were hiked from $5 to $8 and over 15,000 of those bad chairs were scooped up between Holtz's second warning and third magic show. Like I've been telling you, this guy comes on like a Rolls Royce at a used-car auction and marvelous tales about him and his messages are spreading through the Ozarks.

As you might suspect, there's a snappy, New York cut to Lou's clothes. He visited some of the better garment houses when he wasn't giving Joe Namath plays last year in the Big Apple.

His blue-checkered suit, complete with dark necktie and expensive black shoes, made him one of the best-dressed coaches ever to greet a press tour. But the red strap on his red Razorback watch didn't seem to go too well with the outfit. Still, the watch probably kept good time and it most certainly brought smiles to the chops of Razorback rooters wherever Lou went.

By now you might be getting the idea that Holtz is a snake-oil salesman, a dolled-up carnival character. That's not a true picture. There's no doubt that Holtz is a hot salesman, an excellent pitchman who knows a thing or two about showmanship. But he also happens to be a solid coach and a hard worker.

It's nothing short of amazing the way that he's won so many fans and followers in such a short time but, perhaps far more importantly, while winning outside friends he's also managed to collar complete respect from his players. They love the man.

As a matter of fact, some veteran starters heap so much praise on their new coach it begins to look like a mild knock at Frank Broyles in some areas. "He's exactly what this team needed," said one three-year letterman. And to the man, each player explained how Holtz has taught them to respect each other and, in doing so, won great respect for himself.

This fellow could be the hottest thing to happen to Arkansas since the first Geritol truck rolled through years ago.

You've got to take fast notes when you interview Lou. He comes at you with sparkling gems in machine-gun style.

Within a three-minute period he popped up with dozens of good one-liners. Things like, "I'm new here so I really don't know what to expect but I durned sure know what the alumni expects." And, "We should have a good team but we just don't have enough big men who are willing to dive on hand grenades."

Somebody asked Lou if his Razorbacks would be fatally injured should his top quarterback, Ron Calcagni, get wounded. Without hesitating, Holtz answered in no uncertain terms, "No, we would not be fatally injured if Calcagni were to get wounded." Then perhaps 20 seconds later he added, "Of course, we would be listing at a 45-degree angle."

Someone asked Lou about the speed of his running backs and receivers. "Oh, I don't put much stock in those kinds of statistics because over the years I've seen too many 9.1 sprinters caught from behind by 9.8 defensive backs. You see, figures don't lie, but liars do figure."

He might not yet be in a class with Blackstone The Great or Mandrake, but he sure has worked some heavy magic in these hills. All he has to do now is win and fans will be asking, "Frank who?"

December 15, 1977

Racism Still Enters Sports Debates

Why must we always resort to the racial angle? How come color suddenly becomes the most important thing with some after a stupid act of violence between black and white? And, what I'm really leaning toward, why are we writers always called racists after we side against guilty ones who commit violent acts?

The point is, our society is a far more distant piece from true compatibility and integration than most authorities would like to believe. The trouble, however, does not rest with the so-called great majority but, rather, with those from both sides who campaign so hard for fair play and equality.

From here it seems that once they enter the battleground — wherever that ground might be — they get lost in reality and can't locate the forest for the trees. They all appear to be rushing around with chips on their shoulders, reading between the lines, searching for unfairness, begging someone to bounce that chip.

Maybe I just don't understand the big picture but from here it appears that such do-gooders, the front-line scrappers, cause far more overall friction and trouble than the grand wizard of the Ku Klux Klan or the most militant honky-hater in Detroit city.

You folks see where those grand wizard rednecks and Black Panther rebels are coming from and there's no question as to which side of the street they walk. But those who dedicate themselves to equality — both black and white — often think that they're strolling down the street's middle while, in fact, they're so far to one side they can't even see the middle.

By now you might be a little confused so we'll zero in on the meat of the matter. The bottom line is, I'm sick and weary of fielding cards, letters and phone calls from racists who want to take the opportunity to call me a racist for not pointing out "both sides" in those sucker-punch incidents in sports. Folks, it just doesn't make a dip of difference to me whether the puncher is black or white and the punchee is brown or red. There just aren't two sides to those stories.

Yet, you might be surprised — perhaps even alarmed — at the number who have written or called to explain that the black athletes are getting the short end of the stick in these "fights" that have drawn so much attention.

Many claim anger at me for "siding" against Lenny Randle when he busted his baseball manager's jaw early last season. And I wasn't for Kareem Jabbar when he broke his hand while copping a sneaky Sunday punch on Kent Benson. And I sure haven't been for Kermit Washington since he busted up Rudy Tomjanovich's face and head last Friday.

No less than four letters say, "You're always for the white man in such cases." Well, two of them used those exact words and two more came close with the same meaning.

This isn't to go on the defensive because I much prefer to play offense. But, so help me, it never even dawned on me to lump those three incidents together and arrive at the fact that three black men punched out three white men and the three black men were whacked with large fines by white commissioners.

Well, would it make things any better if the three white victims were treated by black doctors? Maybe they were, I sure don't know.

To my knowledge, no story has pointed out the color difference between any of these newsmakers. But it's obvious that a lot of folks aren't going to rest until some white cat plants a bomb on the noggin of a black athlete and then the white commissioner hits the white player with a $10,000 fine.

Let it be said now, however, that the next basketball player to throw the first punch in an NBA game has got to be either mighty rich or terribly stupid. Now that holds whether one is black, white, brown or whatever. Commissioner Larry O'Brien is having great difficulty getting his point across but anyone even the least bit interested should know by now that he's not going to tolerate anymore of those unsuspected haymakers.

Commissioner O'Brien, it should be mentioned, studied all angles and aspects of two tapes of the Washington attack before making a ruling.

I took a look at the same films — five times. Folks, there just aren't two sides to that deal. There's no excuse for the punch that Washington stroked on Tomjanovich.

Some argue that before Kareem creamed Benson the other day, the one who got punched was the tormentor, often, at various times, elbowing Jabbar in the chest and stomach. Maybe so. I sure can't say. But there's no question that Jabbar did lash a sneaky, roundhouse shot flush on Benson's chin. And it's difficult to understand how anyone, black or white, can side with Randle for interrupting a conversation with his manager by bashing the old man in the head.

These things simply don't have anything to do with race. Well, that might not be entirely correct. But the reporting and the rights or wrongs certainly do not have anything to do with race.

Maybe we were lucky that Clint Longley and Roger Staubach are both white. When they got into their series of scraps and sucker punches a little over a year ago there wasn't a single letter or phone call to defend Clint after we sided with Staubach on the incident. I wonder how many letters there would have been if either of the two of them had been black.

January 6, 1978

Old Friend Chats About Color Lines

"Sittin' in the back of the bus was just a pride thing and black people got used to that so it wasn't any big deal. It wasn't, that is, unless the back of the bus was crowded. The real problem, in those days, was finding downtown public toilets and gettin' somethin' to eat out of a restaurant's rear kitchen door."

The speaker continued, moving back 20 and 30 years when he was growing up in San Antonio: "Sometimes it wasn't easy gettin' a drink of water downtown, either. Only the big stores had two fountains, one marked 'colored' and the other marked 'white only.' I suppose if they put a 'colored' sign over a fountain nowadays young people would expect colored water to come out."

I.H. Harvey laughed good on that one. Imagine, colored water. Then, as now, folks called him "Sporty" Harvey and he hasn't changed much since he pulled up stakes here years ago and moved to California. The years have been good to Sporty.

Oh, when he takes his cap off you can see that his forehead has become longer and his hairline has moved back about three inches. Maybe four. But Mr. Harvey is now 50 years old and hairlines have a

147

habit of retreating around that point in life. If not sooner. He continued up memory lane and I listened.

"After I got everythin' changed here — me and Maury Maverick Jr. — I caught a city bus and plopped right down in the first seat. That was fun. Then I started eatin' in the best downtown restaurants, you know, places that I'd never been before. I had to stop that after a spell, though, 'cause I couldn't afford some of those spots, black or white. But I'm the one that got it all changed, right? Changed the whole history book, right?"

Well, partially right. I didn't want to break the spell or slow him down but Sporty's real contribution to society didn't have a lot to do with buses or cafes. It was Harvey, with attorney Maverick, who pushed through the courts to get the color line in Texas boxing busted.

Looking back, it's hard to realize now that during the reign of such champions as Joe Louis and Ray Robinson black and white fighters were not permitted to fight each other in this state. So said Texas law.

In those days, in San Antonio, Houston and Dallas and other Texas points, nearly all major boxing shows opened with four- or six-round bouts between two blacks. Names didn't mean much so usually it was the Green Frog vs. Charley Chocolate or Wildman Willie vs. Sweet Daddy Doodle. On the square, those were the handles of four black fighters who championed in these parts 25 years ago.

In those openers fans didn't thirst for style or class. Finesse was foreign to the first-fight fellows on each program. Fans wanted two things, humor and punch, so that's what they got. Those who couldn't give one or the other didn't get invited back for more work and pay.

The Green Frog might have had potential because he packed a sweet left hook and a cast-iron chin. But fans only seemed to appreciate his hopping antics so the Frog hopped a lot between catching and pitching. Forty straight knockouts couldn't have gotten the Frog an eight- or 10-round bout in this neck of the woods. Promoters seldom risked matching two blacks in a headliner and to match a black with a white would have been, well, it would have been against the law.

Harvey campaigned under his real name, with the Sporty tossed in for good measure, and he wasn't a clown. Oh, perhaps a bit of a showman because he did use a windmill windup for a little hot-doggin' on occasions. But he stayed serious and worked hard most of the time. He must have had at least 40 fights in San Antonio but he went to Dallas for his first 10-rounder.

That was after Sporty and Maverick won their case and broke the state color line. Cashing in on the publicity a Dallas promoter matched Harvey with Buddy Thurman in a 10-round main event. If memory serves, it was a good, close bout and the decision could have gone either way. "They got back at me and gave the decision to Buddy," Sporty recalls.

After that Harvey fought all over the South and must have appeared on at least 15 cards in Mexican bullrings. No more four-rounders, either. Sporty was eight- and 10-round material after he got that big decision from the big judge. Joe Louis didn't toss in his sleep, worrying about Sporty, because Harvey never was a world contender. But he was a hard worker, courageous and eager. His paydays just got bigger and more frequent after that court ruling in 1954.

Sporty was born in Hallettsville and he learned to pick cotton and chop wood before he learned the way to school. His family moved to San Antonio when he was still a kid and his mother still lives here.

Years ago, Sporty moved to Los Angeles to seek his fame and fortune but he returns around Christmas time every two or three years to visit his mom. He keeps me on his visit list, too, so the other day we rehashed the not-so-good old days.

Harvey's last fight was in 1965 but he's been working for the Jones Tire Company ever since he hit the West Coast. It's hard to say whether he's moved up or held the line since the last visit here three years ago but, either way, Sporty is doing right well.

Last time he visited me he parked a new, baby-blue Cadillac out front. This time he rolled into town in a slick camper. Not overly familiar with the price tag on either, I only have Sporty's word that both are nice ways to travel on long hauls.

We finished up on the "tough times" tale and Sporty had to move on. He wanted to include attorney Maverick on his visits this trip. "Can't tell. He might need me to help bust down some more color lines," Harvey said.

Well, I haven't heard of any black polo players but I'm not sure that Sporty can swing a mallet and stay on a pony. But he probably could if he set his mind to it real hard.

Divine Free-Throw Guidance

My children are convinced that when I went to high school footballs were round, basketballs had laces and all the guys parted their hair down the middle and wore knickers to the junior-senior prom. Oh, yeah, a big day for us was Saturday when we all went to the movie and laughed at Charlie Chaplin.

Well, maybe the football was a little fatter in those days but I sure don't remember any laces on my basketball. And they've got the wrong Charlie. It was Charlie Chan, not Chaplin, who got my 30 cents each Saturday, and it's interesting to note that the same slick Chinaman is still solving those same mysteries on television some weekends. And my kids are watching, just like I did.

The point is, some things really don't change much, no matter how it seems. You see, back when I was attending St. Thomas High School in Houston our basketball coach was a priest named A.L. Higgins. Father Higgins taught some unusual methods but he believes in the democratic process so he always gave us an option. We had the choice of doing it his way or turning in our uniforms.

His way on free throws didn't jive with the way most hotshots around town took their charity tosses. But Father Higgins not only was our basketball coach, he also happened to be principal of the school.

Let it be known now that although Father Higgins was blessed with many virtues there was no way he could count patience and a smooth temperament among his collection. Our coach carried a short fuse and after he demonstrated how he wanted us to shoot free throws — a two-handed, underhanded style — heaven help the poor dude who even practiced a one-handed push shot from the foul line.

Man, that was a real no-no. If he caught you trying one his jaws locked and his jowls turned red while you explained that you weren't practicing a free throw, just a little one-handed jump shot that only happened to be near the free-toss line.

Frank Shannon, nearest thing to a boss that we had on our less-than-average club, could hit about eight out of 10 from the free line before

Father Higgins began coaching him. When Frank went to two hands, dipping the ball low while keeping the back straight and bending the knees properly in Rev. Higgins' prescribed manner, the best he could do was six out of 10 in a close game.

To be honest, nobody on our team really wanted to learn the method. It not only seemed awkward but none of the good players on the better teams were doing it that way. Why should we? Well, we should because Father Higgins said so.

Late in my senior season of basketball Coach Higgins, much out of character, tossed in the towel. We were only three points behind a heavily favored San Jacinto team when Shannon was awarded a couple of freebies. He tossed a pleading glance to the bench and Father Higgins hollered, "Anyway you want."

Frank promptly sank the two shots with one-handed push jobs, cutting our deficit to one point.

We still got clobbered by about 15 or 20 points. I can't remember the final score after all these years but it must have been 15 or 20 points because I do remember playing in that game. Father Higgins never sent me in unless we were 15 or 20 points behind late in the contest. I can only assume that he would have also sent me in had we led somebody by 15 or 20 points late but that never happened.

That particular contest lingers in my mind because it marked the night that Father Higgins gave up on his free-throw style. It also marked the night when I won my letter.

This isn't intended as a boast but I had lettered in all sports but basketball and time was running out in that area. It was my desperate ambition to wind up with letters in football, baseball, ice hockey, the whole works.

When I went in against San Jacinto it wasn't 30 seconds before I was fouled while shooting and awarded two shots. Father Higgins had taken the freeze off his underhanded method five minutes earlier but, like a well-disciplined athlete, I strolled to the line and flipped both shots up there underhanded. Both missed. But Father Higgins appreciated my loyalty.

He must have appreciated it because he finally gave me a basketball letter at the end of that season.

By now you must be thinking that I've wasted all this space and your time just to tell you that I once got a letter for playing basketball. Well, not really. That is, it wasn't my intention when I started.

The heavy meat of this matter is Rick Barry, perhaps the greatest free-throw shooter in professional basketball history. The Golden State superstar has won three free-throw titles and he's well on his way to locking up another. His percentage is well over the .900 mark. And you know something? He lobs 'em up there underhanded. That's right, with a straight back, two hands on the ball, a little spin and upsy-daisy, exactly like Father Higgins tried to teach us.

Come to think of it, Barry sounds like Father Higgins when he discusses his free-throw style. Rick says no pro should ever go below the .800 mark in shooting from the foul line. No college player should go below the .700 mark.

Rick says it only takes a little practice, about half an hour a day for a few weeks, to learn the underhanded method and, once learned, a blind man should make six out of 10 if properly lined up.

You know, that's exactly what Father Higgins tried to tell us about 35 years ago. Only trouble, then, like now, hardly any of the good players use the system because it "just doesn't look right." That's why we never spent any real time learning it and why Rick Barry keeps an inside track to the free-throw championship every year.

No wonder they made Father Higgins principal of our school. He had a lot of smarts.

No Words of Wisdom for Dorsett

About seven months ago, during football's off-season, word slipped out that Cowboy boss Tex Schramm planned to call Howard Cosell to seek his help in recruiting either Muhammad Ali or O.J. Simpson to talk with Tony Dorsett. Schramm, it seems, was stuck with the stout idea that, sooner or later, because of his tender age and immaturity, Dorsett was going to box himself into a corner either through deeds or words.

When a veteran reporter confronted Schramm about the plan, Tex replied, "You're 100 percent correct." That was, indeed, his plan. Seems that Dorsett has great respect for both Ali and Simpson and would, without doubt, listen to whatever advice they might offer. But that was seven months ago and Tex's game plan probably fell flat.

Because of their busy schedules and numerous conflicts of interest, it's not easy to catch Cosell to lateral a request to Ali or O.J. for a visit to Dorsett. As a matter of fact, it might be much easier to get Jimmy Carter to ask the Shah of Iran to talk with Idi Amin about stepping on so many small toes. After all, that's their bag. They get paid for doing each other little verbal favors.

At any rate, it's doubtful Schramm was able to follow through on his plan and if that is the case, then Tex must now be agonizing over his lack of pursuit. It was such a good — and probably necessary — idea.

From here, it appears that Tony has just one enemy in Dallas. His name is Dorsett. Nobody has it in for the fluid, flowing running back. His current controversy has nothing to do with racial issues unless, of course, they exist in his own mind. Yet, Tony seems to read between the lines and draws his own conclusions on each story printed about him and his behavior.

Tony is bitter about an opening line in a Dallas Morning News column when, in reality, that line is geared more to his defense: "Before we tar and feather Anthony (I overslept) Dorsett and boo him out of town, before we send him and his million-dollar contract back to the steel mill, let us step into his cleats for a moment."

Tony's response to that was, "Tar and feather, isn't that what they used to do to blacks before they lynched them?'

Well, somewhere down the line, I suppose a few blacks did get tarred and feathered but I don't remember ever reading or hearing of such incidents. As a matter of fact, mobs dead set on lynching seldom wasted time with such a preliminary. Tar and feathers usually were reserved for slickers, con men — almost always white — who duped folks with bad snake oil or phony land leases.

This sick slice of American history really has no place here today. But it does illustrate how Dorsett is going to the offense with a poor game plan. He's whipping out the racial issue, waving the color line, when it shouldn't even be in sight.

And if they had visited, just what do you suppose Simpson or Ali might have told Dorsett to — as they say — get his head on straight?

It's anybody's guess as to what wisdom Ali might have stroked on Tony but Simpson might have advised him to quit being so sensitive, to understand that you've got to take the bad with the good, that life is a push-and-pull, give-and-take deal. Finally, O.J. might have told Tony not to get upset when one newspaperman or one radioman or one TV reporter gets on his case because, in the long haul, the public usually will wind up on the right side.

In short, it's well to keep in mind that a man is no bigger than the smallest thing that bothers him. And, by the same token, if you're ever going to get anywhere in life, you should never stop to step on woolly worms. Woolly worms can't help or hurt you but they sure can delay your progress.

Of course, there's no way of knowing what kind of advice Tony would have received if Schramm had been able to follow through on his idea of last summer. On second thought, it's possible that Tex did make connections and Ali or O.J. did talk with Tony.

If that's the case, one of two things is certain. Either the advice wasn't taken or they offered him some lousy advice.

There's one thing about this business of publicity that has sort of stumped me over the years.

You can spend the better part of 15 seasons writing nice things about the great career of a brilliant athlete and he'll never acknowledge the fact that you're alive. But if you use one paragraph to put the smallest knock on that same athlete, explaining how he might be getting a little lazy, a wee bit old or no longer takes much time for interviews, the odds are heavy that you'll hear from the fellow, complaining about that "unfair knock" given him in print.

So help me, it's happened at least 40 times to me. Nobody expects a thank-you note after nice things are said. But after nice things are said for years and years, writers shouldn't expect notes of complaints after tossing out a mild verbal jab.

This doesn't have anything to do with Dorsett because he's far too young. This is about the veterans. But it does point out the problems Tony is having as, for the first time in his life, he is experiencing a few knocks from the newsmen and boos from the fans.

Up until a few weeks ago, he'd only seen one side of the crowds and the newsmen. It must be confusing to travel so far and suddenly discover that he's on a two-way street.

M a y   3 ,   1 9 7 9

Staubach, Man Without Flaw

Some day, many years from now, somebody is going to write an exposé on Roger Staubach. They're going to dig up all the dirt on him and put it into a book. It'll probably be the shortest book ever to challenge the best-seller list but I'm going to read it because every line will be news to me.

After following his career for 16 years and interviewing him hither and yon at least a dozen times, I can't locate a single fault in the man. Now, that's not normal. It's not that I've been searching and digging for flaws but they usually flash through, whether you're looking or not.

Staubach, however, was the All-America boy next door we talk so much about, who grew up to become the All-America collegian and now stands as the All-America man. Weaknesses? Well, he's not as fast as he was five years ago and sometimes his passes wobble a bit. But when it comes to character and pure warmth, genuine concern for his fellow man and, above all, devotion to and love for his family, Roger stands at the head of the pack.

It was an honor yesterday to introduce Roger to the 10,000 at Alamo Stadium who gathered for the S.A. Independent School District's Achievement Day. Of course, Staubach needed an introduction here about like Mike Ayala needs one at the San Fernando Gym. The whole crowd began to buzz with excitement when he first rolled into the stadium high on the seat of the convertible.

He had no speech notes but for the better part of the 15 minutes, he talked about love, care and concern and he talked without hesitation, without a pause, without a stammer. He came through loud and clear. It wasn't exactly what you'd call a stock, standard talk because Roger often referred to the city, to his Uncle Tom Staubach who lives here and to the Spurs. Staubach changed his plans so he could stay over and watch last night's game at the Arena.

During other parts of the late-morning ceremony, I asked Roger if he ever lost his place mentally and forgot what he wanted to say. After all, he speaks often during the so-called "off-season" and, as mentioned, he had no speech notes.

The Cowboys quarterback thought for a brief moment and then said, "Yes, I went blank once but it was a long time ago." I waited and Roger, breaking into a thin smile, continued.

"It was my senior year in high school, a Catholic school, and I was to recite the Apostles' Creed during the crowning of the Virgin Mary. The whole school was there and we all knew that the prayer starts, 'I believe in God the father, the creator of heaven and earth.' But I started by saying, 'I believe in the creator of God.' The moment I said it, I knew it was wrong and for a long spell, I just went blank. It was terribly embarrassing," Roger said.

See what I mean? The guy's got to go all the way back to high school to recall the last time he goofed in public.

Off-hand now, just how many invitations to speak do you figure a man like Staubach gets in an average week? The answer is somewhere between 25 and 50. About half of them are freebies and the other half carry offers that range from $200 to $2,000 plus expenses.

And which was this one here yesterday? It was a freebie. Roger's appearance and talk didn't cost the school district a dime. As he put it, "There's no way that I can make them all, of course, so I try and pick and choose with care, speaking at no cost to youth-oriented affairs and then taking the better-paying offers from the rest. There was just no way that I could turn down a program like this with 10,000 high school students being honored for their achievements."

The Dallas star has a deep-rooted feeling about his responsibilities and what he might owe in various directions. But that's why he plans to cut "way down" on future talks. He owes his wife and five children a little more of his time.

After years of doing without, Roger confided that he finally broke down and decided to have a swimming pool installed in his back yard. "They dug the hole a week ago and it's rained every day since," he said. "My kids are beginning to think that that's it since we've now got a big hole in our backyard that's filled with water."

Staubach wasn't bragging about his soon-to-be-pool. That story came in response to the numerous apologies about our San Antonio weather yesterday. The two-hour program was presented during a steady drizzle but the rain was forgotten or ignored when Roger talked.

Most athletes I know tend to take things easy during the off-season but Roger is getting a little long in tooth, as they say. He's 37 and he knows that at that age, he's got to work harder to stay in top shape.

Take, for example, yesterday morning. He was a little pressed for time so he didn't run two miles like he does four or five times a week. He did, however, get up at 5 a.m., worked out with weights for almost an hour and then he ate a quick breakfast so he could catch a 7 a.m. flight to San Antonio. Once he arrived here, it was a whirlwind of visits and hand-shakes and his most relaxed moments — if any — must have been at last night's Spurs game.

And this visit, keep in mind, was a freebie.

Being Roger Staubach might be a far tougher chore than most folks realize. Still, it's a shame that he's one of a kind. We need a whole bunch just like him, both in and out of sports.

O c t o b e r   1 2 ,   1 9 7 9

The DH Rule Started Here

It's come to my attention that the main man in baseball needs some help. Again. A week before the start of each World Series, Commissioner Bowie Kuhn is besieged with questions about the designated hitter rule. Will it apply in the Series? If not, why not? How come it's okay for the American League's entire season but never good enough for the game's showcase classic? If it's a lousy rule, not good enough for the Series, why allow the AL to use it all year?

Well, folks, that's what I'm here for today — to help. No longer does Bowie have to hide in his closet and duck such questions. From this day forward, he shall have the answer because I'm getting ready to drop it in his lap.

Normally, I wouldn't bother because a small voice down here, hundreds of miles from Mr. Kuhn's stomping grounds, isn't likely to have any steam left by the time it filters through Bowie's office — if it gets there at all. Yet, there's cause for confidence. You see, two years before the designated hitter rule was even suggested at a meeting of baseball's top mugglywugs and three years before it was actually adopted, the idea was suggested right here in your friendly conductor's workshop.

No, this isn't to tell you that team owners and paid officials sat around a long table, passed a copy of this column around and said, "Hey, this dummy down in San Antonio just might have something." Still, the fact remains that this column did go into great detail to offer the idea, pointing out that some of the dullest moments in professional baseball came when a pitcher stands at the plate and waves his stick at three pitches. It's also durned disappointing when those waves come with two or three runners on base.

As we all know, there are a few good-hitting pitchers but they are in the great minority. About 90 percent of baseball's starting pitchers wind up with batting averages less than their weight. Well, that's what the column pointed out and two years later, the designated hitter rule was suggested and three years later, it was accepted.

As we must realize, the odds are potent against that column having the slightest thing to do with the rule being suggested and adopted. Still, if I want to hold out a ray of hope that words here caused a major change in baseball's rules, well, that's my business. There are some, of course, who wouldn't want such credit, claiming that it's a discredit. Those would be the ones who hate the rule.

Nevertheless, it has stretched the careers of some tough old hitters who no longer field too well and I've got to believe that it's added excitement to the game. So, regardless of who first suggested the rule, let's return to the question of today. If it's good enough for half the leagues in big-league baseball, how come it's not good enough for the World Series?

Okay, Bowie, there'll be no more need to duck the issue. Here's my latest suggestion, another contribution to the cause for more exciting baseball. Starting next year, let's let the annual All-Star Game decide whether or not the designated hitter rule shall be used in the World Series of that year. If the American League stars win, the designated hitters get to bat in the World Series. If the Nationals take the All-Star Game, the DH rule will not hold for the Series.

The real beauty of this plan is that, for the first time ever, something solid will be at stake at the so-called Midsummer Classic. Something, that is, besides pride that we're all weary of writing and talking about. Too many of the game's top stars prove that pride is not a great motivating factor because too many snub the game to go fishing, claiming assorted minor injuries.

Okay, Bowie, the ball is back in your court now. Personally, I think that this is the best idea that I've tossed your way in years, although I realize it's being tossed with a poor approach, having you hide in the closet and all.

But I can't decorate these little gems with whipped cream and ribbon. You've just got to take 'em the way they come and as long as I'm conducting this tour, it's going to be done my way.

As everyone knows, we've got a great World Series under way now but there does seem to be something missing. As a matter of fact, that something has been missing for years. All the loonies are gone from baseball. It's not nearly as much fun as it was when the loonies were on the loose.

It might be that the money is just too great today and all the athletes now read the Wall Street Journal instead of the comic books. Still, there should be at least one or two folks like Babe Herman around.

Babe, whose full handle was Floyd Cave Herman, played with the old Brooklyn Dodgers, and although his bat rattled and cleared many distant fences, his fielding left a lot to be desired. In fact, he was the original Dr. Strangeglove. They took him off first base and moved him to the outfield so fans couldn't be treated to such close views of his bobbles. But, as an outfielder, Babe didn't change the error of his ways. Just the ways of his errors. He missed balls in the outfield like no outfielder before or since his time. He made a routine fly an even-money bet. But for years, he denied the published report that a pop fly hit him on the head.

"Why," he told one newspaperman, "I'd quit baseball for good if a pop fly ever hit me on the head." The reporter thought for a moment and asked, "How about a shoulder?" And to that, a half-bothered Herman said, "Oh, no, the shoulders don't count. Just my head."

Babe, some old-timers might recall, was the key baserunner in that infamous play that saw three — count 'em, three — Dodgers wind up together on third. When two were tagged out, Manager Wilbert Robinson moaned in the dugout and said, "I can't complain because it's the first time all season that they've been together on anything."

Come to think of it, I wonder what happened to baseball's loonies. Probably graduated to the two league headquarters.

THE '80S

If I had my choice of any two people to be with while trapped in a coal mine I wouldn't take Bo Derek and Raquel Welch for a little last-hour happiness. I'd take Earl Campbell and Jimmy Brown because if there was any possible way out they'd find it.

January 16, 1980

Computerized Tribulations

L adies and gentlemen, please bear with me today because this is an experimental run. It's sort of like when Orville and Wilbur rolled the *Wright Flyer* out of the barn in Kitty Hawk or wherever they kept the thing.

I'm coming to you today, I think, from the table in my dining room at home. The only thing on this table is a Silent 700 Electric Data Terminal. That and my 10 fingers that stroll so unevenly across the multicolored keyboard. The Silent 700 is plugged into the wall socket and my fingers are plugged into my nervous system.

You can forget all that 700 jazz. What this really happens to be is a portable computer terminal. If I'm lucky, I mean really lucky and hit all the right keys, then call the right telephone number and poke the phone into the computer's waiting sockets, then this piece being typed on my dining room table will zip right into our main computer downtown at the office and be in our newspaper in minutes. Oh, Lordy, the miracle of it all.

As we know, it's best not to rush into these things. It's like training for the Boston Marathon. You don't just scoot out and start running 20 miles the first day. But my Boston Marathon, the Super Bowl, is just around the corner and I've got to tame and ride this monster starting Thursday. Either that or find a keyboard mechanic who is willing to work cheap.

Learning the in-house terminals downtown was tough. Perhaps you recall how my best pieces kept being zapped off the little TV screen. Some showed up on an Omaha bus station computer while one, I heard, wound up at the stock exchange. Ah, but I finally mastered those little dandies. Why, on a good day when my fingers are nimble, the words are flowing and my juices are running in the right direction, I can bat out a halfway decent column while playing the "Flight of the Bumblebee" on those keyboards. But alas, this portable 700 has me stymied.

This thing has more keys than the dashboard on a large plane. There are three red buttons and they are labeled "Skip" and "Enter" and

"CMD." That CMD is the big bopper because it gives this computer commands. It's the steering wheel, the reins, the only way we have of tapping this little monster on the brain and getting its attention.

You don't jack with that command button without a fair idea of what you're doing. The skip button not only paragraphs these lines but it starts things working after you hit the command. Don't ask me about the enter button because that's heavy. I won't get to that until I finish. That's the Mayday pop that enters all this into the computer, if the wind is right.

By the time I get to the enter button I'm going to feel just like A.G. Bell must have felt when he first tried his telephone. Or did Don Ameche discover the phone? At any rate, the rest of the buttons are three shades of gray and a whole bunch are white. Many of the white buttons are near the bottom right side and have a period, the number three and a tipped arrow pointing to the right. I don't mess with 'em except to hit a period.

By now, you've got the point. You don't have any sports from me but you must be aware of a great ordeal that I'm suffering while pecking on this thing. True to his name, this portable computer is silent but I know that it's alive and well because it's breathing. That's no jive. It's puffing a steady flow of air from the top left side. I'd really like to pop a rag over the airhole and see if I can suffocate it but this little monster, I'm told, cost close to $4,000 and it seems sinful to kill anything so expensive.

Besides, I'm afraid of it. It's so much smarter than I am. There's not the slightest doubt in my mind that if I were to plug up its airhole, the Silent 700 would use its last gasp to tell other computers of my sin. My fingerprints would go into the memory banks of 700 cousin computers and each time I touched a keyboard, I'd probably get arthritis. Or maybe even ringworm. You've heard of Mafia gang wars, tong wars and family fusses like the Hatfields and McCoys. Heaven only knows what the consequences might be if a thundering herd of Silent 700 computers were to seek revenge.

Or, worse yet, this thing might somehow be hooked in to Charles Kilpatrick's office and the publisher wouldn't take kindly to the destruction of a $4,000 piece of company equipment.

No, in my own simple way, I'm going to match wits with this machine. In short, no matter how much it torments me, I shall smile, peck on it gently and act as though we're tight, bosom pals.

And, in a sense, that would be correct. Hey, we're going to be traveling companions. I'm taking this little sweetheart with me to Los Angeles and Super Bowl XIV. She can sleep on the bed if she wants and I'll manage on the floor. I don't even care if she snores. We're going to get along. I've made up my mind. Far be it from me to fight progress.

However, if I don't return from Los Angeles and this thing comes home in its box in 700 separate, not-so-silent pieces, we'll just call it a little lover's spat and I'll look for work in another area that doesn't need computers. Like a neighborhood car wash.

Oh, yeah, in case you're wondering how I know the gender of this Silent 700, I should tell you that it always — and folks, I mean always — gets in the last word. No matter what you say, it always comes back with things like "unfind" and "done." Unfind starts an argument and done ends one.

Trevino's New Titanic Tale

The Titanic Thompson true stories live on and the old hustler's legend continues to grow, seven or eight years after his death. Lee Trevino, in town for the Texas Open, yesterday strapped some "new" tales on me about the old games master.

To begin with, let it be known that Titanic was for real, a living, breathing character who once startled such writers of yesteryear as Damon Runyon and F. Scott Fitzgerald. He startled writers while busting a lot of highrollers from Corpus Christi to New York's Great White Way.

Ti excelled in all wagering games like golf, bowling, pistol and shotgun shooting. If they weren't games of chance then they became such after Thompson made the scene.

That explanation was necessary because so many folks, old and young, have heard so many Titanic Thompson tales that, in the minds of many, there's doubt he ever existed. He was for real. I met him here 18 years ago after using an old friend's influence to get me into a poker game with him. True, that was like sending a lamb into the lion's den but the consequences weren't important because he was such an interesting, legendary lion.

Ti is the one who, many years ago, first bet serious money that he could drive a golf ball a quarter of a mile. Then, after the wagers were placed, he stroked one from a high hill on to a frozen lake. The ball was still sliding forward after 600 yards. More often than not Mr. Thompson rigged or fixed the little propositions that he bet on so often.

Monday, as we sat together during the St. Peter-St. Joseph Children's Home luncheon where Trevino spoke, Lee explained how Titanic once won $5,000 by betting he could place his hat about a foot outside his hotel room door in the hallway, close the door and then flip all 52 cards in a deck through the one-inch crack beneath the door and have at least 15 somehow wind up fluttering into the hat. Ti was known far and near for his ability to flip playing cards.

Did he win the bet? Did he get 15 of the cards in his hat, even though he sailed the cards through a thin crack and couldn't see the hat?

"Yes and no," Trevino said with a sly smile. "He won the bet but the way he did it was to have a partner in the room across the hall, watching through a peephole. After the hat was placed in the hall, the door shut and the cards started flying through that bottom crack, the guy across the hall slipped out and put 15 or 16 of the cards into the hat and then slipped back, careful to be quiet while closing his door," Lee said as we both laughed at the old hustler's cunning.

Lee also told me how so many different movie scripts have been written on Ti's life and how, finally, one was accepted. Trevino pleaded with moviemakers to cast his old pal, Clint Eastwood, in the lead role and it certainly would be perfect casting. Eastwood is tall and thin, like Ti was, and he has the same cold, steely look in his eyes.

Trevino told me something else about Titanic that I didn't know, something Lee suggested for an ending to the movie script if and when they ever get around to filming Thompson's amazing life story.

"He spent his last year or so in a nursing home in Fort Worth but although he had trouble getting around his mind stayed sharp to the end and he didn't change his ways a bit," Trevino explained. Then he revealed, "After reading the script I was the one who suggested the ending for the movie. Can't you just see 20 or 30 folks in the nursing home, sitting in a circle and lightly applauding the death of Titanic? The camera would zoom in, pan around the group and then zoom back for the close. It would be a fantastic close."

He's right. It would be a great ending for a movie that should top "The Sting" if handled properly.

Why would the old folks in the nursing home be applauding the passing of Titanic Thompson? After all, he was a rather personable and interesting sort, not the type who would make waves in a nursing home.

Well, it was sort of like the slaves. They just naturally shouted with joy when they became free.

As Trevino explained, "It took Titanic about nine months to win all the wheelchairs and crutches and other aides in that nursing home. He hustled the other old people in cards, dominoes, whatever their preference happened to be. Then, after winning their wheelchairs, he rented them back to the original owners for 25 or 50 cents a week. So when he finally died at 84 or so they were happy to be free of those weekly payments.

Yeah, it should make a wonderful ending for a movie on Titanic Thompson, king of the hustlers. Trevino swears that's a true story about Ti's last days here.

You'd never get the idea that Trevino is a superstar of the highest level if you sat around and chatted with him for half an hour or so. Once a pretty fair golf hustler himself, Lee is pure class. He's as comfortable to be around as an old house slipper.

You don't ever have to wonder what's on his mind or try to read between the lines at anything he says. He'll lay it out straight for you. You don't have to turn on the light in a dark room to figure where he's standing.

Take, for example, the subject of jogging. Someone asked him how his once-bad back is these days and Lee answered, "It's great now that I quit jogging. I never liked to jog in the first place but I thought it was good for me so I tried it for a long while. Hey, that was my trouble. Now I'm convinced that jogging is lousy for you. Joggers make nice-looking corpses but that's all. Friends view the corpse and say, 'Doesn't he look nice?' Yeah, he looks nice. But he's dead."

Go ahead, pick a subject. Any subject. Lee will give you an honest opinion if that's what you want. No, he doesn't claim to be an expert on all matters but, by golly, he's got opinions on most of them.

Even though he's loaded with wisecracks he's not a wise guy by any stretch of the imagination. He's just a down-to-earth, fun-loving fellow who has great talent. You know something? I hope he wins the Texas Open here this week.

Sizing Up Earl

It's taken three years but Earl Campbell, at last, is beginning to turn a few tongues.

Jimmy Brown, old No. 32 for the Cleveland Browns, still rates on top in most minds but big Earl, ever so slowly, is beginning to cast some heavy shades of doubt.

Just last weekend a couple of veteran TV throats told us how they "still figure that Brown was the greatest running back in pro football history."

But then one of them added, "However, Earl Campbell is about to change my mind." The other dude with the mike added, "Yeah, he could change my mind any week now."

It's interesting to note that the styles of Brown and Campbell look like first cousins. There must be at least 50 defensive backs around today who could dust either Earl or Jim — in his prime — in a 40-yard dash but none comes close in the area that sets Earl and Jim apart from all others. That area covers power, balance, quickness and determination. After the initial impact of a hard tackle, when most running backs are trying to protect the ball while heading down, Earl is digging for another yard while searching for a way out of the trap. Brown was much the same.

If I had my choice of any two people to be with while trapped in a coal mine I wouldn't take Bo Derek and Raquel Welch for a little last-hour happiness. I'd take Earl Campbell and Jimmy Brown because if there was any possible way out they'd find it.

Nevertheless, more than anything else, this is to compare Brown and Campbell and in my book Earl is the winner. Campbell is now and has been for the last three seasons a better running back than Brown ever was.

That kind of talk hurts Brown. He dearly loves the unofficial title of "greatest of all-time" and nobody can blame him for that. It's something that he earned the hard way and now he's reluctant to surrender the prize.

He's especially reluctant to give it up to someone who is not close to him in any way. The lifestyles of Earl and Jim are a million miles apart.

Brown's disturbance at the raves after Earl's rookie season was a bit too obvious. When reporters caught up with Jim and questioned him about the new man on the NFL block Brown admitted that Campbell was "pretty good" but then he went into great detail explaining how a career can't be judged against one season: "Earl still has a long way to go before passing the test of time and he might not make it, the way he sacrifices his body on so many plays."

So said Jimmy Brown and, although he was correct, I got the husky idea that he was at least semi-insulted by the suggestion that Campbell, then just a mere rookie, might wind up on a higher level than he finished.

It should be mentioned that the interview came at a time when Jim was up to his navel in bad publicity. One of his many Hollywood hassles had occurred not too many weeks earlier. Either Jim had thrown some starlet off his balcony or wrapped a 4-iron around a golf pro's head. For a long while it was hard to keep track of Brown's social troubles.

But this isn't to knock Jim for his sometimes-wild ways. He kept his rudder straight during his long term in sports and it might be that some folks just tried to take advantage of him because of the great reputation that he built in football.

I don't remember, however, Brown ever offering any public praise or thanks to his offensive line for helping him attain the lofty heights that he reached in the NFL. Jim raced through almost a decade of pro football without once saying that he wouldn't have done nearly as well if his teammates hadn't blocked for him. He and Campbell really differ on that count.

There've been a few times when some of us thought that Earl was a little too humble after his 100-yard-plus performances. It got to the point that Campbell shoveled so much praise to his blockers some folks figured that it was an act, one of those good-guy grease jobs.

After all, there've been at least a few times when Earl didn't seem to get any blocks, when he collided with three, four or five would-be tacklers but still broke loose for long gains. It seemed silly to thank blockers after solo performances like that.

But that's the way Campbell is geared and we know that he's sincere.

He wasn't looking for publicity when, before the season started, he secretly told his offensive linemen that he would give each of them a Rolex wristwatch if he broke his own rushing record this year.

Midway through the season Earl decided Tim Wilson should be

included in the offer since Tim cleared more than a few paths for the great one. So now Tim and all the fellas up front are eagerly awaiting their Rolex watches. Earl's total for the year went to 1,731 last week — a new Campbell high — and there's one game left in the regular season.

In case you haven't shopped for watches lately you should know that if you get a wholesale price you might pick up an Earl Campbell handful for about $1,600 each.

The way I've got it figured, if you count every play of every game where Earl carried the ball he's paying about $7 for every decent block thrown on his behalf. He might also be paying for at least a few indecent blocks but, what the heck, maybe all the watches won't keep perfect time.

At any rate, we now know for sure that Earl is serious and genuinely grateful when he tells reporters how he "couldn't have done it without all the fine help from his teammates."

Sooner or later Earl is going to have to change at least a little. No man can handle all the pressure being shoved on him without showing some signs of a distinct change.

No, not just the pressure on football fields. That's his cup of tea. He thrives on that. I'm talking about public pressure, the kind that comes from fans, agents, promoters and, perhaps above all, countless reporters who all seek "exclusive" interviews.

It hasn't been easy but, so far, Earl has held his old familiar ground. Other than the normal maturing process he's pretty much the same fellow who first strolled on to the UT campus in the shadow of Roosevelt Leaks. But now, on and off the field, he stands in no man's shadow. He's one of a kind. By now even Jim Brown should be ready to concede.

February 13, 1981

A Big Disservice to Mays

You probably won't believe this but I made a mistake. So did Bowie Kuhn. My mistake was agreeing with him but now it's time for both of us to back up and right a wrong.

Today's topic here is prompted by a brief news dispatch out of

Atlantic City.

Perhaps you saw the story. It told how Willie Mays had collapsed on the stage of a junior high school auditorium as he prepared to address a large group of students.

Willie was treated for fatigue, given a few sleeping pills and told to get some rest. About 48 hours worth of rest.

Maybe that's all it was, fatigue. Let's hope so. But you don't have to log long hours in a medical school to know you're getting a serious warning from your body any time that you conk out cold while performing a routine chore. Addressing a group of youngsters has got to be the most routine thing in the world for the baseball star of yesteryear.

True to his old form and style, Willie vowed that he would return to the school "a little later" to talk to the students. He explained that he "owes it to the kids."

Commissioner Kuhn and everyone even close to baseball might be wise to consider the collapse of Mays as a last chance to right a wrong. He's got a great attitude but Willie Mays doesn't owe nearly as many baseball-related debts as he seems to think. Much to the contrary, baseball is deeply in debt to Mr. Mays.

Several years ago, when Willie was offered a lucrative job as a greeter and public relations man for Bally's Park Place Hotel and Casino in Atlantic City, he was told by Commissioner Kuhn that if he accepted the position he would have to sever his ties with baseball.

In all probability Willie wasn't making more than 40 or 50 thousand a year as a batting instructor, but he loved the job. He's always loved every job that he's ever had with baseball, and after his playing days were all used up he couldn't imagine himself not having some kind of job in baseball.

That's why Willie was shocked and hurt when Kuhn told him that if he accepted the job in the gambling house he would have to give up his job in baseball. In so many words Kuhn told Mays that baseball was too sacred and, above all, had to stay above any suspicion, to allow any salaried employee to work in or around a casino.

The thought rolled around my brain barrel for an hour or so and, perhaps a little reluctantly, I agreed with Kuhn.

No, Mays wouldn't do anything to hurt baseball but his double-dip job would give bleacher boo-birds something to exercise their lungs about. Whenever his team hit a mild slump, as all teams do sooner or later, people might talk. "Psst, this game's in the tank. Last night I seen Willie talkin' with Greasy Fingers Ferrachimo at the casino…"

Well, that was my reasoning. It must have also been the reasoning of Commissioner Kuhn. That and tradition. Baseball is heavy on tradition, and ever since the Black Sox scandal of 1919 the sport has strained hard to walk a straight and narrow line.

Be reminded that almost any other player would have sought the advice of an attorney and probably sued Kuhn. But not Mays. Like I told you, Willie would never do anything to hurt baseball. With a few tears in his eyes he accepted Kuhn's ruling and resigned his job as a batting instructor.

The Bally Casino people offered him the financial chance of a lifetime, three or four times what he was making as a baseball coach.

Now, so many months later, I've had a lot of second thoughts. Lord, I should have known better than to agree with Kuhn. He's a stuffed-shirt nincompoop who can be relied on to make the wrong decision at least four out of five times.

What the heck, Willie doesn't have a piece of the gambling action. He's not dealing blackjack or even steering suckers toward the dice tables. He's simply meeting and greeting folks in a perfectly legitimate house of business. Besides, his long track record in baseball is a whole lot better than baseball's record.

Forget about the fixed World Series. That's ancient history.

Closer to the present, seldom does a week slip by that another active player doesn't admit to using or having used hard drugs. Bowie doesn't know what to make of it all.

Ferguson Jenkins got nailed with a small satchel full of funny powder but since the federal folks in Canada allowed him to cop a plea and walk free the commissioner decided to also overlook the matter and let it slide. Of course, if the truth were known, Kuhn would be a harsher judge were it not for the fact that he's afraid. He's afraid of (1) the players association and its attorneys and he's afraid of (2) the individual players and their attorneys.

But he wasn't afraid of Willie Mays. He had a long talk with Willie and he knew that the legendary superstar wouldn't sue, so he whacked him.

Look, times change. Maybe not always for the better but, by golly, they do change. What was considered terrible 20 years ago is now acceptable.

Rogers Hornsby was once chewed on by a commissioner for spending too many of his days off at a racetrack. Now, on a given day, you'll find the so-called cream of society and the nation's top politicians sitting in the best boxes at Churchill Downs, Santa Anita and Belmont. Another commissioner once banned Leo Durocher from baseball for a whole year because he was keeping some bad Hollywood company, bumming around with people like George Raft. That came at a time when Bobby Riggs was also considered "bad company," a cheap sports hustler.

Today, Riggs is a celebrity for doing the same things that he used to do, but on a larger scale. If any manager were even threatened with a year's ban for keeping bad company a swarm of legal eagles would land on the commissioner's desk and pick him apart.

Kuhn is painfully aware of this, moreso than most fans.

So why doesn't he reinstate Willie Mays and let him keep his better-paying job at the casino before it's too late? Willie deserves a better hand than baseball dealt him. There's no sense in waiting until he's gone for all the old baseball heads to nod and agree that Mays got a bum break.

March 20, 1981

Out-of-Sight Salaries

The newspaper ad says that Mark Haroldsen, millionaire and well-known author and lecturer, wants to teach us his techniques that can take us from scratch to financial freedom.

The ad tells us about a free, two-hour lecture that promises to "wake up the financial genius inside you."

It's a tempting announcement that for long moments stirred some old rays of hope in my greedy soul.

But alas, I know better than Mr. Haroldsen that there is no financial genius inside me. None in my family, for that matter.

My brother Frank wound up as vice president of a Houston bank but that's the absolute best that we could have expected of him because when he was in the second grade he once purchased a pecan for a nickel. Some fat pecans may now be selling for a nickel but in 1933, a year of great depression, you could get a dozen walnuts and two Tootsie Rolls for a nickel if you shopped around a bit.

It didn't matter that the seller of the pecan was a little older and a mite larger than Frank. Our dad hit the ceiling when he heard about Frank's pecan purchase.

But that was long ago and the only reason I bring it up now is to explain how my brother, the pecan buyer, has far more financial smarts than I possess. As a matter of pure fact, he's probably the closest thing to a "financial genius" our family has had in many decades. I rate right at the bottom of our family chart in that and many other areas.

The only real qualification I have to be a good candidate for millionaire Mark Haroldsen's seminar comes under the No. 1 pitch in his newspaper ad: "How to start without cash."

What all this amounts to is an act of fairness. It seems only fair that I forewarn you of my knowledge of high finance. Now that you've been given that message in clear tones you might want to turn to the crossword puzzle because I'm about to offer some free financial advice to some of our great captains of industry.

This is directed at the owners of professional sports teams.

More than anything else it is directed toward owners of baseball and basketball teams but, for good measure, you can also toss in the top NFL brass.

The message is: gentlemen, you are nuts. Together you look like so many ripe bananas on one great stalk. Most of you are captured in an egotistical web of your own weaving. You are doomed to draw the nation's sympathy and scorn, laughter and ridicule.

Most unfortunately, there is no way out. There isn't, that is, unless another banana, even riper, can be located to fill in and bail one out.

More than anything, this is aimed at single ownership propositions. But before moving to that we can touch on the Spurs' setup here, a deal that has 70 or 80 owners.

At least 90 percent of those who invested in the Spurs did so strictly as a civic gesture, sort of like backing the symphony orchestra. The "main" investors put up $100,000 or more and there are only a handful of those. A very few tossed $200,000 or more into the big pot. Nearly all of these people can easily afford to tie up that much money without earning a dime's profit. They'd better be able to afford it because in all the years that the basketball franchise has been in San Antonio, there hasn't yet been a single dividend. Not one owner has made a thin dime on the investment.

If you figure that's a fair shake, nothing for the team owners while players balk on fat contracts and demand more and even more, then you probably qualify as a federal baseball arbitrator.

But, as mentioned, this really isn't intended for those in multiple ownership deals. It's directed at those who have 12, 15 and 20 million dollars tied up in a team and continue to compete for average or slightly-above average players with big-buck bids.

If a person wants to make a contribution to his or her community and take on a $100,000 hobby that's one thing. But when wealthy people wrap 15 or 20 million around one of those teams and pay individual salaries of a million a year, it's a serious business deal.

Why, you may ask, is there a difference between one person putting up $15 million and paying skyrocket salaries and 70 or 80 people chipping in to do much the same thing?

Good question. The main difference rests in the future. When these fatcat owners get ready to toss in the towel, or when they die, it's going to be durned near impossible to replace them. Let's face the fact that not all multimillionaires dream of owning the New York Yankees and hassling with star players over future contracts.

What I'm trying to say is that the team owners of today, out of control as they bid against each other, are screwing up sports for the future — the not-so distant future at that.

Nobody is going to make me believe that wealthy businessmen are lining up out there to invest millions in a team and then pay players with .280 batting averages $1.3 million a year.

We've got a lot of nuts in this country but not that many nuts with big money.

Dave Winfield, the newest Yankee, has a contract that calls for $1.3 million each season. He's just one of seven baseball players who will be getting more than a million a season. In all, there are 40 players who will be getting in excess of half a million a season. Folks, there are 40 more who are crying and trying to make that much.

Maybe in years past the old owners did put the shaft to a lot of their players. Maybe they pocketed far too much and paid out far too little. But a financial idiot can put a pencil to a pad and quickly discover that one of the lousiest investments in the world today is ownership of a professional sports team.

The Spurs, it certainly seems, form one of the most successful franchises in the whole NBA. A lot of teams would love to do as well financially. The Spurs are breaking even. That's progress?

Well, it is for today. I didn't even have to go to Mr. Haroldsen's free lecture to learn that an even break on the books is a financial victory. But, somehow, I get the feeling that Haroldsen doesn't embrace that theory.

March 31, 1981

Knight Runs on 3 Flat Tires

The question is too complicated. We need some slick shrink to tell us why so many who display pure genius in one area of endeavor often don't have enough common sense to pull the plug on a tub of dirty water.

We all know that General Patton was a brilliant tank commander. Yet, in some ways, he was nuts.

Vincent Van Gogh was one of the greatest artists of his time. But when he discovered that one of his lady friends was a hooker he used a razor to cut off one of his ears. Later on he really got angry and killed himself.

Stop and think about it. Almost every person in our society who sashays around with special brain brilliance in one particular area seems to be running on four flat tires in other areas where just average intelligence is needed. It seems to be the good Lord's way of making Abe Lincoln's statement true. Maybe we all are created equal. It's just that we have to do a lot of adding and subtracting before we finally arrive at the point of equality.

That, if you haven't already guessed, leads us to Bobby Knight, the coach of Indiana's great collegiate basketball team. Mr. Knight, you must agree, is one of the nation's top coaches. Some even say that he's a genius when it comes to making X's and O's on a blackboard and teaching young men how to put a ball through a hoop. Bobby, however, isn't wrapped too tightly. He hates prosperity. He despises calm seas. He's the kind of guy who would take an ocean voyage and jump the rail just to hear folks scream, "Man overboard!"

Somewhere in Puerto Rico there's a policeman who called Knight a "pop-off troublemaker." That was in 1979 when Knight was coaching the United States team in the Pan American Games. The matter became an international incident when Knight refused to apologize to the policeman after the run-in. Most of us, I'm sure, felt Coach Knight was just the victim of a tense political problem. That's what we thought in 1979.

But not anymore. Now we realize that the poor policeman probably was 100 percent right.

It might not be altogether fair to say that Knight is a ham, that he does dumbo deeds to propel himself into a spotlight that's usually reserved for the players on his team.

It might not be altogether fair, but it durned sure appears to be first cousin to pure truth. Seems each time one of Knight's teams does great and earns national or world attention, it's the coach, not the players, who somehow hogs the headlines. So it was this past weekend, right after Indiana demolished LSU and gained the national finals.

By now you must have read or heard how Knight got into a word hassle and then a shoving match with an LSU fan. Almost without fail, when those things happen we're treated to two entirely different versions from the two main characters.

But Knight's version alone — in my book — is enough to pour all the blame on Knight. He tells the story like some kind of martyr who has accepted all the verbal abuse that he's prepared to take from those who watch his teams. Yet, as Bobby tells his tale, the hard, cold facts as he presents them indict him as a dummy who really shouldn't be allowed to run loose after dark. He shouldn't, that is, if he hopes to continue to represent a reputable institution of higher learning.

Let's ignore any other explanation or version of the matter and deal only with Knight's words. But first, keep in mind that for many years now fans of LSU Tiger teams have taunted all foes with a chant that goes, "Tiger bait, Tiger bait."

It's not an insulting chant. Not nearly as bad as the yells and songs some other schools hurl at opponents. More than anything else it's an intimidating chant and it does work wonders. Especially in Baton Rouge. I've talked with a lot of football and basketball players who've told me how they felt "spooked" when entering the LSU arena and heard thousands chant, "Tiger bait, Tiger bait..."

Any collegiate coach of any sport who hasn't heard of the LSU tradition is either stone deaf or hasn't been around much.

There's nothing wrong with Knight's hearing and he's made far more treks around the nation than most college coaches you know. Now then, let's return to Bobby's version of that little incident.

A few hours after the game Knight and several friends were strolling into a hotel lounge when this man dressed in LSU's colors approached the coach. The man said, "Congratulations." That's all. Nothing more. To that, strictly according to Knight, the coach replied, "We weren't really Tiger bait after all, were we?" The LSU fan was surprised at Knight's answer — as well he should have been — so as the two parted the fan cursed the coach. Knight returned to the man in great haste and asked him to repeat the insult. The LSU fan said, "I just gave you a compliment and you were sarcastic." Knight then said that he "wasn't sarcastic" and the LSU fan repeated the insult. It was at that point that the coach grabbed the stranger and pinned him to a wall.

Now that's Knight's version. To my way of thinking, Bobby got exactly what he asked for — the center of another silly, needless controversy.

Almost any level of common sense tells us that when a winning coach is approached by a rival fan who has just seen his team whipped, the fan should be handled with kid gloves.

When that fan says "congratulations" to the coach who just beat his team, the most obvious reply is a quick "thank you." A quick "thank you" and then keep on moving. The last, absolutely last thing a winning coach should do is taunt the fan who evidently was trying hard to be a good sport.

Bobby's not going to change. As you can tell from his own statements he doesn't think he does anything wrong. He was just a victim of circumstances and that LSU fan picked on him and made him lose his temper.

The sad part is that he really won't understand it when, sooner or later, school officials are forced to fire him. Woody Hayes is still trying to figure out why Ohio State tied the can to his stubborn tail.

NOTE: On Sept. 10, 2000, almost two decades after this column was written, Knight was fired by the University of Indiana after a confrontation with a student.

No Time for a Toilet

PONTIAC, Mich. — Before I tell you this story I've got to bring you up to date on Jack "Hacksaw" Reynolds. His gears run a wee bit on the rough side. He's not like most folks you meet at the Bingo parlor. If somebody hollers "Bingo" after N-32 is announced it would not be out of character for Mr. Reynolds to chew up his cards and the arm of the winner.

He dearly loves to win. As a matter of fact, most of his waking hours are devoted to his next challenge, whatever that might be.

As veteran football followers know, Jack didn't get his nickname by sawing his way out of somebody's jail. It arrived after an act of deep-rooted frustration. That was shortly after Reynolds' Tennessee team lost a big battle against Ole Miss.

Reynolds' disappointment at being deprived of the victory was so great that he went home, took a hacksaw in hand and, for the lack of a better target, sawed his 1953 Chevrolet in half. Yep, that's right. He started on one side between the front and back door and cut that little dude smooth in half in a matter of two hours.

Reynolds spent what most folks feel is the better part of his pro career with the Los Angeles Rams. For 11 years he wore a Rams uniform while busting up ball-carriers and slapping down passes. But in 1981 the Rams figured that old Hacksaw was over the hill so he was given his release. San Francisco coach Bill Walsh felt otherwise so he signed him in late June. Walsh felt that such valuable experience and undying spirit were needed items for his green defense. Reynolds spent most of last season and all of Sunday afternoon proving Walsh correct.

So now that you've got the picture we're going to proceed to my story for today. Keep in mind that at a sports spectacular such as Super Bowl XVI, the classic that became known as Sweet Sixteen, there are all sorts of interesting little sidelights. This is just one of them.

Okay, you may recall that late in the third period the 49ers made a fantastic goal-line stand to deny Cincinnati a touchdown that probably would have later led to a Bengal triumph. Twice, big Pete Johnson slammed into the middle in search of 14 or 15 inches but twice the middle slammed back. Reynolds was there both times to plug the hole and the 35-year-old veteran simply refused to buckle or bend. On one of the occasions he met the 249-pound Johnson head-on and the result would have been the same if the fullback had run into a loaded cement truck.

But when that gallant stand was over, after the defensive unit had retired to rest on the sidelines, Reynolds called his group together and they formed a tight circle around him. As I sat in the press box I wanted more than anything else to know what was being said. I kept a mental picture of that small circle in my mind and jotted down a notation in my notebook, a reminder to inquire after the game was over.

It could have been that the TV cameras also closed in on that little meeting and I felt that some of you would wonder what was being said. By golly, it was my honor-bound duty as your agent here to report back with the details. Were they complimenting each other for the fine stand or were they rededicating themselves to more such play in the immediate future?

So after the game I asked. And I learned.

You're not going to like this but I went to a lot of trouble to get the story so you are going to get it, too.

It seems that after extending himself almost beyond belief Hacksaw Reynolds was in need of relief. He called eight or nine of his teammates to form a tight circle around him on the sidelines and then he . . . well he, dadgum it, he urinated on the green floor of the Silverdome.

A first question might be, why not dash a clear path 40 or 50 yards to the nearest team toilet instead of handling the problem before 81,237 witnesses and countless millions watching on TV? After all, they use those zoom lenses on TV to poke their cameras everywhere these days.

But Hacksaw knows that it takes only three or four seconds to turn the football over on a fumble or pass interception and he was well aware that if that happened his services would be needed immediately. If Cincinnati had scored a winning touchdown while he was standing in somebody's bathroom he might have sawed the team bus into five sections before cooling down.

Well, gang, I'm sorry to disappoint you but all sorts of unusual things happen on those sidelines during big games. It's not just a pacing coach and a bunch of "Hi Mom" waves like TV would have you believe.

So help me, when I started on the trail of this little tale it was my intention to offer a revealing insight into the character of some manly souls dedicated to defense. It's always said that the legs go first on old athletes. How was I to know that the kidneys of Hacksaw Reynolds went first while his legs are still doing right well?

Gervin's Ultimatum Game

George Gervin stands tall among the most amazing men ever to play sports in San Antonio. It's unbelievable how he can maneuver his rail-thin body through masses of mean muscle and execute precision shots with unmatched skill. And it's unrealistic how he can show such fantastic timing on the court and such terrible timing for contract negotiations.

The bitter bite of playoff defeat — four straight losses — was still in everyone's mouth when one of George's messengers was sent forth to seek more pay and years for the one we call Ice.

We all realize that the franchise is now built around George, but there's got to be some kind of pecking order for negotiations that doesn't show him first in line each time the line forms.

For Pete's sake, there are five free agents and two coaches to deal with but Gervin, as usual, has jumped to the head of the line again with his "gimme or trade me" routine.

George is a great athlete and a nice guy but I'd hate to be with him in a life raft, dying of thirst and see him in charge of the water. He has a bad habit of losing count on when his turn comes.

But even if George does feel the need to pad his pact and ensure his future, it would have seemed a lot wiser to at least wait awhile as the Spurs tried to collar the coaches and free agents. Or, if nothing else, at least wait until fans got used to the idea that this season is over and the team lost four straight in the conference finals.

This "gimme or trade me" jazz is beginning to burn bad feelings in the minds of many. It's not only creating sour tastes for Gervin as an individual, but it's beginning to hurt the team as a group. Times are hard. Some of the biggest companies in the nation are folding and we're all beginning to feel the pinch. But each time folks turn to our only big-league team for mental relief and a change of pace, they're greeted with more bad news that includes demands and threats. You might be surprised at the number of fans who are throwing up their hands in disgust.

If nothing else, it divides the Spurs into two camps at a time when there is too much division already. Management and performers, it seems, will always be at odds because the main link is money. But when a guy's got four years left on a contract he should be able to sit still for a few weeks while others with less talent and no time remaining try to straighten out their business arrangements.

It can't be that Gervin is worried about the Spurs giving too much money to too many and there not being enough left for him. It's highly unlikely that any of those free agents, the coaches included, will get more than two- or three-year contracts and, like I told you, George has four years left on his written and legal agreement. So why jump to the head of the line so soon?

I can't answer that. Maybe it's habit. Perhaps as soon as a season is over and players start wondering what they're going to do for the next few months, George just thinks that he should start arguing for more money. Or maybe he looks around and counts noses at the close of each campaign and gets scared, worrying about how he'll take care of his growing family and old friends and agents who keep their hands in his pockets.

At any rate, Ice might have been wiser to have waited at least a few more weeks before making his newest pitch. But that's only from a popularity viewpoint. It's well to keep in mind that he's undefeated at the "gimme or trade me" game. He's gone to the well about five times now, and on each occasion he's come away with a fresh bucket of water. There's no sense in even hinting that the well could be running dry.

It's a solid 8-5 bet that in the last five days at least five Spurs have taken pencils in hand and done some quick-stab figuring.

"Let's see now, 41 home games plus four playoff games. Average attendance was about 11,000, so 45 times 11,000 is 495,000. Hmmmmm. Average ticket price was about $10 so 495,000 times 10 bucks is . . . hey, honey, whatever happened to that little calculator the insurance guy gave us last year? And what's the name of that airlines dude who was telling us how much each trip costs a team? I need a little help here."

Ah, well, maybe I'm just envious. Last week I went into the boss' office and told him that I wanted to renegotiate my working agreement here, and he just laughed. I left pleased that I could make him feel so good. Not everybody can make the boss laugh like that.

Cooney-Holmes: One for the Ages

He doesn't know it but I've got a foot-high stack of money that belonged to Michael Landon. It's no big deal to him — it is to me — because he'll make a thousand times that amount with his next episode of "Little House on the Prairie." He'll do even better with his next commercial for Kodak.

A couple of strange things happened to me just as I arrived in Las Vegas and then, three days later, when I left the heavyweight title fight scene. Your tour conductor flew in on a large DC-10 and even though over 300 were on that flight, my bag was the first to roll down the baggage train. Really now, how many times have you had your bag come out first after a long, one-change, two-plane flight?

Then, as I departed Saturday morning, I sat in the same Vegas airport and watched a handful of movie stars pour silver dollars into slot machines. Since it would be my last fling at legalized gambling for a husky spell, I decided to sashay over to the one-armed bandits for a few farewell pulls.

The little change lady in charge of the area, a talkative woman between 50 and 60, asked me if I was there to waste time and money, or was I eager to make money. Naturally, my reply was "make money." I was offering the lady a $10 bill for a roll of quarters.

"Forget the quarters and play that dollar machine," she said. "Michael Landon just put $200 in that number four machine over there and he didn't get anything in return. The machine is ready to hit."

I nodded and held my hand out. Instead of the requested quarters she dropped 10 silver dollars in my hand. Ah, well, no sense in leaving Vegas with an argument. I went to the number four machine. Sure enough, on my seventh pull of the handle the three-bar jackpot hit. Lights went on, a whistle blew and for the next two minutes that machine sounded like a 90-lane bowling alley as it burped out $150, one at a time.

Michael Landon's warm fingerprints were still on most of them, I'm sure, but I still cashed them all in for paper. My first thought was to tip the nice change lady $10, but then it dawned on me that she probably was a slot machine tout. Realizing that in 10 minutes I would leave and never see her again, and not knowing the proper way to deal with slot machine touts, I just gave her $5. She seemed grateful enough.

So the beginning and end of that trip defied all odds to favor me, and in between I sat on press row to watch one of the greatest heavyweight championship fights of all time. There will be some who'll argue that last statement, but for the life of me I can't think of a better bout between two big dudes with the championship at stake.

Some always trace back to the days of Dempsey, Tunney and Johnson, but none of the battles involving those men got the world eye-witness exposure given the meeting between Larry Holmes and Gerry Cooney. It's never the same when you listen on radio. For one thing, radio announcers — now as then — have a habit of making an event sometimes sound better than it really is. Some feel that it's part of their job, to hold the interest of listeners. Partly for that reason the good fights of yesteryear somehow get magnified in the minds of many and after proper aging they become great fights. A little later they become all-time great fights.

But the Holmes-Cooney war had everything from round one to the end. Cooney, the big Irishman, was down, stunned and almost out in the second. Yet he returned to win round three on all the judges' cards. He was hurt again in the sixth, desperately hanging on, but he returned stronger in the seventh to again sweep the round on all three cards.

From the sixth round on Cooney spurted blood from a left eyebrow cut that was later to take 17 stitches. Yet that wound had nothing to do with the outcome of the bout.

Holmes took a low blow in the ninth, a wicked hook that threatened to change his gender. He doubled up and groaned with pain. But Larry came back to win the next round on points. It was a seesaw war and, going into the 13th with blood pumping badly from that eye cut, Cooney looked a lot like a late-round Rocky — I, II and III all lumped into one pathetic picture.

But this was for real, not a movie with artificial gore. This was sport in its roughest, rawest form.

There are some who now say that Victor Valle shouldn't have

jumped into the ring to catch Cooney and call a halt. But those who say that either wagered on Gerry and have wallets for hearts or they know nothing about boxing and the maximum punishment a man can absorb. At that late stage in the fight, eight seconds remaining in the 13th round, Cooney was in no condition to continue. He had given it his best shot and was then wobbling on rubbery legs, about to be seriously and maybe even permanently injured. Those who argue that "only eight seconds remained in the round" should use a stopwatch and see how many bombs a good fighter can explode off an easy target in eight seconds.

Eight seconds might have been a lifetime. Cooney's lifetime.

Looking back, I can't recall any bad parts in that Vegas trip. I particularly enjoyed my first and last moments. Imagine, first bag off upon arrival and a $1-machine jackpot upon departure. Lordy, what a parlay that would have made.

December 16, 1982

Bear Adjusted, Survived

It was a year ago when I leaned forward in the Alabama dressing room of the Cotton Bowl, straining to hear the words of Coach Bear Bryant. He was talking in near-whispers and sometimes mumbling answers to routine questions.

Some said he took that day's defeat hard, suffering a 14-12 upset to Texas, and that he was often like that after losing a bowl game.

But that line of thought wouldn't fly in my book. I once saw him in the Cotton Bowl drop an even bigger upset to Texas A&M, and after the game he raced across the field and personally lifted and carried the opposing coach, Gene Stallings, 10 or 15 yards. But that was another day, another time. And Gene, of course, had been one of his players, one of his boys. Fred Akers was not "one of his boys," and this last bowl loss came late in his career. Until Wednesday when Bear announced his retirement nobody knew just how late.

Nevertheless, Bryant looked, seemed and sounded old to me on the first day of 1982 in Dallas. Sure, we all knew that he was on the far side of 60 and leaning heavily toward 70. But he had never before come through to me as an old man, as he did early this year.

He wasn't in a hurry to leave. He didn't avoid any questions or appear angered by some of the silly ones. He just sat there on a small stool, glared at an empty locker and whispered answers that few if any of us could hear.

Yeah, he seemed mighty old that afternoon and as I left I wondered how much longer Bear Bryant would continue to call the football shots at Alabama. Now we know.

It's been said that Bryant is a dinosaur from the Ice Age who gracefully galloped into the Space Age. An excellent description because of all the great coaching qualities the man possesses it might well be that the thing that carried him so far for so long was his ability to accept change, to adjust to changing times.

Bryant had only one low period during his 25 years as head coach at Alabama. After an amazing string of successes his Tide team fell to 6-5 in 1969 and then went 6-5-1 in 1970. Word went out that Bryant was "too old," that he couldn't cut it anymore. So what did he do? He changed his system.

The Bear took a plane ride to Austin and sat down with Texas' Darrell Royal for many hours, studying the wishbone offense that had been devised by Longhorn coaches. Bryant was later to say, "It fit our material just about perfect. I made up my mind that we were gonna sink, swim or drown with that Texas stuff."

The first time the Tide used that "Texas stuff" was Sept. 10, 1971, against a heavily favored Southern Cal team in California. The Trojans had whipped 'Bama 42-21 the previous year in Birmingham and they were favored to do it again on their home grounds. But Bryant did a whale of a job polishing the 'Bone in a short time and his Tide shocked Southern Cal 17-10 with that triple-option attack. For many years later — even a lot this season — that attack that swirls around a quick quarterback has served Bryant and 'Bama well.

It's amazing that in 38 years as a head college coach, Bear had just one losing season. That came at College Station in 1954 when he used an iron will and a heavy hand to sweep clean the old program while installing his own methods at Texas A&M. Bryant took his squad to Junction for spring training, to escape the eyes of sympathetic boosters, and there he ran a concentration camp designed to chase away all but the strongest who dearly wanted to play and win.

More than half the squad left after two weeks and the Aggies endured a 1-9 record in the Bear's first season at A&M, the only black mark on his long report card. But from that strange start came following campaigns of 7-2-1, 9-0-1 and 8-3 before Bryant left for Alabama. He knew what he wanted and he — and some of the Aggies — paid the price to get it.

For years I harbored a semisecret anger for Bryant. That came after I read in Sports Illustrated where he had said, "I never met a sportswriter that I couldn't buy with a bottle of bourbon." I hated the man for that. Not just for saying it but for even thinking it. That's like telling me that I'd sell my soul for a bottle of booze.

But long after that line was published, after I'd pouted for half a decade, Bryant and I discussed it one afternoon and, as memory serves, he tossed out lines like, "I guess I've said a lot of things over the years that I later was sorry that I said," and "I wish people would quit paying so much attention to silly things that I say when I get angry at somebody."

With such small words as that the man, suddenly in my mind, became even bigger than his legend.

May 10, 1983

Baltimore Waylaid by Elway

George Steinbrenner, former football coach and current owner of the New York Yankees, told us an interesting tale when two of us reporter types cornered him at the Kentucky Derby last Saturday.

It was an hour before post time and George was strolling through the peon section, making his way toward the heavy-wallet area. "On the square, George, how much money did you offer John Elway to play baseball instead of football in the NFL?" That was the question and Steinbrenner paused and made ready to emphasize each word by pointing a finger into the palm of his other hand.

The moment was used to poise pencil to pad. Then came this statement:

"John Elway is a fine athlete and a nice person. I'm sure all the

Elways are nice people. However, I did not make him an offer — not a firm offer or a loose offer — to play professional baseball. He simply handled his own business in his own way and it now looks to me like he's ruined future football drafts."

Now then, in case the full impact of those words doesn't start your car clock, be reminded that Elway is the Stanford quarterback who was drafted No. 1 in the recent National Football League raffle. The handsome young man had made it crystal clear that he preferred football over baseball but he did not want to play in Baltimore, location of the team with the first draft pick.

But Baltimore drafted him first anyway. So Elway, it now seems, then ran a bluff. He told the Baltimore people that he would not play for them, that he preferred to play football out West, but before pulling on a pair of knickers and shoulder pads in Baltimore he would accept an offer to play baseball for the New York Yankees.

Rumors being what they are these days, word spread that Steinbrenner had offered Elway $200,000 a year to play baseball. Hours later the figure was upped to $300,000. Within two days Yankee players — first stringers on the big club — were being questioned by reporters about the $500,000 being offered to the rookie from Stanford. Steinbrenner himself said nothing. But one Yankee starter went on TV and said, "I don't care if Steinbrenner gave him a million a season. Elway or whatever his name is will still have to make this club and I doubt if he can."

Baltimore football officials, feeling they had wasted their No. 1 pick, bought the bluff and hit the panic button. They traded Elway to Denver for a few players, a few future draft choices, a small sack of gold and all the Johnny Unitas photos that could be found in Colorado.

Elway then caught the next plane to Denver and signed immediately. There was no dickering about the contract, no hesitation for lawyers to take some second looks.

We can now assume that the reason for the swiftness of that Denver signing was because Elway was afraid that Steinbrenner might not continue to hold his breath and maintain his silence much longer. After all, when you're bluffing with a pair of fours you don't show your hand to sweaters and wait for laughter. Besides, George is not known as the greatest secret-keeper since the Sphinx.

But Steinbrenner obviously enjoyed the word game that Elway

played with the football people. Elway, to my memory, always said that he "would accept baseball offers" before he would play football in Baltimore. He never exactly said that he would play with the Yankees, although he had tested a Yankee farm club earlier and reports say that Steinbrenner gave him $140,000 for that short season.

So everyone just assumed that a much greater offer would be made by George if the young athlete chose baseball and although he had big-league potential in both sports he prefers football. Maybe even football in Baltimore if it ever came down to that.

Now I'm thinking that he also has even more big-league potential in politics. He said just the right thing at the right time and didn't lie but didn't tell the whole truth to get exactly what he wanted. Now if that isn't a perfect picture of a present-day poiitician then my observations are garbled beyond belief.

November 2, 1983

Halas Tallest of All in NFL

It was 13 years ago, at the airport in Miami, when I first met George Halas, one of the most amazing men in sports history. We were five steps apart, waiting together at a baggage ramp, so I strolled over and introduced myself.

The thing that impressed me most at that moment was the size of the man. He was ramrod straight, easily 6 feet and probably weighed a slender 170. He had always looked so small on the sidelines. But then in those TV scenes he was always standing beside his players, those giants we called the Monsters of the Midway.

We were also in Miami the last time I saw Mr. Halas, four years ago. No, he didn't remember my name but after several sessions in between those first and last meetings he did recall the state. "Texas isn't it?" he asked as we shook hands. He was 84 at that time and still ramrod straight. George had just bounced back from a serious operation, and he allowed that his doctors may have missed something or other because he still didn't feel up to par.

George Stanley Halas, the one so many called Papa Bear, was a gruff, tough old gent, but he stayed loaded with compassion and loyalty and his tireless efforts to promote pro football didn't end until his death Monday night.

There was only one bad knock on George throughout his association with the Chicago Bears, the team that he founded, played for, coached and owned. They said he was too tight, too close with a buck to hire enough great players. He wouldn't shell out the many thousands needed to hire a first-rate NFL quarterback. So, for the last 10 or 15 years when the price tags became ridiculous, Chicago went without first-rate quarterbacks.

It was Mike Ditka, Chicago's current coach, who once said that George "threw nickels around as though they were manhole covers."

But those who rapped Halas for a tight wallet should have considered the battle that raged in the man's mind. We can all adjust to paying a quarter for a nickel candy bar or even putting down $300 for an $80 lawnmower. But giving a young man over $200,000 for one year to play a game that he should love was something that Halas found distasteful, immoral and maybe even illegal. It was the young turks around him, those in closer step with the times, who pried open the Halas pocketbook to keep Walter Payton in a Chicago uniform because, after all, Walter has been the franchise for half a dozen years.

So in the end, it was the grand monster that Halas helped create that robbed the old warrior of his winning ways. The NFL, a pitiful, struggling pauper when Halas entered for lifetime service, is now equal to any corporate giant in America.

Ten times more money is spent on a single pregame cocktail party today than franchises cost when Halas was a player. The price of a one-minute TV commercial during any NFL playoff game today is higher than all the franchises together were worth when Halas began to coach in the league.

There were long seasons when George did it all. He played and coached the Bears all week and then on Saturdays he stood before the front gate of University of Chicago games and passed out handbills advertising the Bears' game the following day. Then, on Sunday, he helped sell tickets on the few occasions when help was needed, taped his own ankles if there was enough tape to go around and then gave his boys a fight talk before taking the field to play and coach. He pinched every dime he could because, as owner, he had to if his franchise was to survive. He played because he wanted to and he coached because he felt, rightfully, that he was the best man for the job.

Knute Rockne and Gus Dorais generally are credited with popularizing the forward pass in football, but it was Halas and Curly Lambeau of Green Bay who turned the pass into a major offensive weapon and not just a desperation play reserved for third-and-long.

And it was Halas who started the man in motion in pro backfields after he noticed the defensive players' reaction to a sub who was racing for the sidelines, trying to get off the field before a play started. Five defensive players, not sure that the extra man really was attempting to reach the sidelines, began to make wild adjustments to compensate. Two weeks later the Bears started sending backs in motion, players who weren't going to leave the field.

As fate would have it, Halas got into football after a disappointment in baseball. An all-around athlete, he sought his fame and fortune with the New York Yankees in 1919. He got in only 12 games, managed two hits in 22 times up and finished with a "lifetime" big-league batting average of .091. Now that had to bend the ego of a young man who was burning with desire, talent and ambition.

But that same year, in the salesroom of Ralph Hay's Hupmobile agency in Canton, Ohio, a new football league was started as seven men met, chipped in $25 each for "operating expenses" and then elected Jim Thorpe as their president. The next year, after a less-than-successful start, a bigger group reorganized and that time Halas was present as the athletic director for the Staley Starch Company. The team was named the Decatur Blues but everybody called them after their sponsor's name, the Staleys.

That's right, it was that same Staley's Starch team that Halas eventually purchased and moved to Chicago as the Bears.

Once you consider all that, it's a little bit easier to understand why old George had trouble comprehending why any player should be paid half a million for just half a year's work. He kept pace with modern times, but he died thinking pro athletes are overpaid and underworked.

Now I wonder if George ever figured that it was largely because of his early efforts and stubborn struggles that the National Football League became the great attraction it is today, big enough and rich enough to provide all those handsome salaries?

Super Sitdown With Nagurski

TAMPA, Fla. — The Hogs and Smurfs and big, bad Raiders can wait for another day. This one belonged to one of the greatest legends football has ever known.

He was brought here from the cold country, hundreds of miles away, just to flip a coin Sunday to determine which team will kick and which will receive. But when word spread of his arrival, more than 60 newsmen juggled their plans and regrouped for what was billed as an "informal press conference." It lasted more than an hour.

Bronko Nagurski, one of the last of the great legends, now walks with a cane and wears thick glasses over his piercing blue eyes, but even at 74 there's evidence enough to detect the power and strength that his body once carried. He looks a little like an old lumberjack who just retired last month. The size 19 neck still looks strong as a bull's and his large shoulders and arms are solid, offering no visual evidence of the arthritis that pains him when he moves about.

And his hands, good Lord, those hands, are massive tools that must have been meant for a giant at least two feet taller. When he became a charter member of the Pro Football Hall of Fame, Bronko needed a size 19H ring, the largest ever cast for anyone inducted into that house of honor.

But his ring finger is now even larger, swollen by arthritis, so he can't wear it anymore. He still carries it in his pocket.

For many decades the name of Bronko Nagurski has symbolized the raw power and brute force of football. It's a name that once struck terror in the hearts of opponents and now stays on a privileged level with only a few of his time, a few that would include Jack Dempsey, Red Grange and Babe Ruth.

Doc Spears, his coach at the University of Minnesota, once said that Nagurski could have made All-American at any position. For that matter, he did make All-Pro at two positions, fullback and defensive tackle. He also played guard and linebacker, when needed, for the Chicago Bears.

Grantland Rice, once king of America's sportswriters, wrote that

Bronko was the greatest of the great. "Eleven Bronko Nagurskis could have beaten 11 Jim Thorpes or 11 Red Granges," Rice wrote. When asked about that yesterday, Bronko smiled and said, "I guess he just liked me because I played more positions than the others did."

It might be hard or even impossible to find an athlete who was so aggressive in competition but so shy and introverted otherwise. He seldom leaves his home on Rainy Lake in International Falls, the cold attic of America that's sometimes known as the nation's icebox. It's in northern Minnesota, just across the border from Canada, and right now the natives are enjoying an unseasonal warm streak, just 35 below zero.

Since Bronko seldom strays from his own backyard, he's known in some circles as the Recluse of Rainy Lake. On the rare occasions that he does leave, they say that he'll talk football but never about himself.

We changed that pattern Thursday. Strange as it seems, he said that the 60 of us who cornered him made up the largest press conference — by far — that he'd ever sat through or even seen.

Why this visit? And why did he agree to this Super Bowl visit after so many years alone with his family?

"I just wanted to take a little break from the cold weather and see what this was all about, this Super Bowl," Nagurski said.

Did he ever think that football would grow to such an event?

"Not in my wildest dreams could I have ever imagined anything like this."

Bronko's first contract with the Bears called for $5,000 a season and he had a great season. But the Depression caused a cutback, so the next year he only got $4,500. He had an even better year, but the Depression was still there, so Nagurski was paid just $3,000 for his third season of double duty at fullback and tackle.

So, as fate would have it, the five-day expense tab for Bronko and his family party of 13 will cost the NFL much more than he ever earned in a single season of playing pro ball.

Does he have any regrets about the salaries then and now?

"No, none at all. When I played we only had 18 to a team. Later, I think we went to 20 and then 22. But we were a close-knit group, great friends, and we enjoyed playing and we enjoyed each other. We had fun. I don't think the players today enjoy the game as much as we did, and I know they don't have nearly as much fun," Bronko said.

Are the players today as tough as the players when he played?

Bronko thought on that one for a moment. He didn't want to knock the NFL, his host for the trip. Finally, he started slowly, "I don't think they have to be as tough today because none of them plays more than 15 or 16 minutes each game. You know, with all the teams and the offense and defense platoons. We had to play 60 minutes, both on offense and defense, and if you weren't ready to go all out the whole game then you didn't have a job the next week."

Bronko handled that one well with a neat sidestep, something that he never used when he played. He much preferred to run over people.

Then came time to check out a few of the old Nagurski legends, incredible tales that are now accepted as pure fact.

Did he actually put a crack in the concrete wall at Chicago's Soldier Field, when he ended a 40-yard touchdown run and hit the barrier at full speed?

"I don't see how I could have. A lot of people — Fran Tarkenton was the latest — say they saw the crack but I honestly don't know. I do know, however, that I hit it mighty hard. Just couldn't stop," he said.

And the plow? Was he recruited by Minnesota after a coach stopped by his farm and asked for directions and he pointed with the plow? Was that true?

Bronko just laughed. "The coach came down to see me and we went fishing together. That was all. I did a lot of plowing in my time but I don't recall ever pointing one."

The old man would have stayed longer but an NFL official mercifully called a halt after 70 or 80 minutes and we all applauded. Bronko seemed pleased and surprised. He was even more surprised when some of us asked for autographs.

"I never knew that newspapermen ever asked anybody for an autograph," he said to me. "Every 10 or 20 years some of us make rare exceptions," I said. That put a wide smile on his face — and a thrill in my heart.

Remember the Clown

B uffalo Stadium was the biggest ballpark in Houston and Allen Russell had just worked himself up from parking cars to general manager of the Texas League Buffs. It was almost 40 years ago, long before the San Diego Chicken was to be hatched.

The average crowd at Houston Buff baseball games then was about 5,000 but on that hot afternoon so long ago, more than 4,000 made it to the stadium at least an hour before post-time. Al Schacht, the clown prince of baseball, was to perform there that night for the only time during the long season.

In those days, he wasn't just the funniest clown in baseball. He was the only one. The original.

Other Houston writers with more experience were to cover the game but my assignment was to cover the clown — "in six paragraphs or less." My editor's emphasis came on the "or less" line so I was stuck with the notion that anything over four paragraphs became an instant favorite to get chopped.

Sending a reporter across town for a four-inch story is like calling a plumber to tighten a screw on your toilet seat. But the editor realized my need for experience was greater than his need that night for office help to answer the phone.

For more than an hour, I visited with the zany baseball clown in the dressing room and then the dugout. He seemed old to me but all of the young players either knew him or wanted to know him. At 52, Al Schacht had made a complete baseball swing — a 20-game winning pitcher in the minors, three years in the majors, one year of coaching — and now he was drawing great crowds while pioneering a new baseball endeavor.

He had played with some of the game's legends and was pals with most of the old stars but when I met him, his closest associates were general managers who negotiated for his services as a clown.

And just how funny was he? Well, he used a lot of props that ranged from stooges in the stands to a live goat that followed his every step. The goat followed him closely — that is, until all the cabbage was eaten from Al's back pocket.

But even at 52, the man still had a far better-than-average arm and although it wasn't good enough to handcuff young batters, he still amazed crowds by sending sweeping curves from home plate into a peach basket propped over second. The zinger to that act came on the fourth or fifth toss that appeared to be far off target but Al would jerk it back in mid-air with the help of a strong but thin rubber string.

We talked for almost an hour but he ribbed so much, I never knew which answers were serious. For example, he told me that his parents came from Russia after they learned what a fantastic throwing arm he had as a tiny child and it would be wasted in Moscow since there was no baseball over there.

I later learned that there was a degree of truth in that tale. Schacht's parents were immigrants who fled czarist Russia but Al was born in New York and grew up on the streets of the Big Apple. None of his family moved two blocks because of the strength of his right arm.

But Al did. He moved from the minors to the majors but that really came on the strength of his right hand's penmanship. You see, he posted a 20-game victory season in 1919 with New Jersey and then flooded anonymous letters to Clark Griffith, owner of the Washington Senators. Those letters told of the great feats young Schacht would perform if just given the chance in the majors. Some were signed by "old scouts" and others by "just veteran fans."

Some later said that Griffith made a terrible mistake in signing Schacht because after three years in the majors, Al's record was just 14-10. But what the heck, a lot of pitchers who had 14-10 records last year are playing this year for $350,000 or more.

Griffith got a bargain because Al never made more than $2,000 a season.

He got a lot more than that, however, for one World Series appearance as a clown. In all, Schacht performed at 27 World Series and 29 All-Star Games. He took his act all over the world, wherever professional baseball was played. For 50 years, he performed as the funnyman of baseball, a forerunner to Max Patkin, the San Diego Chicken and all the others who now follow.

Schacht died the other day at the age of 91. One of the great tragedies of long life is that you outlive your friends and most of your best acquaintances. He entertained many millions throughout his career but only 19 attended his funeral. Six were pallbearers and all the others were family members. There wasn't a single representative from baseball in attendance.

I just thought that you might want to know a little more about the man who introduced humor to serious professional games. Besides, during that initial visit with him so many years ago, I gathered much more information than could possibly be packed into four paragraphs. This seemed like a good time to use the rest.

J u l y   2 5 ,   1 9 8 5

Too Much Blame on Budd

It's a sad situation but the do-gooder nuts are beginning to outnumber the folks who carry average loads of common sense and fair play.

As you know, Zola Budd is a skinny little teen-aged girl whose greatest love in life right now is running, a feat she performs rather well but not well enough to rank among the world's top two or three.

For whatever sins against sports and society that Zola may have committed — if, indeed, any — she's been subjected to more insults, ridicule and pressure than any one athlete should ever be forced to face. Her greatest sin, it seems, was to have been born and raised in South Africa. Her second-greatest sin was to have tangled a foot with America's Mary Decker Slaney during the Olympic Games.

Well now, that's two strikes on the little girl so let's get her. We'll write her nasty letters, threaten her life, boycott her races, pull our advertising off any TV networks that show her in action. By golly, we'll even rush out on the track and threaten her physically if she continues to compete. We'll show that sneaky, skinny runner from the land of unfair racial laws.

To make matters worse, Zola runs barefooted so the Adidas, Nike, Converse, Kaepa or Puma people won't even stand on her side. She's about as alone as any athlete can get. Even a boxer getting his brain barrel busted has a referee ready to step in and corner hands eager to offer a seat and words of advice.

Zola has nobody. Just the other day, her dad, Frank Budd, advised her to give up her running career and return home to South Africa. That was right after Zola was whipped by Slaney and several others in a Saturday race in England, an event that was televised live here in the States.

But Zola continues to hang tough and I like that. Tuesday, she ran one of her greatest races ever — just three days after the "Slaney-Budd return match" loss — and scored a victory in Scotland. Was it a satisfying triumph?

Far from it. Those protesting the violence against blacks in South Africa booed her throughout the race, spread banners of protest across the scoreboard so nobody could see the contestants' names or times and several "fans" even leaped onto the track and actually tried to attack the tired winner, chasing her to the protection of security guards.

It's easy to get steamed up over unfair policies that cause suffering and deaths in other countries but it's far beyond my understanding how anyone fighting for fairness can put the blame on a little girl and use her as a target for some of the unfairest treatment ever displayed in track and field.

In one way, it's a compliment to the great interest in sports today but I wish those with political axes to grind would build their own platforms and quit using a sports spotlight to air their assorted opinions. Generally speaking, the biggest problem with holy wars is that the combatants get so consumed with their crusades, the holiest often lose touch with holiness.

September 11, 1985

Tight-Lipped Ty

"Mr. Cobb. Wake up, Mr. Cobb. There, that's better. Mr. Cobb, what do you think about Pete Rose busting your career hit record in this season of '85? Do you have any congratulatory remarks for him? What? Mr. Cobb, I can't print that in a family newspaper. Would you mind toning your reply down a wee bit?"

It was what radio people call "prime drive time" the other morning, about 8:35, when the voice came through the dashboard of my Oldsmobile and stated in a clear voice, "Ty Cobb would be the first to congratulate Pete Rose if he were still here today because Ty loved a competitor and Rose long ago modeled himself after the great one from Georgia."

That's what the voice said but music followed those words so I don't know who owned the voice.

This simply is to explain that the owner of that voice knew as much about Tyrus Raymond Cobb as I know about the sex life of a Pittsburgh prairie chicken.

Cobb probably was the greatest baseball player ever to buckle a belt but he was not a nice person by any standards accepted by society today. A competitor? Oh, yeah, he was that and much more. A standup double to him should have been stretched to a triple and one of his great pleasures in life was branding rookie infielders with deep spike marks when they tried to tag him out.

Cobb went to his grave in July of 1961 "knowing" that no player would ever equal or break his career hit record of 4,191. If he hadn't felt confident of that, he wouldn't have died without playing at least a few more years. It was then considered the greatest of all baseball marks, the one that never would be matched. Grantland Rice himself said so in print. So did all the other writers of that time. Hey, we were still saying it right up until two years ago.

The Georgia cracker was 65 years old when I met him in Beaumont during a celebration for Spindletop week, the 50th anniversary of the first great oil find in Texas, a field that still pumps the black gold today after eight decades. Cobb, they said, was paid a princely sum for the visit to East Texas but he was far from friendly and he cared nothing about oil except the kind you rub into the pocket of a new glove. In short, he was gruff and cold but some said that he was showing his very best behavior.

I was one of the more fortunate ones in that a Chamber of Commerce-type dude presented me to Mr. Cobb with a flowing intro, lying a little by explaining that I was a bright, young reporter. Ah, well, two out of three isn't bad. I was young and I was a reporter.

But old Ty didn't give me much to report on that afternoon. He listened to the introduction, looked me in the eyes, said "hello," patted me on my left shoulder with his right hand and then whirled back into his hotel room and slammed the door.

It wasn't exactly the highlight of my week or even that day but, what the heck, how many can say that Ty Cobb patted their shoulder — and then slammed the door in their face? I'm sure that he just had to go to the bathroom and intended to return to visit with me. Well, I'm pretty sure. But after waiting 30 minutes for his return, I left — to go to the bathroom.

The next day, the greatest downtown crowd ever assembled in Beaumont gave Ty Cobb the biggest hand during a long parade. Even for those of us who had been "close" to him, patted on a shoulder, it was a moment to remember as the greatest of the great made one of his last public appearances.

This isn't to belittle Rose's record but you can't really compare the two players and keep the bottom lines close. Cobb, as mentioned, may have been the greatest of all time. Pete won't rank among the top 20 or 30 but he does have stamina and good health so in his 23rd season, he'll fracture the mark that Cobb needed 24 seasons to set.

But the key comes from times at bat and Rose has had hundreds more chances than Cobb, and it's well to remember that Ty wound up with a lifetime average of .367, far, far above the average that Rose will someday have when he closes his career.

But, more than anything, this is to contradict that radio voice that told us how Ty Cobb, if he were here today, would congratulate Pete. Yeah, he'd congratulate him — by slipping scorpions into Rose's shoes and stretching piano wire across the first base path.

J a n u a r y   1 7 ,   1 9 8 6

Four Horsemen Were Special

Some sports legends cool and fade as the years mount and memories are dulled. Others seem to grow as time passes, their deeds magnified in the minds of many. The Four Horsemen of Notre Dame belong to the latter category. Their destiny was determined by a popular sportswriter who was helped with a great idea.

Notre Dame, like the Aggies with their 12th Man, will never let us forget. Each time the school faces a tough struggle on any field of play, the ghosts of Knute Rockne, George Gipp and the Four Horsemen are called into service.

Grantland Rice, like all writers of his time and ours, was not above lifting an idea from any available source. The day that he wrote his memorable lead on a game story, he had earlier noticed a theater marquee that advertised a movie, "The Four Horsemen of the Apocalypse."

Thus, while others in that press box scratched their heads for a beginning, Granny wrote, "Outlined against a blue-gray October sky, the Four Horsemen rode again. In dramatic lore, they are known as famine, pestilence, destruction and death. But these are only aliases. Their real names are Stuhldreher, Miller, Crowley and Layden."

Chances are good that those words formed in Rice's mind long before halftime of that lopsided game. But it doesn't matter and never did.

A few days later, the sports information director at Notre Dame, or whatever they called the paid school tub-thumpers in those days, suggested to Rice that he rent four horses and pose the four Irish backs in saddles, in full uniforms and each holding a football. There was great discussion over who would pay for the horse rental, and some say that the school and Rice's paper split the total cost of $15, a whopping $7.50 each.

It was that photo, combined with the earlier words that immortalized the Four Horsemen of Notre Dame.

Forty-five years later, a lot of us Texans had the honor of meeting the surviving three of that group after Notre Dame ended a long fast from bowls and agreed to meet Texas in the Cotton Bowl.

It was one of those rare thrills that even veteran sportswriters get just ever so often, maybe two or three times a decade. It was bigger than my first meeting with Joe Louis, Jack Dempsey or even Babe Ruth. The Horsemen were a group who had done their things before I was born, but their stars continued to grow as their stories were told and retold by old and young alike.

Two days before the game, most of us arrived early for the press conference in that downtown Dallas hotel room that would hold 40 or 50 newsmen within listening range. It seemed sort of funny calling them the "Four" Horsemen when only three were there — quarterback Harry Stuhldreher passed away several years earlier. And most of us realized that it might be the last gathering for those three survivors. They were all closing in on 70, when Father Time often picks up his pace of pursuit.

Don Miller, I recall so vividly, stood apart from Elmer Layden and Jim Crowley. Not just in five yards of distance during that interview but in his thoughts that he relayed. Don wasn't eager to play down the deeds that he and the others performed while winning the national championship in 1924, Notre Dame's first such crown. He seemed a little hurt when Layden and Crowley insisted that none of the four, in their primes, could have made either the Texas or Notre Dame squads that would be playing there in a few days.

It was a time to recall that Miller was a businessman, looking every bit the part in his three-piece suit, a fellow who was foreign to the new breed of athletes. Crowley and Layden had been bonded closer as long-term jocks, coaches who kept careful eyes on football's progress.

Layden coached Notre Dame at one time and Crowley developed some of the last great Fordham teams. They knew of what they spoke when they explained how none of the Four Horsemen weighed over 170 pounds, how none could have stepped the 100 in under 10 seconds and how none of them could have made the starting lineup on any good team of that 1969 season.

Miller frowned in disagreement. Or, perhaps, it was disappointment as he sat and listened to his old pals rub the glitter and greatness from their ancient legend. Little did he know that they were only adding honesty to a chapter in sports that may live forever, as long as the game is played.

Don was the next to leave. And then Layden. Crowley, the one they called Sleepy Jim because of his drooping eyelids, often remarked how lonesome he felt, being the last survivor of that famed football foursome. But then Wednesday morning, at the age of 83, Sleepy Jim went to eternal sleep.

So now, they're all gone. But don't get the idea they'll soon be forgotten. Maybe President Reagan, in his first movie appearance, helped kindle the fires of the Great Gipper. And perhaps Pat O'Brien, in the same movie, pushed the successes of Knute Rockne. But for whatever reasons, those legends live beyond the lives of the men and they won't be soon erased.

Notre Dame and football history will never let us forget.

I'm just glad that I was at that 1970 Cotton Bowl and had the good fortune to shake hands and visit with three of the Four Horsemen. But now, I'm wondering if it would have been that great of a thrill if old

Granny Rice hadn't passed that movie marquee and got the idea to create the legend. It's funny how lasting greatness sometimes develops from the push of a small idea.

March 6, 1986

The Allure of Bad Guys

Fans never change. They're quick to forgive any athlete who uses body and exceptional athletic skills to hit homers, score touchdowns or dunk basketballs — no matter what their crime might be. But they stay forever united against a front-office hand who has somehow piqued their anger.

Most of the calls and letters were for Duane Thomas and against Tom Landry back in the early '70s when the running back got his brains scrambled in drugs and spoke publicly only to knock those who paid his wages.

About the same time, the best pitcher in baseball, Denny McLain, pulled a six-month suspension for running an illegal bookmaking operation in the Tigers' clubhouse, often accepting and making wagers over the locker room phone an hour before game time.

When Denny was permitted to play, a near-capacity crowd turned out for his first home game of the season and he was given a standing ovation. You got that? A standing ovation.

One month later, a respected Detroit star named Al Kaline, a gentleman who had put in 17 starting and spotless seasons in the majors, was honored with a day in a well-organized team promotion. The crowd was 25 percent smaller than for McLain's return and not nearly as enthusiastic.

It was on that occasion that McLain, the cocky outlaw, turned to teammates and offered the sad but sometimes-true observation, "Good guys never draw."

That, by the way, was the same McLain who last year drew a long prison term for bookmaking, loan-sharking, drug-dealing and physical threats while making collections.

But you know something? If McLain were to be released tomorrow

202

and somehow thinned 50 pounds from his overweight frame and tried a pitching comeback with the Tigers, he'd almost certainly receive another standing ovation. Two of them if he happened to win the game.

Now, let's move to present days and turn to basketball.

Micheal Ray Richardson was given a standing ovation last season after he returned from a drug rehabilitation center and assumed his old starring role with the New Jersey Nets. Many sportswriters frowned on that scene but last season Richardson was voted, by sportswriters, the league's comeback award, an honor usually reserved for someone who returned to greatness after whipping a disease, surviving a car wreck or getting sidelined with a broken leg or arm.

The runner-up for that fine honor the season before was John Drew.

Now, as we visit today, Richardson and Drew stand as the only two active players ever to draw a lifetime ban from the NBA for repeated drug abuse.

Nevertheless, lifetime NBA bans are a lot like death sentences and life jail terms. They seldom mean what they say. Richardson and Drew can both appeal after two years so both loom as candidates to repeat as "comeback players" in 1989 or thereabouts.

Willie Wilson, outfielder for the Kansas City Royals, was sentenced to three months in a federal penitentiary for possession of cocaine, and just before the hammer fell the judge jumped on Willie for not handling his responsibilities to his community and to the children who looked to him as a role model.

Wilson later told a reporter, "That's a responsibility that I never asked for. Some of the people asked for it and baseball asked for it. All I did was sign to play baseball. I didn't sign a contract to take care of anybody's kids or to be a role model for anybody."

He's right, too. Policemen who join the crooks and ministers who join the devil violate their oaths but athletes never make such pure promises.

For the most part, athletes are judged by the fans who pay to watch them perform, and a little law-breaking only endears some superstars to many fans.

Thousands thought it was funny when Tim Raines of the Montreal Expos admitted that he slid headfirst while stealing second so he wouldn't break the vial of cocaine in his back pocket.

Some were sickened by that admission but a lot of fans who pay to watch Raines slide thought that was cute or funny.

That tells you a lot about the blindness of some wild-eyed fans. And it tells us even more about our society today, and the way it started to turn in the '70s when McLain and Thomas were nearing the peaks and the ends of their careers.

This isn't to cop a holier-than-thou attitude. We're all in this thing together. But the time must be near when fans start demanding a little more from the athletes who they support so well.

We know they can't all be role models, but any young man who becomes a millionaire by working just two or three hours a day should be expected to stay inside the laws of the land the other 21 hours of each day.

May 21, 1986

A Rare Boxing Jewel

The private jet touched down here Tuesday shortly after noon and a long limo, a dark blue job with a uniformed chauffeur, loaded the seven passengers and made haste for the Marriott North on Loop 410.

Mrs. Josephine Abercrombie was right on schedule for the press conference that she had called. Fifty minutes later the lady was ready to leave, whispering to aides that the plane would be ready to take off in 10 minutes.

The plane, of course, belonged to Mrs. Abercrombie so it got ready to leave whenever she said. But the Houston socialite was on a tight schedule. She had left her home base early in the morning, visited Fort Worth around 10 in the morning, popped into San Antonio for a one-hour session and was scheduled in Corpus Christi at 3 p.m. Her plans called for dinner back home in Houston before sundown.

The string of press conferences was to announce a series of cable telecasts for Texas. June 5 is the first date here and that card will feature San Antonio's Aaron Lopez, who was also at the conference here, against Alvaro Ramos of Arizona. But more on that in other areas of this sports section. This is about the lady promoter.

Over the years there have been other women who promoted boxing across the country. Eileen Eaton, who took over when her husband, Cal, died in California, was the best known for more than a decade. Yet, never in the long history of the ring game has there ever been anybody like Josephine Abercrombie.

First off, she's high Houston society and has been since birth. She's got more millions than most kids have marbles, and even today she's got more Kentucky thoroughbred horses on her farm in Lexington than she has boxers in her gym.

She knows which fork to use first at one of those formal, four-fork dinners, but she also knows a left hook from a jab, a right cross from an uppercut.

Josephine is a slim bantamweight, an attractive lady who, at 60, has allowed a little gray to slip into her blondish hair. She was raised to say the right things at the right time to the right people, but once she makes up her mind to do something a tad of fire crosses her blue eyes and she sets her jaw in a determined way. She knows what she wants and how to get things done.

Perhaps, above all, Josephine is her father's daughter. As one of the founders of Pin Oaks Stables in Houston, he often took her to horse shows. And, when she was about 13, he took her to boxing matches. "I don't really remember which I enjoyed more in those days but I feel that I knew more then about boxing than most kids my age," she told me Tuesday.

It was three years ago, about this time in 1983, when she shocked her wealthy friends and announced that she was forming the Houston Boxing Association to promote cards in her hometown.

"They all thought that I was crazy," she laughed. "Some of them still do, but you know what? They're all there at ringside, taking up the first few rows for most of our fight cards."

Mrs. Abercrombie then told how next week in Houston she and her boxing people will be conducting a clinic for women who want to learn more about the sport. Naw, not a clinic to teach them how to fight. It will be a school to teach them what a left hook is and the value of the punch, to explain the art of clever footwork, what it's all about between two men once the bell rings. "About 13 of my best friends have already signed up for that session," she said with a degree of pride.

A whole lot of veteran promoters, matchmakers and managers must have licked their chops and reached for telephones when Josephine first announced her entry into boxing. Wow, a multimillionaire rookie promoter and a lady, no less. The odds on her surviving two years in that jungle of double-cross must have been longer than Ferdinand's 17-1 in the Kentucky Derby.

But survive she has and now her goals are even greater. She's about to try something that's never before even been attempted in boxing. The lady is getting together a small handful of promoters around the state to form a boxing coalition for a series of bouts to be telecast.

Boxing has never needed any enemies because it nourishes a hatred from within. Managers bounce back and forth from one promoter to another, wherever the biggest buck is to be made, and those on the inside of a big show automatically become targets of all those on the outside of that particular card. That's the way it has been since somebody strung ropes around a squared platform and the Marquis of Queensbury presented his rules.

But now comes this lady, straight out of the top 10 of Houston's social register, and she's going to unite a bunch of promoters into a coalition and improve the sport while building it bigger than ever before in this state.

Can she do it?

Well, as they say, she's off to a flying start and I sure wouldn't bet against her. But only one thing seems certain. The lady needs another million in her purse about like I need another wrinkle in my forehead.

November 5, 1986

Ice's Timely Trade

It's no secret that a few thousand fans kicked the Spurs habit a year or so ago when the wheels wobbled on the franchise and losses outnumbered the wins.

We all love a winner and it's durned difficult to support a loser.

It's amazing, however, the number of one-time fans who write or call to explain that they gave up on the local team when the coldhearted front-office folks traded George Gervin.

Folks, that old dog just won't hunt anymore. It's a phony excuse, although none is asked for here or required. It's as if to say, "I was a loyal, ticket-buying fan but, being of such high, loyal character, I can't overlook the way they treated our beloved Iceman."

That story wore well a year ago. But not anymore.

Hey, we all had or have strong feelings for Gervin. He was, without doubt, the franchise-maker for many years here. He also was the greatest single athletic attraction this city has ever known. A rare and gifted athlete, he thrilled local fans and awed opponents.

But George was never the least bit timid about seeking more and more money and pleading for trades when the raises weren't immediately offered. When the Spurs sent him to Chicago last season there was one year left on George's contract and the Bulls had to pay Gervin in the neighborhood of $800,000.

If you think that Chicago got $800,000 worth of service — or even $400,000 worth — from the Iceman last season then you weren't paying close attention.

This year, as a free agent, Gervin could make his own deal with any NBA team. Sure, Chicago would have wanted something in return. But not much. Maybe a second- or third-round draft pick somewhere down the line. Perhaps even less.

Not one NBA team made a serious effort to sign the 34-year-old Gervin.

The silky smooth Iceman, once the league's greatest point-maker, was over the hill, not only through as a superstar but finished as an NBA starter.

San Antonio officials had tried hard earlier to get Gervin to accept a sixth-man position, to come off the bench and, hopefully, spark rallies in key spots. But George wouldn't buy that package and most fans sided with him when the offer became public.

So after just one season away from the Spurs, in a Chicago uniform, Gervin accepted a contract for $250,000 to play this year in Italy. That's the end of the basketball line for old NBA performers.

This isn't to throw rocks at Gervin, to cheapen his great image here. Not only do I consider him a friend but without any doubt, he was an NBA superstar and for several seasons he was one of the game's all-time greats.

But this is to point out that time has proved the Spurs' front office 100 percent correct in last year's trade of George. As a matter of fact, perhaps the two wisest moves that management ever made were (1) getting Gervin and (2) getting rid of Gervin at the proper time.

So use whatever excuse you want — if you want to use any — for not attending the games here anymore but please, don't bug me about "giving up on the Spurs because of the way they treated George Gervin."

No excuse is needed and none certainly would be better than that lame line.

You might be surprised at the number of folks who ask why Sugar Ray Leonard is coming out of retirement — again — to fight Marvin Hagler.

"Why is he doing it? He doesn't need the money."

That's the talk around town and the nation and those two lines are almost always followed with, "He could lose an eye or maybe even his life."

So why is he doing it?

First off, he's doing it for $11 million guaranteed and probably more. Never in the history of the human race has there yet been a rich man who wouldn't pause to do his thing — whatever that thing happened to be — to pick up a purse like that.

Secondly, and most importantly, it's something that has been burning on Leonard's mind for six years and it obviously won't go away. Sugar Ray has always felt and sincerely feels now that he can whip Hagler.

Yeah, I know. You and I don't think so. Not anymore. Not after such a long layoff, with just one poor fight in the last four years.

But the more he hears that from friends, fans and family the more he wants to prove them wrong. As Leonard says, he's not trying for a comeback. He just wants this one more fight, against Hagler.

It's well to keep one thing in mind. Leonard turned 30 last May and Hagler is four years older. On top of that Hagler had a long, tough brawl with John Mugambi in his last bout and that one could have taken a lot out of the old champion.

If Sugar Ray can shake the ring rust he just might have a much better chance than many fans figure.

As I've said and written before, I'd be happy to accept a bout against Magilla Gorilla for a lousy $1 million as long as somebody pulled him off me each time that I went down.

Two Teams Too Much

It was a clear Tuesday night and the Spurs were on a five-game victory streak, the hottest team in the NBA. And the locals stretched their string to six straight that evening as an Arena crowd of just 5,926 watched.

Hey, don't you think that it's about time for us to quit kidding ourselves about the big pie in the sky, a $50 million to $100 million sports complex?

We're at least 15 years away from having the support required to keep two major-league franchises alive and flourishing.

For two years now the conductor of this tour has purposely avoided the subject of a new, multimillion-dollar stadium for an NFL franchise. It's never wise to turn down the volume on enthusiasm, to pour cold water on the anticipation and excitement of others.

It's even worse, perhaps, to act the role of a prophet of doom, to present reasons why something can't, won't or shouldn't be done. The popular champions of our society are the movers and shakers, the progressive people who buck odds and get things done.

Sure, we'd all be proud and pleased to have a large, magnificent stadium here, one of the NFL variety. We'd like that no matter who paid for it.

But, by the same token, we were just as proud and pleased when the Spurs came to town and, eventually, graduated into the NBA.

We got the team because Angelo Drossos seized the moment of opportunity, because Dallas folks were too sophisticated and preoccupied with their highly successful Cowboys to waste time with the ABA, a major-league pretender.

The ABA survived here because (1) George Gervin developed into a silky-smooth superstar and (2) because the Spurs wound up with the concessions for HemisFair Arena.

The NBA Spurs prospered because (1) they were winners, always title contenders in the playoffs and (2) because they were the only major-league professional team of any kind within 200 miles.

Ah, but for every winner there's a loser and some bad years always follow good ones. The Yankees, Celtics and Cowboys, in three different sports, can offer testimony to support that fact.

When the bad years hit here, fan support evaporated. Within just a few months, the San Antonio franchise became a strong contender to lead the league with the lowest attendance figure.

Nothing has changed since the fan drought arrived.

The team has a loyal, die-hard group of about 5,000 and another 700 or 800 might be expected to make last-hour plans to attend. That won't cut it on a big-league basis.

Only when the Celtics or Lakers play here, or when promotional gimmicks are offered — like two-for-one nights — do 10,000 or more file through the doors.

This is major-league support?

But please, don't bother to write or call to explain your assorted reasons for not attending games here. They've all been aired, from "owners too cheap to pay big salaries" and "the policy of no-smoking in the Arena stands" to the "new parking problems."

But, by golly, thousands more make the scene on gimmick nights, when hot dogs are a dime or wristbands are freebies at the door.

The bottom line shows that the only major-league team in town is getting terrible fan support, clearly indicating that this area is far from ready to support two big-league teams in different sports.

City Manager Lou Fox arrived at the Arena 30 minutes before last Tuesday's game. He seemed pumped up and a bit excited when he strolled by Drossos' box and predicted a crowd of "about 11,000" for the evening.

Drossos replied, "I sure hope that you're right but a friend of mine guessed that we'd have about 8,000 tonight and I'd settle for 7,000."

Fox left immediately after the game, shortly after the attendance figure of 5,926 was announced.

I'm not blaming Mayor Cisneros for getting behind the stadium drive here. All politicians dearly love to see big things accomplished while they're in office. Don't forget that it was Henry who accompanied Clinton Manges to New York to secure the Gunslingers' USFL franchise for San Antonio.

At this point, however, Cisneros looms as the best thing the pro stadium people have going for them. He's their lone big gun. But from here it appears that he's dictated more by his political ego, image and ambitions than by his common sense, not to mention his business sense.

It's the personal opinion here that the NFL stadium plan will not leave anybody's drawing board for at least 10 years. But one thing is almost dead certain. If a stadium is built and an NFL team does come here in the next six or seven years, the NBA franchise will be forced out.

Like it or not, this area simply will not or cannot support two big-league teams and that situation doesn't figure to change for at least a decade.

––––––––––––

June 2 4 , 1 9 8 7

Walking in Big Dave's Shoes

It was a wise old Indian, I think, who first said that you can't know another man's problems until you've walked in his moccasins.
Of course, if his moccasins don't fit you, then you've got an even bigger problem.

This is with regard to David Robinson's reluctance to get excited about being San Antonio's No. 1 draft pick.

He's admitted that "there are other teams" that he "had hoped to play for ahead of San Antonio." That, coupled with cracks from "experts" like Rick Barry, who went on TV and twice said that if he were Robinson he wouldn't play for San Antonio, have left a lot of local fans disappointed.

Barry was a great player but he's a lousy one to be advising anyone about choosing a team. His career stops look like a Greyhound bus schedule. He played for Oakland, Washington, New York, San Francisco, Golden State and Houston.

Folks are already writing and calling to complain about David's reluctance. But I'm on his side.

To begin with, he hasn't said a single negative thing about the Spurs or this city. He's often said that he wants to keep an open mind, that he plans to visit San Antonio, that he wants to come here, meet people and look things over first-hand.

So what's wrong with that?

As mentioned here before, the big center is in no hurry because it

211

will be months before he can sign and two years before he can play. We're the ones who are rushing things.

Now then, let's slip on his moccasins and walk his trail for a few furlongs.

There's no such thing as a draft for plumbers, carpenters, insurance salesmen, realtors, lawyers or sportswriters.

But in this slice of fantasy, I'm going to make believe that I'm a talented young sportswriter, just coming out of college. I made a straight-A average for four years and I have my heart set on working and living here in beautiful San Antonio.

Hey, quit laughing about the talent and the straight-A average. I clearly stated that this was make-believe.

Now then, if I can't work here in San Antonio, I'd sort of lean toward Dallas or Houston.

But alas, Buffalo drafted me. They picked me in the first round. I've never been to Buffalo and a visit there doesn't rate among the top 20 things I'd like to do. Working and living there seems out of the question.

I once read that a magazine contest offered as first prize a one-week, all-expense trip to Buffalo. Second prize was two weeks in Buffalo.

I even heard that the publisher in Buffalo is so tight his shoes squeak. He wouldn't chip in on a new drum for the Salvation Army 10 days before Christmas.

But, facing reality, the Buffalo Bugle has drafted me so I'll hide my disappointment as much as I can and then sashay up there and meet those people — whenever I get a little time. I'll even force a smile and be nice to that tightwad publisher when he offers me slave wages.

And to think I went all through college and made those great grades just to wind up in Buffalo.

See what I mean about those moccasins?

As mentioned, I've never been to Buffalo. Robinson has never been to San Antonio. I might like it up there. I'm betting that he'll like it down here.

Yet, at this moment, there's no good reason why he should get excited about San Antonio using its No. 1 pick to draft him. Everybody who has ever dribbled a basketball knew that he was the pick of this year's crop, that some NBA team would make him a rich man.

When you're in military service, you don't have much say about where you'll live and work. But when you leave the service and become your own person, the choices often become countless.

That isn't always the case for professional athletes, no matter what Rick Barry says.

All I'm saying is, let's not be too hasty just because Ensign Robinson isn't jumping with joy over the opportunity that San Antonio is offering him.

To be honest, when I rolled a few hundred miles across South Texas and came here in 1952, it was my intent to stay one year — and no more. It was my firm plan to be working for a newspaper either in Chicago, Los Angeles or New York before I was 30.

Offers finally came from Chicago and San Francisco (close enough to L.A.) when I was 32 and it took Katy and me about 30 seconds to reach the decision to stay here.

Of course, there are some who'd like to see me leave but that's their problem. My one-year stay in San Antonio has now turned into 35 years and I hope to still be here long after David Robinson has completed his NBA career — hopefully in San Antonio.

December 25, 1987

Coaches' Sour Holiday Mood

Here's wishing that you got it, whatever it was you wanted for Christmas. And here's wishing that you don't have to take it back and exchange it for a different size.

Santa Claus is not a bad old dude but he's getting old and his memory does slip a peg every few years.

But, like the rest of us, he's learned a lot from experience.

Exactly 35 years ago I learned that a waffle iron is not a great gift for your first Christmas with your wife. It's not a great gift, that is, to give your wife.

Oh, she tried to hide her disappointment. But I got real suspicious by early February after that iron had failed to produce its first waffle.

On the other hand, it takes different strokes for different folks so if you happened to give your lady a waffle iron this morning she might treasure it as a wonderful gift. She might, that is, if she stays starving-wolf hungry for waffles in the morning.

At any rate, this is a holy day for most of us, a happy time or, at least, a time to reflect on happy moments.

That's a small signal to explain that there'll be only a few sour notes typed in this space today.

Instead we'll touch on the lighter sides of semiserious matters.

Basketball coaches, for example, provide the lightest side of sports this side of mud wrestling. And it's been a hard week on some from that group.

The Miami coach met this Christmas Day with his arm in a sling. Monday night he was "coaching" from the bench, flapping his arms like a wounded fly, screaming at the ref to call a foul against an opposing player.

The poor man dislocated his left shoulder and became the only casualty of the contest. Not only that but he also lost his voice.

And pity the poor Manhattan cage coach who took his New Yorkers to Beaumont for Lamar's tournament. He went bonkers on the sidelines, cursed the ref in a booming voice that could be heard all across the arena and finally was ejected.

Then, to compound his problem, he stole a page from Bobby Knight's basketball book of etiquette and removed his team from the floor and the tournament.

Well, Bobby Knight got away with it and was given a standing ovation prior to his next outing. Ah, but Bobby Knight has won national titles and Manhattan's trophy case is . . . well, let's just say that there's plenty of room for more.

Turning to football, we learn that losing has a way of changing the personalities of some who seem destined for hall of fame honors.

Chuck Noll, a tough old dude who never had a single complaint while his Steelers dominated so many Super Bowls, has learned that living in the low-rent section can juggle a gent's nerves.

Chuck all but challenged Houston coach Jerry Glanville to a fistfight after the Oilers completed a two-game season sweep of Pittsburgh last Sunday. Dirty play, unnecessary roughness, tactics used for intimidation — those were the charges against the Oilers.

Imagine, the double-tough Steelers, the ones who rolled their battle-scarred helmets onto the field and whipped most teams for many years, crying about rough play.

Jack Lambert and Mean Joe Greene must have giggled aloud when they heard those charges from their old coach.

But losing changes most men. It does, that is, unless you happen to be Tom Landry.

The Dallas coach has suffered through his worst season since the Cowboys' first year of existence, hearing from fans and newsmen who want him fired and listening to criticism from his team president and his team owner.

But he hasn't changed a lick. There must be fires roaring in his mind and his gut but you'll never detect it from his speech, his step or his manners.

What did he get for Christmas? Probably a new hat that he hasn't yet unwrapped. I just hope that he didn't give Mrs. Landry a waffle iron. The poor guy has enough problems already.

March 4, 1988

Let the Ladies Speak

This is ladies day here. There won't be any free tickets to the ballgame and the first 100 ladies to read this column won't even be offered wilted carnations.

It's just that the mail satchel, for reasons unknown, dropped a large load on my desk and 80 percent of the dispatches are from women.

Sure, there are a few dandies from dudes with axes to grind but we've never before had a "ladies-only" gig here and the time will never be riper.

Yeah, I know, it's sort of illegal, tossing aside all letters from men. At least, however, this is a new form of discrimination.

Dear Dan:
There was a time, not too many years ago, when I admired you because I thought that you were filled with understanding and compassion for fallen athletes. But in recent months I began to have doubts and now I am wondering why I ever thought so highly of you.

You have continually low-rated fans for giving standing ovations while welcoming back baseball and basketball players that fell to drugs and then returned after beating the terrible disease. You show no compassion whatsoever for the athletes that beat their drug problems or for the fans who welcome them back.

The final straw came Tuesday when you questioned the Spirit Award being voted to skater Dan Jansen because he fell twice in his two events.

Some grow mellow in their old age but you, Dan, obviously have hardened. It is not at all characteristic.

Oralla Sims

To begin with, if drug addiction really is a disease then it's a self-inflicted one that comes after countless warnings. Secondly, I have far greater compassion for the men who left an arm or a leg in Vietnam than for the jocks who waste fabulous salaries on destructive drugs. Yet, we give bigger, warmer welcomes to the self-destructing athletes, knowing that most of them really aren't cured. Finally, skater Jansen has my sympathies, but I would have admired his spirit much more had he taken his tumbles, hopped up and at least tried to continue. When he lost sight of the gold he lost his competitive spirit.

Dear Mr. Cook:

I can't understand why so many are expressing so much disappointment in the way our American athletes did in the Winter Olympics.

In the previous Winter Games in Yugoslavia the United States won just eight medals, only two more than this year. Why do so many in America think that we should be on a par with those from countries that keep snow-covered mountains and frozen lakes six or seven months out of every year?

It is my guess that more than 90 percent of our population does not know what a luge is and couldn't care less. So what's so bad when one of our luge competitors finishes 15th or 20th in the Winter Olympics?

Do you know any little boys anywhere in this country who want to grow up to be bobsledders? I understand one of our bobsled teams many years ago won an Olympic title but does anyone remember any of their names or were they just weekend heroes?

Mrs. Sylvia Stuart

Well, Sylvia, I guess we just think that we're better than anyone else at almost any game and it chaps us to find out differently.

Dear Dan:

Our son, Richard, is 11 years old and preparing for his second season of Little League Baseball. His great ambition is to get his name in your column.

We have often told him that the papers here only print the team results and seldom mention the names of many individuals. Will this change this year?

You should remember that young children also like to see their names in print and they may grow up to be your future subscribers.

Mrs. Donald Watson

Yes, ma'am, but we'll probably lose a lot of present subscribers if we use the sports space for too many Little League names. Meanwhile, your son's ambition just got filled up there in your letter. Now tell him to raise his sights and aim at bigger things.

Dear Mr. Cook:

There are a lot of things that I do not understand about the Spurs and pro basketball and I hope you can help me.

Why do professional athletes have such a hard time winning road games? Does fan favoritism really mean that much to men who perform for big salaries while playing a game that they've played most of their lives?

And please explain why the Spurs have not done anything since George Gervin left us. Other teams get new stars every few years but our owners seem to use each new season as some kind of training period to introduce unknowns.

Angela Villarreal

The home crowd is only half the problem for visiting basketball teams. The officials who also listen to the crowd are the other half. As for our "unknowns," I'll check with Angelo Drossos on that the next time I see him. I'm sure that you'll love his answer.

Rose's Bum Rap

Pete Rose just came out on the bad end of a three-play parlay. That is to say, the Cincinnati manager is the victim of three errors made by National League officials.

You no doubt read about Rose's 30-day suspension for bumping an umpire, the longest ban handed a manager since 1947 when Leo Durocher was thumbed for an entire season.

Leo, it was said, sashayed about with a bunch of shady characters so he was deemed guilty by association. That ban of 40 years ago by Commissioner Happy Chandler would never have happened these days. Any lawyer who can get a postponement on a parking ticket hearing would punch all sorts of holes in that kind of charge.

Pete's situation, of course, is of an entirely different nature.

Last Saturday, umpire Dave Pallone blew a close call at first base by not making a call.

He came up with a correct decision, finally, but during the delay of four to five seconds — a long wait in anybody's league — the Mets scored the winning run.

That was mistake number one.

When Rose rambled from the dugout and began to argue the delay in Pallone's call, he did no more or less than hundreds of managers before him. He flapped his arms, showing how the safe signal should have been made and he did a heap of jawing about 15 inches from Pallone's face.

Now these times and distances on the call at first and the debate that followed are mighty accurate because I studied tapes of the whole incident many times, in slow motion, something that we can only assume that league officials also did.

Rose never came within 15 inches of touching the umpire until Pallone leaned forward in Pete's face and began barking his own opinions on the matter and the debate. While shouting at the Cincinnati manager he emphasized his claims by pointing a finger down in Pete's face — hard. At least one of the three points caught the manager high on his left cheek, just below the eye.

That was the umpire's second mistake.

It probably was an accidental poke but, by golly, the umpire did make the first contact and that husky finger point left a small mark on Rose's face.

Then, and not before then, Rose shoved the umpire. He shoved him hard, twice.

National League commissioner Bart Giamatti, in announcing the 30-day suspension of Rose, claimed that the manager "forcefully and deliberately" shoved Umpire Pallone.

Giamatti was correct with that assessment.

But the league boss failed to mention that Pallone poked Rose near the eye to initiate the physical contact.

That strange oversight, plus the long suspension that followed, marked the third error committed against Rose on the subject.

If Giamatti reviewed the tapes, as so many of us did, then he had to notice his umpire's pokes so close — too close once — on the manager's face.

If Umpire Pallone is as honest and sincere as he claims — dedicated to the high standards of his profession, he says — then he should have slept on the matter and then admitted that (1) he was a little slow in making the call at first and (2) he accidentally made the first contact on Rose.

Instead, Pallone said that his honest opinion was that his call at first was handled in a proper way. He refused to comment on the incident with Pete and the manager's 30-day suspension.

As mentioned, Pete got a bad rap.

So what should the league boss have done about the 15-minute fuss that ignited fans, almost caused a riot and forced all four umpires to leave the field while trash from the stands was collected?

Well, if he was looking for fairness and real baseball justice, he should have called Pallone and Rose together on his carpet, shown both men the tapes, chewed on both their cans and then given Rose a three- or four-game suspension and either fined the umpire or placed him on probation for several weeks.

Dropping the whole load on Rose with an unprecedented 30-day suspension and not offering even a lukewarm public word to the umpire casts a horrible reflection on Giamatti's wisdom and brand of justice.

After all, the umpire is one of his personal employees. Rose is not, although Giamatti has authority over all who work and play in the

National League.

By now you may be harboring the idea that Pete Rose in one of my favorites.

Not so.

Over the years I've admired the spirit and talents of the one they call Charlie Hustle, but I felt that he stayed too long as a player, seeking more and more headlines while thriving on his own publicity.

With a haircut fashioned after a Raggedy Ann doll, Pete spent all of his adult life visiting the largest cities in America. But once removed from baseball, he seemed to have the IQ of a banana.

Nevertheless, the old pro certainly is entitled to a fair shake and the National League boss and one now-silent umpire have teamed up to give him a long shaft.

May 24, 1988

The Mysteries of Indy

After 11 consecutive trips to Indianapolis for annual 500-mile races, countless hours in Gasoline Alley and long conversations with drivers and mechanics, there are still a number of things about that event that I don't understand.

Maybe you can help.

1. We know that drivers push their cars to the limit to try to qualify but they're on the track all alone during that part of the show. They also push their cars as hard as possible at times during the actual race when jockeying for the lead or improved position. How come so many veterans crash in qualifying?

It would seem that driving five or six miles an hour slower in traffic with 32 other cars would be far more dangerous than going the car's limit all alone on the track.

Pancho Carter, a veteran of more than a dozen Indy races, has now crashed three different cars in his last three attempts to qualify, one last year and two this month.

Johnny Rutherford and Tom Sneva, both former Indy winners, also crashed during practice or qualifying runs this month, not to mention half a dozen less-experienced drivers.

On my last count, 21 drivers — many of them veterans — died during qualifying or practice runs while only 14 have been killed during the actual race.

I don't understand that.

2. Every car that qualifies costs more than the most expensive Rolls Royce and some of the world's finest mechanics tune each car with the latest equipment. Yet, next Sunday when the order comes, "Gentlemen, start your engines," it's an even money bet that at least one car won't start. Sometimes they have to push the stubborn starter and let the driver catch up with the pack on warmup laps.

Sometimes, during practice and qualifying runs, the cars are pushed back into the garage because they won't start.

Yeah, I know, those light rockets are tuned to the finest degree and far more time is spent milking an extra two or three miles of speed from the engine than checking the ignition.

But I still don't understand it.

3. Why is tradition so important to Speedway officials and that one race run there each year around Memorial Day?

They still have a "carburetor test" day but, since all of the cars are now fuel-injected, there hasn't been a carburetor in an Indy car in at least 15 years.

Also, oldtimers continually refer to the track as "The Old Brickyard" but most of the bricks came out close to 50 years ago and all of the track was resurfaced with asphalt 12 years ago.

Only a small strip of the original bricks, 36 inches wide, can be seen at the start and finish line, to help preserve tradition.

Just for the records, the original track was "paved" with crushed stone and tar but then 3,200,000 bricks were used to smooth the 2H mile oval.

I understand the "Old Brickyard" handle is a term of affection or admiration but I don't understand the "carburetor tests" that are misleading to all new fans and just mildly interested parties.

Traditions often are worth preserving but not at the risk of inaccuracies.

4. This is something that you can't help me with because it's sort of an emotional problem.

We all understand how some children follow their dads, big brothers or uncles into a particular line of business. That often holds true for sports.

But when one dangerous sport heaps tragedy upon a family and causes years of problems and grief it's hard for me to understand how the little ones follow the same path, take the same risks and court the same dangers.

For example, Bill Vukovich won the Indy 500 in 1953 and '54 and was leading the race in '55 when he crashed and died.

Yet, in 1968, Bill Jr. ran in the Indy race for the first time. He finished second in 1973 and third in 1974.

Now his son, Billy III, is in the field for Sunday's race.

Tony Bettenhausen died on that Indy track in 1961 and his oldest son, Gary, raced in the event for the first time seven years later. Gary lost an arm while racing in 1974 but still competed at Indy for many years after.

This year, Tony's youngest son, Tony Jr., will be in the field again, starting in the eighth row.

We all know about Bobby and Al Unser but not many remember their older brother, Jerry, who was killed on the Indy track in 1959.

Al is the defending champion and he'll start from the first row. His son, Al Jr., will start in the second row.

My question is, don't the memories of those relatives who died there ever haunt the men as they circle the old track in the name of business and sport?

The answer must be no or they couldn't compete so well there. And I don't understand that.

October 22, 1988

A Late Entry's Campaign 'Promises'

It probably won't come about but just in case I happen to be elected president of these United States on a write-in ballot this seems like a good time to explain some of the things that I plan to do.

First off, let's remember that campaign promises don't really count. They don't count as lies or pledges. They're like morning dew before sunrise on a hot day. They'll soon be gone and forgotten.

After all, we vote for presidents, not dictators, and our Congress carries the heavy hammer on nearly all issues unrelated to matters of national emergencies. If or when a president acts on his own he often catches more heat than he can handle.

So don't bother to even consider that my election will not give me the right to make most of the changes that I'm about to promise. These simply are planks in my campaign platform, teasers for the many who forget that our president isn't all-powerful and capable of fulfilling all promises.

Now then, should I be elected, the first thing that I promise to do is pass a law to jail all politicians who serve two years without fulfilling at least 70 percent of their campaign promises.

That'll cut future TV debates down to 30 minutes and leave more time to view serious things, like reruns of "Three's Company," "Family Ties" and "The Jeffersons."

Then I'll change the stupid basketball rules that reward trailing teams for intentional fouls near the end of each game. Instead of making a lousy foul shooter take free shots, he'll be allowed to keep possession and take the ball out of bounds. No athlete should be rewarded for fouling.

That will prevent the final 90 seconds of many games from being stretched to nine minutes. It will also allow fans to get home in time to watch "Three's Company," "Love Connection" and "The Jeffersons."

My next move will place the NCAA under authority of the FBI and the IRS.

It's sort of silly to keep half of the NCAA's investigating team camped in the Southwest Conference while coaches of other schools in other leagues order Trans-Ams by the fleet for their athletes.

And we're going to check into the finances of that sweet aunt in Florida or the kindly uncle in California who agree to purchase those slick wheels for their dear nephews.

Oh? You say that the ACLU won't allow such peeks into personal records? Don't bet on it, buster. When I get to be president we're going to hear a lot less from the ACLU.

The FBI will train 50 more NCAA investigators and all of those jocks who get caught catching goodies under the table will be sent directly to the IRS for a full accounting. They'll be given six months to pay their taxes or six months in jail, whichever comes first.

Oh, yes, my next move will be to build more jails.

What's that? Will I raise taxes? I'll promise not to, but you can bet your grandmaw's Sunday church coat that I will. The tooth fairy sure isn't going to build those jails.

Moving right along, it will become a federal law requiring every athlete who spends two years in the NBA or NFL to take $30,000 from his third-year paycheck and return it to the school that gave him an athletic scholarship.

It's ridiculous for the pros to feed and get fatter off the colleges while the schools have to beg for more money to stay afloat. Baseball has always paid for its own farm systems to develop new talent but football and basketball just use the colleges as feeding grounds and give nothing in return.

If, for some reason, the pro is unable to pay the $30,000 in a lump sum when it becomes due, his pro team will be forced to pay for the athlete.

It's amazing how many of those jocks who make $300,000 a year or more are often late with payments on their Cadillacs and Mercedes, not to mention child support.

Say what? You want to know who my vice presidential running mate will be?

I'll let Katy handle that and I'd dearly love to hear any of those four other dudes try to debate her. In 35 years I haven't once come close to winning a debate against her.

Well, that's it for openers, gang.

Your semihumble candidate here is heavy on the shorts for campaign funds and we're mounting a late push purposely, allowing those front-runners ample time to shoot themselves in the foot while letting their mouths overload their ambitions.

But we're looking for a strong finish to this write-in drive. Now then, does anybody have the address of "Thirteen Percent Undecided?"

I think that it might be wise to start by grabbing a husky percentage of folks who haven't been paying close attention.

College Monster Too Tough to Tame

Suddenly, everyone is searching for a solution to the sick situation that has infested so many of our collegiate athletic teams with robbers, rapists and assorted other rogues.

Fingers of blame are aimed in countless directions as the national scandal continues to spread like a dreaded disease.

The Southwest Conference long ago became a national disgrace — the butt of a thousand bad jokes — as teams took turns on probation.

But, if truth were known, the SWC was one of the lucky leagues. The culprits were caught before their programs raged out of control, like the sad scene created by Barry Switzer in Oklahoma, where goons rule the school's athletic dorm.

After all, most Southwest Conference offenders stayed on a level with teams like . . . well, like Iowa of the Big Ten. Iowa isn't on probation, but some Hawkeye football players continued to play while on "academic probation" and two of their courses were billiards and bowling.

So what's to be done? What corrective measures will provide a longstanding solution? Should each jock factory be forced to cut back on scholarships and entrance exams be made tougher for jocks with free rides? Should the plush athletic dorms, those great recruiting tools, be converted into study halls and library extensions?

The monster grows as the masters meet — and worry.

Hey, let's back up a bit and be realistic.

There is no longstanding solution and never will be as long as the accusers, the disgusted ones who now stand in shame, head up the groups looking for cures.

Sooner or later we'll all have to understand and accept the fact that the Barry Switzers of college football today came to power as the answers to prayers of those who now accuse them. They simply were extensions of the feelings and desires of so many who now stand embarrassed by the publicity from the messes they've made while winning.

Their methods were well-known and tolerated while they and their successes were hailed. Happy and knowing winks and giggles overshadowed and muffled any protests and all charges that couldn't be proved.

Any exposé on any star, any publicity on any player who drove a sports car he couldn't afford, brought screams of "media bias," complete with organized plans for retaliation. Run the rascal out of town — that actually happened once in Oklahoma — cancel subscriptions, cut out all advertising.

But now, as the rape, robbery and assault charges mount among college jocks across the country, as drug scandals in athletic dorms produce shootings and deaths and police reports that can't be buried or hidden, the high and mighty boosters accuse and seek solutions.

Most of those now pointing fingers of accusation should point at mirrors.

Nobody ever looks at Iowa State as a football title contender but the coach at that school, Jim Walden, diagnosed the problem better than anyone.

It was Walden who said, "Very often, the people who went to the school for the reasons the buildings were put up in the first place — chemical engineers, the botanists — are the same ones who on Saturday dress up in funny clothes and blow their stupid horns at games. They don't just want to see their team play. They want to see their team win. It's odd. The people to whom academics mean the most end up being the ones who perpetuate non-academic attitudes."

The late Walt Kelly, who drew the comic strip character Pogo, once summed up a similar situation in one of his panels with a classic line: "We have seen the enemy — and it is us."

Naw, no longstanding solution will be found. Far too many of those now looking will never be satisfied with any answer that places their team in a losing situation.

We all love winners, and after suffering a lot of losses we don't mind wearing blinders to watch our guys become winners.

While on the subject of needed change, this should be a good time to mention a needed alteration of some NCAA rules.

Nearly all new and old rules place strong restrictions on recruiting but few, if any, favor the recruit. When a high school athlete signs with a certain college because he's impressed by the head coach he should be given an opportunity to play for that coach.

But coaches move around, often leaving on short notice.

Jimmy Johnson, for example, signed some of the hottest blue-chip stars in the nation for Miami, telling each one how he'd love to coach them to greatness. Then he left for Dallas, to coach the Cowboys.

Most of those kids now feel cheated and want to change schools. They can, too, if they stay out of athletics for a year or two.

That's wrong. It's a rule that sends a young man to college with a bitter attitude.

The solution there is obvious and simple. When a recruit signs his letter of intent he should also list a second choice, to be used only in the event that the head coach he signs with leaves before his sophomore season is completed. If the coach resigns to take another job that young man should have the option of transferring to his second choice without losing one week of eligibility.

But that probably won't be considered because the NCAA is made up of school officials — coaches, athletic directors and school presidents. Right now they're not looking for fair deals for their future student-athletes.

They're too busy trying to figure out how to tame and control the ones they've got.

———

Saddles and Scriptures

L OUISVILLE, Ky. — The world's smallest minister, with self-made preaching credentials, also happens to be America's No. 1 jockey.

Pat Day, national riding champion the past two years who rode five straight winners here Saturday before finishing second in the Kentucky Derby on favored Easy Goer, got himself born again five years ago. He's been reading the Bible and preaching it ever since.

For a long while it appeared that Day would become the first jockey ever to win all six races of a Big Six Picks — the kind of long-shot gamble that got Pete Rose so much publicity from the wagering end.

Day booted home five straight winners, to the delight of his backers, but his sweet Saturday turned sour in the big race when he finished a disappointing second to Sunday Silence.

It was like a great pitcher throwing two hours of batting practice and then getting knocked out of the box in a World Series game.

But, as he put it, "You just do your best and Jesus will take care of the rest."

The little rider saw God's light in a dark Miami hotel room in 1984 and at first he thought it was an unwanted intruder. We'll let him tell his story:

"The first thing I do when I walk into a hotel room is flip on the TV and that day Jimmy Swaggart was on, preaching as usual. I was tired, really worn out, and since I wasn't due to ride until the next day I listened to the preacher for a few minutes and then jumped into bed for a long nap."

Day paused and then inserted a moment of confession.

"I wasn't doing things right. I drank too much, fooled with dope a little. Of course, even a little is way too much. That was one of the few times that I went to bed without first taking a drink."

Then he continued his story of conversion on the late, strange afternoon in that Miami hotel room.

"It seemed as though I had been asleep for a long while but when I woke up I had the feeling that I wasn't alone in the room. It was scary because that hotel wasn't located in the best part of Miami. I kept looking around and then I noticed that the TV was still on and Rev. Swaggart was still preaching. He was making an altar call, asking those who wanted to be saved to come forth."

Pat raised his head a notch, looked the small collection of newsmen in the eyes and said, "Then I knew. I knew that Jesus had been in the room with me. I got down on my knees and cried and asked forgiveness."

But he did more than that. The tough little jock says he gave "serious thought" to leaving the horses altogether and studying for the ministry.

"It got to be a burning desire with me," Day explained.

After a few weeks, however, he said that God helped him decide that his ministry was "right here in the racing industry, preaching His word whenever possible."

Now he reads the Bible every night so he can, as he put it, "learn more to teach more."

That was five years ago. Today — and each day since that "close encounter" in his hotel room — Pat stays away from booze and drugs and preaches the evils of those "tools of the devil."

Since then he's become a better jockey, the best in the nation. He's also become a much better person.

But he missed on the big one Saturday as he got boxed at the head of the stretch and couldn't overhaul the winner, Sunday Silence.

Meanwhile, they overlooked the old man this time.

Wee Willie Shoemaker long ago rode to the level of legend but nobody wanted the 57-year-old jock for the Derby run this year.

Twenty-six times the tiny Texan has been aboard a Derby entry when the band struck up "My Old Kentucky Home." That's five more Derby starts than any rider in history and 11 more than any other active jock.

But nobody wanted his services this year. Instead, the 16-horse field got a bunch of Derby rookies and only one in the field, Laffit Pincay, had ever before felt the blanket of roses.

Well, maybe The Shoe has slipped a little. He figures to after sitting in saddles for 40 years. But he got his fourth Kentucky Derby win just three years back, aboard Ferdinand in 1986.

A lot of trainers say that Willie can still rate and ride a horse better than any of the young hotshots making their marks today.

None of those trainers, however, had horses in Saturday's Derby.

In 1910 the first airplane flight in Kentucky took off from and landed in the infield of Churchill Downs. But that didn't create near the excitement that the annual roses run generates.

Now known in not-so-affectionate terms as "The Snake Pit," the racetrack infield is always the wildest area in Kentucky on the first Saturday of every May.

The only difference this time was a marked scarcity of naked bodies in the infield. Morning and early afternoon rains wet the grounds and unseasonal temperature readings from 42-45 made warm clothes preferred items.

Little Items, Big Bucks

D ad, tell Junior to save all of his baseball cards, ticket stubs to sports events and any other memorabilia that he might come across. That stuff suddenly has become pure gold.

It's only a wild guess but I've probably given and thrown away more than $20,000 worth of collectible sports items in the last 25 years.

Of course, when I discarded most of the junk, there wasn't any real market for any of it although I realized there was some value to the baseball autographed by Babe Ruth when I sent it to a very ill youngster.

Before moving any deeper into this subject let it be known up front here that a Honus Wagner baseball card recently sold for $115,000.

You may argue that old Honus struck out from this earth years ago so the cards of dead superstars become more valuable as time passes. After all, Honus hasn't been able to sign any autographs since 1945, the year he died.

But Mickey Mantle is alive and well and his original 1953 Topps card sold for $110,000 two years ago.

When I was a kid I thought the cards were just little bonuses and the chewing gum was the main item of my purchases. See? Even then I was on the shorts for business smarts.

It wasn't until four years ago when an attorney from New York first wrote me that I realized how valuable the stuff was that I had been tossing aside. It looked like a personal letter but I later learned that he had written similar letters to just about every sportswriter I knew.

The guy was "very interested" in purchasing "any sports memorabilia" that I might have saved over the years.

He was particularly interested in Super Bowl items, such as press pins that allow reporters entrance to the hospitality room, and Super Bowl press box tickets. As he put it, "Anything with the Super Bowl name and insignia on it draws my interest."

Since I didn't know the guy from a judge's gavel I tossed his letter with the one that offered me a new TV set if I'd just visit the waterfront sites on beautiful Lake Gotcha.

He second letter, however, got my attention.

The New York lawyer said that he'd be "happy to fly to San Antonio" to look over my collection of old sports items if I had enough and was "interested in selling."

Now either that dude couldn't hack it as a lawyer — probably get you off for a $200 fine and a year's probation on a parking ticket — or he knew something that I didn't know.

The latter was about a 500-1 favorite.

After contacting some others in the sportswriting fraternity, I learned the truth. A complete set of Super Bowl programs now sells for $1,100 and the price rises by 15 percent each year.

Even if you have just four or five old Super Bowl programs those might be the ones that will fill out somebody else's collection so they could be worth $50 each.

Folks, for 40 years the first thing I've done after taking my press box seat at any football game was to kick my program under the table. The cardboard speed charts with names, weights, positions and ages are all I use while working a game.

Over the years I've been photographed with such legends as Jack Dempsey, Babe Ruth, Joe Louis, Bobby Layne, Phil Rizzuto, Rocky Marciano, Darrell Royal, Richard Petty and Jimmy Brown — to name a few.

I can't find a single one of those pictures.

My treasures of those moments are all in my memories, which are valuable to me but they're not worth a single Big Mac at any McDonald's.

The point is, my work kept me in position to collect a truckload of such valuable goodies and I came up empty.

No, I'm not looking for a sympathy vote. This is just to let you know that old programs, pins and ticket stubs are becoming more valuable with each passing year.

Hang on to them.

I do have one item ratholed away at home that I plan to give to our Texas Sports Hall of Fame.

After the Steelers edged Dallas in the 1979 Super Bowl — following the '78 season — I was interviewing Mean Joe Greene one-on-one.

But then some local TV crew butted in and asked Joe for a "few words." He left me as if rattlesnakes were jumping from my pockets.

Before departing, however, he handed me his lineman's gloves that he'd worn during the game and said, "Hold these and I'll be back."

But as his TV interviews went on and on and my deadline drew nearer and nearer I left — with his gloves.

If you run into Mean Joe Greene don't tell him that I'm the thief who swiped his gloves.

Theft of a pair of well-worn lineman's gloves shouldn't draw more than 90 days in the jug but I'd hate for Mean Joe to be waiting for me when I got out.

1990

The poor man looked as though he suddenly had been stricken with a cross between constipation and diarrhea, with a headache tossed in between.

April 14, 1990

When Ray Met Lee

It was Sunday afternoon when the TV announcer mentioned that Lee Trevino and Raymond Floyd were old friends and they'd both be back at the Masters next year.

Floyd was leading the tournament by three strokes and Lee had just finished among the top 24.

The announcer's line about those two being "old friends" made me wonder if he had any idea about the circumstances when they first met so long ago.

Then I began to wonder how many of you out there, if any, knew the details of that unusual introduction.

Well then, let's go back to when Floyd and Trevino were in their 20s, back to when a berth in the Masters was just a dream for both men. Lee was living in El Paso, in a rent-free condemned tourist court while trying to get his PGA card. At that time he was a little closer to starvation than he was to golf fame as he hustled $10 and $20 bets while working on commission in a club pro shop.

His best hustle was using a tall Dr Pepper bottle as his only "club" while betting on par-3 holes.

Titanic Thompson, a legendary old hustler and the most interesting character I've ever known, learned that some wealthy golf enthusiasts in El Paso would back a "chubby Mexican kid" against almost anyone.

The call went out for a young smoothie named Ray Floyd, a second-year man on the PGA Tour who was about as well-known nationally as a fifth-year caddie.

When Floyd arrived in El Paso, Titanic insisted that he tour the course to be played although Ray was reluctant, figuring he had a soft pigeon to be plucked. Besides, in his early travels, he'd played the course before. Still, he humored Ti.

When their golf cart rolled toward 18 Trevino was pointed out as "the enemy" and then Floyd just knew that he had a "fat pigeon" ready to hop into his broiler. He bubbled with confidence. Even more than usual.

But so did the El Paso natives, the ones who were backing Lee, after they viewed this young kid who had been imported to challenge their champ.

It turned into a three-day affair — with Titanic and his people trying desperately to get even after the first two days.

Floyd opened with a 69 and lost by one stroke. Titanic lost $12,000. The second day, a Sunday, Ray hunkered down with his best strokes and fired a 67. He lost by two shots and Titanic dropped $17,000 more.

Thompson was furious that evening as he planned a final assault on Monday — hoping just to get even.

Floyd insisted that he was distracted by the unorthodox style Trevino displayed.

"Then quit watchin' him and tend to your own game," screamed the old hustler.

After extracting a promise that Ray would give the next day's match his best concentration and top skills, Titanic returned to the clubhouse to get down more wagers on his man.

However, some of the big bettors had taken their profits and left.

The next day, Floyd shot a 65 to nose Trevino by two and Thompson picked up $20,000 of the money he had dropped earlier.

Still, he left El Paso a $9,000 loser, beaten by a "little fat Mexican kid nobody ever heard of." He complained of that setback for many years.

It's been said that the sickest financial setback a hustler can feel comes when he gets hustled at one of his own games.

But old Ti must have felt some consolation when that "fat little Mexican kid" with the unusual style went on to win the U.S. Open about four years later.

Thompson lived to 86 and he must have absorbed a tinge of pride when Raymond Floyd and Lee Trevino blossomed into two of the greatest golfers in the world.

After all, he matched them in El Paso when neither one of them had a credit card.

And that was his first "promotion" that allowed others to perform with his money riding. As an expert golfer, bowler, pool shark, pistol and shotgun marksman, he spent most of his years betting on himself — and silly proposition bets that he had fixed.

But the TV announcer was correct. Ray and Lee are old friends.

It's just that they didn't seem destined for a long friendship when they first met so many years ago in El Paso.

————

Fabled Pool Shark is Hobbled

There was a time here when the old guy used steady nerves, keen eyesight and a smooth stick to become a world-class pool shooter. In those days, he carried a fat roll, part of the necessary working tools, while looking for challenges. Far more often than not the roll was much fatter after toiling long hours over a hot table.

But that was long ago, several decades back.

Now hard times face the one known as Skinny Grant.

He'll soon see his 73rd birthday in the VA hospital, recovering from a hip that was shattered in three places.

They say in sports that the legs go first but in pool, it's usually fading eyesight that kills a career.

Skinny, whose proper handle is Merald B. Grant, walked thousands of miles around hundreds of tables until new aches pierced his bones and he graduated from reading glasses.

But it was his legs that put him in the hospital as he stumbled on a curb and busted his hip.

A world-class pool shooter? Is his name in the record books?

No, but it could have been had he chosen the tuxedo circuit.

Most of Skinny's best work was done in old, smoke-filled parlors as he thinned the wallets of small-town champs, visiting hustlers and old pros who loved to clip young chargers. Finally, he became the old pro who gave expensive lessons to the young.

The popular thought that you should "never hustle a hustler" was forever planted in Grant's mind when he was a young man.

That happened when he played a smooth-stroking stranger for hours, until it became obvious that there was nothing to be won — or lost.

In those days, photos of old and current champions decorated the walls of many billiard halls so the best compliment a stranger could be paid was to tell him, "Your picture might be hanging on the wall."

After 40 games that night, Skinny and his unknown foe were dead even, 20 wins each. So Grant called it quits and said, "I'm gonna leave you because your picture might be on the wall."

To that, the stranger pointed his stick toward the wall at a dust-covered photo and said, "It is."

Skinny had just spent the night playing an elderly gent who had been world pocket billiards champion five times in his younger days — Thomas Hueston.

It probably was the first time that Grant ever left a pool hall happy after failing to make expenses.

Hollywood makes a habit of picturing all pool hustlers as less-than-honest thieves at heart, if not in fact.

Skinny's word has always been solid. When he was a kid, some high rollers would hear about a hotshot shooter up East who had rich backers. They'd send Skinny off with a load of cash to pluck the pigeons and nobody ever worried whether he'd return with an honest count.

If he owed you money and said he'd meet you at the Gunter Hotel, you could set your watch by his arrival.

Of course, if you owed him money, he might get there 10 minutes early.

When he was near the peak of his game, younger players often asked Grant for advice. In the '40s, he took a liking to an up-and-coming and confident player named Robin Johnson.

One night, Johnson called Skinny from Corpus Christi.

"I'm about to play this guy that mentioned that he knows you. I think I can beat him like a drum but I need to know how many balls I can spot him and be safe."

Robin then gave an accurate and detailed description of his foe, even explaining how the man carried a red bandana in his back pocket.

Finally, Skinny asked Robin where he was calling from and when he was told the location of the phone booth, Grant replied, "When you leave that booth, walk two blocks north and then one block east and you'll be at the bus station. Get on the next bus to San Antonio and don't look back. You were about to play Bananas Rodriguez and he'd eat your lunch."

In almost every business, the good ones know each other, either from past experiences or by reputation.

Bananas now owns and operates a sleek pool parlor here on San Pedro. He's far off the form of his youth but on occasions, he still fascinates customers by making tough shots look easy.

Skinny is now nursing a mangled hip in a hospital that probably doesn't even have a pool table.

But if they've got one, he'll find it and other patients would be wise to let him play alone or he'll wind up winning their crutches.

August 25, 1990

This Space Sponsored By . . .

This is going a tad too far, the Poulan Weed-Eater Independence Bowl. The John Hancock Sun Bowl was bad enough and the Mobil Cotton Bowl still hits a harsh ring in my ears. Then there's the Federal Express Orange Bowl and the USF&G Sugar Bowl.

Is there no end to this sports dollar derby, the sudden romance with corporate America? Does everything we own and treasure now carry a price tag?

For many decades, every car entered in the Indianapolis 500 has been a flying billboard, zooming about with anywhere from 10 to 50 commercial messages.

Most of those ads can't be read, however, until the race is over or the car gets special attention for winning — or crashing.

But it's still the Indy 500 and not the Red Man Chewing Tobacco 500.

This chase to make more money to pay more money has become insane.

Now the NCAA, the collegiate rules enforcement agency that for years frowned on corporate tie-ins, calls for bowls to give each partici-pating team a minimum of $600,000. It's either that or get out of the bowl business.

Figure it out. A crowd of 50,000 paying $20 a head can't come close to cracking the nut on that egg. So, without a great TV contract, most bowls would fold and only a handful of the current 19 bowl games have good TV pacts.

Oh, in case you're wondering, the Poulan Weed-Eater Bowl is in Shreveport, La.

And this top part of today's column here was brought to you by

Mac's Service Station, which keeps my car rolling in excellent condition. If you have to wait for more than 90 seconds for an attendant at Mac's, your first gallon of gas is free.

Advertising sales people keep folks like me in business — bless 'em — but those marketing gangs with charts, surveys and strange conclusions are forever searching out new areas to conquer, fresh places to drop old ads.

Agents for Budweiser recently opened a door that promises to lead them into a temptation that carries a gold mine — and countless boring moments for millions.

Framed in red, with the action thinned down by 20 percent on your TV set, we're told, "This kickoff is brought to you by Budweiser, the king of beers."

How long will it be before Schlitz wants to bring us all the replays? Then, "This extra-point try is brought to you by Miller Lite."

The cheapo advertisers will then start elbowing each other in network lines to bring us huddles and shots of the scoreboard.

There's no limit to it, now that Budweiser has crashed down the doors.

Before long, after football players start making more money than baseball players because of the added TV revenue, it will only be a matter of time before outfield plays are brought to us by car companies.

The NBA won't be far behind once its ratings rise.

Now then, this second chapter of today's piece here was brought to you by the good folks at Growl and Grow dog food. They keep my little Jubilee healthy and happy.

Sure, by now some of you are pointing fingers back and telling how this newspaper in your hand is loaded with advertisements.

But, as you know, it's your choice when and if you read them. It's up to the advertisers to make their ads appealing and attractive enough to merit your attention and time.

The only complaint here is that there's never enough money around to satisfy the individuals and teams in sports so everything in sight, sacred or not, is sold to outrace the competing groups.

Even the golfers and tennis stars now sell space for patches on their work clothes. And don't get the idea those gimme caps on the golf tour were just handed out by the Ace Nut and Screw Company.

Old Ace had to pay a price to sit his hat on the head of Two-Putt

Parker.

You've probably heard that one of the biggest businesses in sports right now centers on the feet of basketball and tennis stars. Only the lonely and the lousy buy their own. Even some NBA benchwarmers get $30,000 to wear certain brands.

None of this bothers the average fan too much but that's the scary part. It's going to get worse.

In conclusion, the last segment of this piece here today was brought to you by Katy's Sugar Cookies, a specialty in our house. Katy's cookies have no cholesterol. She's now working up a price list for the recipe so watch this space for more details.

November 4, 1990

An Ongoing Experiment in Reality

Sometimes a few deep thoughts in a shallow brain barrel create confusion and cause undo concern.

In case you haven't figured from that opening bit, there's nothing revealing here today.

Yeah, I know, so what else is new?

It's just that many years ago my first and last physics teacher tossed me a semi-insulting line and now, ever so often, it comes back to haunt me.

I'm probably wrong but it seems like a good idea to just toss it out on the table here for no particular reason.

Mr. Pope (I forgot his first name if I ever knew it) was a whiz at physics and he couldn't understand why I couldn't understand his teachings. He seemed shocked when I explained that I had no real interest in the subject.

In a stern voice he asked, "Just how do you expect to make a living when you leave school?"

"I hope to become a sportswriter," I said.

The poor man looked as though he suddenly had been stricken with a cross between constipation and diarrhea, with a headache tossed in between.

"Is that all you want to do with your life, waste your years following stupid games?"

Now, after 46 years in this business that I love so much, the thrills still come and the excitement and interest are always near.

Nevertheless, off and on for the past few decades, there've been rare occasions when my mind had bugged my body by asking why I and so many others chase around the country and race deadlines to tell others about fun games.

Mr. Pope's words keep popping into my head, his question is asked over and over.

Can it really be considered honest, productive, meaningful work?

The first time that strange idea entered my head was in the 24th inning of a Texas League game at old Mission Stadium.

It was a weekday night game but at 3 the next morning, with the 24th inning about to start, I began to wonder about the true importance of my job.

Already far past deadline for our morning paper, I wondered how many might read our stories in the afternoon editions. How many cared? Why was I still there at that silly hour, sitting in a press box high atop the roof of a ballpark? Was Mr. Pope right?

The last time those thoughts hit me was in Las Vegas a week ago, shortly after the Holyfield-Douglas fight.

With our time zone two hours later than Nevada's, I rushed my story, sent it through to the mother computer back home, and then began to look around the large media room in the Mirage hotel.

Suddenly, the whole scene began to seem ridiculous.

Some of the greatest writers from all over the world were still banging out adjectives and reaching for greater phrases to describe a one-punch knockout.

If you stacked all of the awards won by all the journalists in that room they'd stretch beyond the Las Vegas strip, topped off by the Pulitzer Prize earned earlier this year by Jim Murray of the Los Angeles Times.

Jim was busy putting humorous but hurting digs into Buster Douglas for coming into the ring overweight and "robbing" us all of a good fight.

Murray's syndicated column almost certainly hurt Douglas more than the one right cross that Evander Holyfield used to put the big guy to sleep.

But Buster's critics were on his case because he entered the fight about 10 pounds too heavy. It wasn't, however, a belly punch that put him away and he wasn't tired or even breathing heavy when the end came. One crunching right on the chin and 246 pounds of floored humanity were about our only real topics for that evening.

There was Blackie Sherrod of Dallas to my right, close to Furman Bisher of Atlanta, and Galyn Wilkins of Fort Worth at my left, Bill Lyon of Philadelphia in front of me.

All old friends of mine and talented wordsmiths, they struggled to tell their tales of how one guy had knocked another out with one punch.

Then fresh news arrived and the tempo quickened.

Word reached our media room that the winner, Holyfield, would bypass Mike Tyson for six or seven months and take on old George Foreman.

A dozen hands grabbed telephones to have this new development inserted in their stories.

Ah, more news 10 minutes later. Those idiotic impersonators of ring authority, leaders of the WBC, WBA and IBF, just announced that they might not sanction a Holyfield-Foreman title fight. As a matter of fact, they're even giving thought to stripping away the title that Holyfield won 20 minutes earlier.

An usher in a crowded theater probably holds a more important and much more necessary job than the presidents of those assorted boxing groups.

Still, we quote them as though their words mean something.

Mr. Pope's words returned again. Is this all I want to do with my life, waste the years by following games?

It does, at times, like the moments just described, seem like a weird way to earn my keep.

But I enjoy it and it sure beats working for a living. Besides, Mr. Pope didn't turn out too many rocket scientists and he probably never knew a right cross from a resin bag.

Sweet Holiday Plan Turns Sour

This is a true Christmas story with a sort of sad ending, but it might help you to get more enjoyment from the coming holidays. It's got a Scrooge angle with heavy reverse English.

You should know up front that there's no real sports involved here today, other than the fact that some former jocks played leading roles in the story. They'll all go unnamed.

This dates back about 25 years and, like Scrooge, the theme is timeless.

Now then, once upon a time, a quarter of a century ago, a friend in the candy business told me he was overstocked with more candy bars than he knew what to do with — good stuff that might not be so good in four or five months.

Hey, 'twas the season for giving so I got this great idea. At least, it seemed like a great idea at the moment.

"Let's give it away and make a lot of poor kids happy on Christmas Day."

That was the original seed that grew almost instantly.

Children don't live by candy alone. Their teeth durned sure don't.

The next day I used this space to write a column that explained how many charitable groups, through necessity, use small percentages of donated dollars for employee salaries and expenses.

I told how a group of my friends was planning a Christmas Eve trip to help needy families and we needed financial support. Not one dime would be used for anything but food and toys, I promised.

My small but eager crew would spend Christmas Eve making our rounds and not even a gallon of gas would be paid for with donated money.

The checks rolled in and we raced around looking for bargains. We got wholesale prices — or better — from a kindly meat packer and friends in the toy business.

Then, from a welfare worker, we got names and addresses of large, desperate families with many children.

Folks, we loaded up two trucks and a car with turkeys and hams, packages of rice, beans, bread and, of course, toys and candy.

Not since I was 5 years old had I been so excited on a Christmas Eve. We packed our caravan and moved out around 10 a.m.

It's hard to even imagine the warm feeling that we all shared.

And did we have fun?

Positively not. It was one of the worst, most depressing days of my life. By late afternoon, we were all suffering from varying degrees of depression.

The only small consolation was that we knew exactly where we went wrong, a mistake that was far too obvious.

You don't have to be real smart to figure that when you go to visit a very poor family with a lot of children you're going to stop on a very poor street with other such families.

But we hadn't taken that into consideration.

Oh, sure, when three or four of us carried dolls, baseball gloves, candy and food into one home we attracted attention from others in the neighborhood.

We never stopped at a house without three, four or five next-door children asking if we had anything for them.

"Yeah, kid, here's a candy bar."

By the time we left each street, at least 10 children crowded the back of our trucks, looking over the goodies that they wouldn't get.

Each time we drove away we left sad faces that were downright haunting.

Yeah, there really is a Santa Claus, but not for you guys.

Some parents even came out and asked if they could just "share a ham or turkey" between them. One girl, about 7, pleaded so hard for a doll she saw in our truck, we gave it to her.

That brought begging cries from a half-dozen others in the growing crowd, others who weren't on our list.

For each person we made happy, we broke the hope and hearts of 10 others. Santa's helpers became a crew of Scrooges.

After making our final stop we had a few toys left over so we dropped by the Salvation Army's main station to leave them.

There we saw real veterans at work, an assembly line of toys going into large trucks.

There were at least 30 efficient workers labeling and loading. It was a beautiful sight that made us feel like the idiots we were.

The point is, you should and will feel better after giving. But give to the people who know what they're doing.

The Salvation Army and Elf Louise are now my choices this time of the year but there must be a dozen other organizations who also do great work.

Send a check today, if not for others, then do it for yourself. But whatever you do, don't send it to me.